AUTISM

AUTISM

Diagnosis, Instruction, Management, and Research

Edited by

JAMES E. GILLIAM, Ph.D

The Department of Special Education
The University of Texas at Austin
Austin, Texas

CHARLES C THOMAS · PUBLISHER
Springfield · Illinois · U.S.A.

Published and Distributed Throughout the World by
CHARLES C THOMAS • PUBLISHER
2600 South First Street
Springfield, Illinois 62717, U.S.A.

*With THOMAS BOOKS careful attention is given to all details of
manufacturing and design. It is the Publisher's desire to present books that are
satisfactory as to their physical qualities and artistic possibilities and
appropriate for their particular use. THOMAS BOOKS will be true to those
laws of quality that assure a good name and good will.*

Library of Congress Cataloging in Publication Data

Main entry under title:

Autism, diagnosis, instruction, management, and research.

Bibliography: p.
Includes index.
1. Autism. I. Gilliam, James E. [DNLM: 1. Autism.
WM 203.5 A937]
RJ506.A9A922   618.92'8982   80-29129
ISBN 0-398-04072-9

Printed in the United States of America
C-1

This book is dedicated to
Sarah Alice Gilliam, a
truly special educator.

CONTRIBUTORS

ANONYMOUS is a parent of a near normal adolescent autistic girl. She is an officer in the Texas Society for Autistic Citizens.

BRUCE BALOW, Ph.D. is a Professor of Psychoeducational Studies at the University of Minnesota. He is a well known researcher and writer in special education and was formerly the head of the personnel preparation branch of the Bureau for the Education of the Handicapped. He has recently written a monograph on autism.

SUSAN JOHNSEN DOLLAR, Ph.D. is a private consultant but formerly was an Assistant Professor of Special Education at the University of Kentucky. She is well known for her work in concept teaching and developed and co-authored *Learning Opportunities for Teachers* (LOFTS).

KITTY DORSEY is a private consultant who specializes in curriculum for severe and profoundly handicapped populations. At the time of her presentation, she was a consultant for the Texas Area Learning Resources Center of the Texas Education Agency.

STEVEN FEARING works for the Texas Society for Autistic Citizens as a Case Manager. He provides assistance and support to families of autistic children and functions as an advocate for the family as they seek and receive services for their child.

B. J. FREEMAN, Ph.D. is Associate Professor of Medical Psychology at the U.C.L.A. Neuropsychiatric Institute. She is the author of numerous publications in the area of autism and co-authored the National Society for Autistic Children's definition of autism. She co-authored *Autism: Diagnosis, Current Research and Management* (Holliswood, New York, Spectrum Publications, 1976).

JAMES E. GILLIAM, Ph.D. is Assistant Professor in the Department of Special Education of The University of Texas at Austin.

MAUREEN IVEY was formerly a researcher at Children's Psychiatric Unit.

HARRIETT KABERLINE is a curriculum consultant for the Statewide Project at the Texas School for the Deaf. She has strong classroom teaching experience and has conducted many workshops on differential diagnosis of hearing impaired and autistic children.

MELVIN KAUFMAN, Ph.D. is a Professor of Special Education at Georgia State University and HELEN M. CLARK, Ph.D. is a professor at Clemson University. Both have been active researchers and writers in special education and autism.

PAMELA A. KIMBROUGH is Supervisor of Education and Training at the Beaumont State Center for Human Development.

MARTIN KOZLOFF, Ph.D. is a Professor of Sociology at Boston University. He has written two books on the education and treatment of autism and is widely respected for his work with families of autistic children.

DAVID KRUG, Ph.D. is Associate Professor of Special Education at Portland State University, Portland, Oregon. He is the author of numerous publications on autism and is particularly well known for his work on identification of autism. He and JOEL ARICK and PATRICIA ALMOND developed, researched and disseminated the Autism Screening Instrument for Educational Planning. Arick and Almond are on the staff of Portland State University and direct a project on autism for the Portland Public Schools.

DONALD MARBURG, Ph.D. is a psychologist at Children's Psychiatric Unit of the Austin State Hospital.

ANITA MARCOTT-RADKE is a Speech Clinician for the Developmental Learning Program of the Wayne County (Michigan) Intermediate School District and Garden City Public Schools. She has made several presentations at state and national conferences and has produced a manual on teaching sign language to autistic children.

WESLER H. PERLMAN, Ph.D. is in private practice but formerly was involved at North Texas State University in training teachers to work with autistic children.

EDWARD R. RITVO, M.D. is Professor in the Division of Child Retardation and Child Psychiatry at the U.C.L.A. School of Medicine. He is the Chairperson of the Professional Advisory Board of the National Society for Autistic Citizens. He is an internationally recognized scholar and researcher on autism and is co-author of *Autism: Diagnosis, Current Research and Management,* New York, Spectrum Publications, 1976).

RANDALL SOFFER is a consultant with the Texas Education Agency and RICHARD LA VALLO is a doctoral candidate at The University of Texas at Austin.

BEVERLY SUTTON, M.D. is a psychiatrist and Director of the Children's Psychiatric Unit of the Austin State Hospital.

PREFACE

*A*utism. Until recently the word itself was likely to be undefin-
able by the general public and large numbers of health
caregivers. Often misdiagnosed or not recognized at all, autism
was permeated by an aura of uncertainty, confusion, and even
mystery. Great strides have been made in recent years to provide
new information about this behavioral disorder. A number of
professionals and parents have sought to dispel some of the
confusion by concerted efforts to provide the public and health-
care systems with information to raise the level of awareness
about autism. This book was designed to assist in that endeavor.
As editor, my goal was to organize a book of readings that
presents current information that can be utilized by persons
responsible for diagnosis, instruction, research, or other aspects
of care giving. The book is broad in scope covering a wide variety
of topics. An attempt was made to balance the offerings so the
information would be relevant and interesting to parents, professionals, and the general public.

The first section is concerned with diagnosis and assessment.
The Ritvo and Freeman chapters provide detailed information
about the characteristics of autism and review the state of the art
of assessment of this disorder. Assessment for educational planning is addressed by Krug, Arick, and Almond. Their work on
identification and educational planning is based on extensive
research and development of the Autism Screening Instrument
for Educational Planning. The problem of differential diagnosis
of autism and auditory disorders is examined by Kaberline. A
process is described to help the practitioner and clinician evaluate the functional hearing of the autistic child.

Instruction is the focus of the second section. Radke's article
describes a communication system designed for autistic students. Generalized imitation is offered by Dollar as a process for
teaching relevant concepts and developing curricula. Perlman

xi

provides a systematic instructional procedure to teach simple discrimination without errors. Dorsey offers the reader an extensive list of curricular materials and programs useful with autistic children.

Section three is concerned with the care and management of the autistic child. Kozloff describes a methodology for working with parents and families to assist in their treatment. Case management and advocacy issues are explored by Fearing in an attempt to provide third party interventions. Issues of concern to parents are addressed in the next two chapters. Soffer and LaVallo examine the role of the parent in the educational planning process and offer suggestions to help parents increase their participation. An anonymous parent offers a poignant plea for help and attention for the autistic child who functions at a high level.

Current research on autism is presented in the fourth section. Balow describes important research on autism and childhood schizophrenia and criticizes various research methods commonly used to study aspects of autism. Kaufman and Clark review research concerned with how autistic children learn. The various sensory mode preferences of autistic children are evaluated by Sutton, Ivey, and Marberg. Finally, Gilliam and Kimbrough report on caregivers' questions and concerns related to autism.

The reader will find this book a valuable reference on autism. The material presented offers a complete and well-balanced look at various aspects concerned with this disorder. Hopefully this text will answer many of your questions and, perhaps more importantly, prompt you to seek more information about autism.

CONTENTS

AUTISM

I.
DIAGNOSIS AND
ASSESSMENT

Chapter 1

CURRENT RESEARCH ON THE SYNDROME OF AUTISM

EDWARD R. RITVO AND BETTY JO FREEMAN

INTRODUCTION

The National Society for Autistic Children's Definition of the Syndrome of Autism

As AN INTRODUCTION to this special section, we first give a brief overview of the needs for and potential uses of a behaviorally based definition of the syndrome of autism. Over the past decade, clinicians and researchers have reached a consensus that autism is a behaviorally definable syndrome and that it should be included in our standard diagnostic manuals. Before reaching this agreement, however, the term underwent several changes of usage. As we have detailed elsewhere (Ritvo, 1976), "autism" was introduced into the adult psychiatric literature by Eugen Bleuler as an adjective to describe self-referential qualities of certain pathological thought processes. When introduced into the child psychiatric literature by Kanner (1943), it was also used as an adjective to characterize "autistic" disturbances of affective contact. During the 1940s and 1950s the adjective subtly metamorphosed into a noun, and "autism" became referred to in the literature as a disease, or specific illness. Descriptive terminologies and proposed etiologies ranged from psychoanalytic and psychotoxic formulations, to genetic and/or congenital factors, early expressions of adult schizophrenia, postviral encephalopathies, and a host of other more exotic models. Despite extensive research efforts over the past two decades, unfortunately no documentation has been found for the psychogenic

From Edward R. Ritvo and Betty Jo Freeman, *Current Research on the Syndrome of Autism*, 1978. Courtesy of the American Academy of Child Psychiatry.

models, no biological markers identified, and no specific pathological processes pinpointed (Ornitz and Ritvo, 1976).

Thus, we are at the state of medical knowledge where we must
accept our ignorance and yet account for the confluence of our
clinical data. We can best do this by using the concept of a
"syndrome" to characterize autism. Syndromes in the history of
medicine have served as theoretical way stations for investigators
who have identified similarities of clinical phenomena among
patients, but who have not yet identified etiological or pathological variables that could allow for more specific grouping or
subtyping.

We are at this point with autism in the late 1970s. Patients with
strikingly similar behavioral and developmental disabilities have
been carefully documented to exist throughout the world. Their
natural history is remarkably similar despite their cultural, social, and geographic heterogeneity. The symptoms often occur
in association with others which are known to be indicative of
different syndromes (epilepsy, mental retardation) and/or other
specific diseases (e.g. rubella, Down's syndrome).

As a consensus concerning autism was slowly emerging in the
medical community, pressures for a behaviorally based definition arose from two different quarters. First, certain educational
systems in the United States and elsewhere systematically ex-
cluded children who did not have precisely defined diagnoses.
Conscientious educators were demanding that we physicians
decide such issues as: is autism a disease, a symptom (autistic-like
symptoms), a mental illness, an emotional illness, a type of brain
disease, a developmental disability, and/or a form of mental
retardation? These labeling criteria are essential since they are
used by educators to determine if a child is eligible for school
placement, and if so to which school, to which class, and which
funds will be used to pay for the special educational program.

Second, pressure arose from parents who had vainly sought
services for their children and who organized resistance to the
"exclusion merry-go-round" they had been on. They demanded
through public educational efforts, legislative action, and successful antidiscrimination lawsuits that "autistic citizens" be
granted diagnostic treatment, and educational services to which

all citizens are entitled. Their success over the past few years in these efforts has placed the responsibility on child psychiatrists — where it now surely rests. At present, we are responsible for "defining" the syndrome of autism to state legislators, federal regulatory agencies, school districts, community medical clinics, and insurance companies. These agencies are in need of medical guidelines to determine whom to serve.

In response to such needs for a practical definition of the syndrome of autism, the Board of Directors of the National Society for Autistic Children (NSAC) sought advice from its Professional Advisory Board. An initial definition was provided in 1976 when the term "autism" was formally introduced into the Federal Developmental Disabilities Act. A subcommittee of the Professional Advisory Board was then established and a new draft circulated to members throughout the country and abroad. Suggestions were collated into a second definition and this was reviewed and modified by the NSAC Board of Directors and the NSAC Professional Advisory Board during the 1977 annual meeting in Orlando, Florida.

Appendix A contains the definition as adopted by both the NSAC Professional Advisory Board and the National Board. We must stress that it contains the qualification that it is a working definition and will be modified as indicated by the results of future research.

The NSAC definition obviously can be of help to researchers, clinicians, and administrators. Researchers have long been hampered in comparing data by the lack of behavioral guidelines for defining patient populations and subgroups. It is hoped that the NSAC definition will mitigate this problem, though obviously it cannot be eliminated until a biological marker or markers are identified that are etiologically or pathologically associated with specific symptoms. Obviously there are other benefits for researchers, but they are beyond the scope of this discussion.

From the clinicians' viewpoint, the definition's chief advantage lies in the fact that it can aid in the differential diagnostic process. Identifying the syndrome of autism, or establishing its coexistence with other syndromes (mental retardation, epilepsy), and being able to monitor behavioral changes are obvious first steps in providing long-term medical management.

Third, from an administrative point of view, the NSAC definition can prove invaluable to child psychiatrists when called upon to provide an "expert opinion" or "current consensus" as to what is the syndrome of autism. The arenas for such questions are varied and range from federal, state, and local governments, to community mental health planning committees, local school districts, and parent groups. For such uses, the NSAC Board requested a version of the definition in nontechnical language which could be easily understood by sophisticated, but not medically trained, individuals. This appears in Appendix B.

The NSAC Professional Advisory Board was fully aware of the DSM III Committee's mandate and deliberations when drafting its definition (American Psychiatric Association, 1978). If the DSM III definition had been completed, it undoubtedly would have been recommended by the NSAC Professional Advisory Board for adoption by the NSAC Board of Directors. Unfortunately, however, for reasons previously elaborated, the NSAC Board requested a revised definition in early 1976 and the Projected DSM III completion date at that time was 1978 or 1979. When it does appear, however, it is most likely that the two definitions will overlap in the main and thus serve a complementary purpose.

Ritvo, E.R., & Freeman, B. J. (1981). Current research on the Syndrome of autism. In G.E. Gilliam (Ed.), Autism: Diagnosis instruction, management, & Research (pp. 5-16). Springfield, IL: Charles C. Thomas.

APPENDIX A

National Society for Autistic Children
Definition of the Syndrome of Autism

I. Essential features: Autism is a behaviorally defined syndrome. The essential features are typically manifested prior to 30 months of age and include disturbances of: (1) developmental rates and/or sequences; (2) responses to sensory stimuli; (3) speech, language, and cognitive capacities; and (4) capacities to relate to people, events, and objects.

(1) Disturbances of developmental rates and sequences. Normal coordination of the three developmental pathways (motor, social-adaptive, cognitive) is disrupted. Delays, arrests, and/or regressions occur among or within one or more of the pathways: (a) within the motor pathway: for example, gross motor milestones may be normal, while fine motor milestones are delayed; (b) between pathways: for example, motor milestones may be normal, while social-adaptive and cognitive are delayed; (c) arrests, delays, and regression: for example, motor development may be normal until age 2 when walking stops; some cognitive skills may develop at expected times, while others are delayed or absent; imitative behavior and/or speech may be delayed in onset until age 3, followed by rapid acquisition to expected developmental level.

(2) Disturbances of responses to sensory stimuli. There may be generalized hyperreactivity or hyporeactivity and alternation of these two states over periods ranging from hours to months. For example, (a) visual symptoms: these may be close scrutiny of visual details, apparent nonuse of eye contact, staring, prolonged regarding of hands or objects, attention to changing levels of illumination; (b) auditory symptoms: these may be close attention to self-induced sounds, nonresponse or overresponse to varying levels of sound; (c) tactile symptoms: these may be over- or underresponse to touch, pain, and temperatures, prolonged rubbing of surfaces, and sensitivity to food textures; (d) vestibular symptoms: these may be over- or

underreactions to gravity stimuli, whirling without dizziness, and preoccupation with spinning objects; (e) olfactory and gustatory symptoms: these may be repetitive sniffing, specific food preferences, and licking of inedible objects; (f) proprioceptive symptoms: these may be posturing darting-lunging movements, hand flapping, gesticulations, and grimaces.

(3) Disturbances of speech, language-cognition, and non-verbal communication. Symptoms may include: (a) speech: for example, mutism, delayed onset, immature syntax and articulation, modulated but immature inflections; (b) language-cognition: for example, absent or limited symbolic capacity, specific cognitive capacities such as rote memory and visual-spatial relations intact with failure to develop the use of abstract terms, concepts, and reasoning; immediate delayed negative echolalia with or without communicative intent; nonlogical use of concepts; neologisms; (c) nonverbal communication: for example, absence or delayed development of appropriate gestures, dissociation of gestures from language, and failure to assign symbolic meaning to gestures.

(4) Disturbances of the capacity to relate appropriately to people, events, and objects, manifested by failure to develop appropriate responsivity to people and assignment of appropriate symbolic meaning to objects. For example, (a) people: absence, arrests, and/or delays of smiling response, stranger anxiety, anticipatory response to gestures, playing "peek-a-boo," playing "patty-cake," and waving "bye-bye," reciprocal use of eye contact and facial responsivity, and appropriate reciprocal responsiveness to physical contact; failure to develop a relationship with significant caretakers or excessive reliance on caretakers. For example, caretakers may be treated indifferently, interchangeably, with only mechanical clinging, or with panic on separation. Cooperative play and friendships (usually appearing between 2 and 4) may not develop. Expected responses to adults and peers (usually appearing between 5 and 7) may develop, but are superficial,

immature, and only in response to strong social cues; (b) objects: absent, arrested, and/or delayed capacities to utilize objects and/or toys in an age-appropriate manner and/or to assign them symbolic and/or thematic meaning. Objects are often used in idiosyncratic, stereotypic and/or perseverative ways. Interference with this use of objects often results in expressions of discomfort and/or panic; (c) events: there may be a particular awareness of the sequence of events and disruption of this sequence may result in expressions of discomfort and/or panic.

II. Associated features: Associated clinical features vary with age and include other disturbances of thought, mood, and behavior. Mood may be labile; crying may be unexplained or inconsolable; there may be giggling or laughing without identifiable stimuli. Delusions and hallucinatory experiences have been reported. There may be a lack of appreciation of real dangers, such as moving vehicles and heights as well as inappropriate fears. Self-injurious behavior, such as hair pulling and hitting or biting parts of the body, may be present, and stereotypic and repetitive movements of limbs or the entire body are common.

Current research estimates are that approximately 60% of autistic children have measured IQ's below 50; 20% between 50 and 70, and 20% of 70 or more. The majority show extreme variability of intellectual functioning on formal IQ testing. They perform poorest on tasks requiring abstract thought, symbolism, or sequential logic, and best on those assessing manipulative or visual-spatial skills and rote memory.

Recent studies indicate that the incidence of EEG abnormalities increases with age, as does the possible onset of seizures.

III. Impairment: The syndrome is severely incapacitating. Periodic medical, neurological, psychological, educational, and behavioral reassessments are necessary. One must monitor the course of the syndrome to keep treatment planning apace with physiological and behavioral changes. Special educational facilities are almost always required. Behaviorally structured, functional, individualized programs have been demonstrated to be most helpful. Counseling families regarding total living planning is often desirable. Individual supportive psychotherapy and symptomatically targeted pharmacological therapy may enhance social-adaptive functioning in selected persons. The severe form of the syndrome may include the most extreme forms of self-injurious, repetitive, highly unusual and aggressive behaviors. Such behaviors may be persistent and highly resistant to change, often requiring unique management, treatment, or teaching strategies.

IV. Age of onset: The exact age of onset is unknown, but symptoms have been reported and observed during the first months of life. Families may be unaware of early symptoms until the child fails to pass major developmental milestones (i.e., onset of walking, speech, socialization with peers). They may then date the onset of the syndrome to these missed milestones, whereas careful history taking may reveal that subtle symptoms were present earlier.

V. Etiology: The symptoms are best explained as expressive of a physical dysfunction within the central nervous system (CNS) — the exact nature and type of which has yet to be determined. This physical dysfunction of the CNS occurs independently or in association with other disorders which directly affect the central nervous system (i.e., maternal rubella, PKU, Down's syndrome, epilepsy). In such cases, the diagnosis of autism is made on Axis One, and the coexisting organic condition coded on Axis Three.

VI. Incidence and sex ratio: The syndrome has been identified in all parts of the world. It is very rare, with an incidence of approximately 4 to 5 per 10,000 births. It is found four to five times more commonly in males.

VII. Complications: Major complications are self-induced physical injuries, infections related to improper hygiene, dental problems related to persistent bruxism, and physical injuries due to inadvertent exposures.

VIII. Differential diagnosis:

(1) Mental retardation, etiology unknown and known. Here, developmental delays usually occur in all areas, and developmental sequences (motor, social, and cognitive) remain coordinated. Responses to sensory inputs, people and objects, and speech and language development are

appropriate to the overall developmental level of cognitive functioning.

(2) Specific sensory deficits (e.g. deafness, blindness). Here compensatory behaviors may be confused with symptoms indicative of autism: e.g., hyperreactivity to auditory, proprioceptive and tactile stimuli in blind children (i.e., blindisms); hyperresponsivity to visual, proprioceptive (i.e., head shaking) and tactile stimuli in deaf children. When auditory and visual deficits are accompanied by mental retardation, speech, language, and the ability to relate to people and objects are appropriate to the overall developmental level of cognitive functioning.

(3) Congenital, developmental, and acquired disorders of central processing of language (aphasias). Here disturbances in language development and central processing are not accompanied by disturbances of responses to sensory inputs, dissociation of other developmental courses (motor, social), relatedness to people and objects. Aphasics may imitate and use gestures and other means to communicate symbolic content. If these disorders are accompanied by mental retardation, then it must be assessed independently of the disturbances of central processing of language.

(4) Sequelae of physical or psychological trauma (e.g., syndromes previously described as hospitalism, maternal deprivation, anaclitic depression, sequelae of a chronically traumatizing environment). Here syndromes include failure to thrive, infantile apathy and withdrawal, physical illnesses secondary to malnutrition or toxin ingestions and physical abuse, specific psychological fixations (psychogenic psychoses, severe neuroses, pathological character development), and all degrees of mental retardation. The patterns of symptoms and developmental delays are specific to the syndromes described, are related to specific etiologic factors in psychological and social environments, and respond to specific therapies if instituted before permanent changes have resulted.

(5) Schizophrenia, childhood type. Here, the disorder is char-

acterized by the presence of a thought disorder. Certain persons with the syndrome of autism also may fit the criteria for childhood schizophrenia, particularly at a later age (ages 5 to 12). In this case, both diagnoses should be listed so that subsequent researchers can objectively test the two main hypotheses regarding the relationship between these two syndromes, i.e., autism is the earliest form of schizophrenia as manifested in late childhood or early adulthood or that autism and schizophrenia are distinct syndromes with different etiologies, family histories, and courses.

(6) Degenerative organic brain syndromes (e.g., Schilder's disease, Heller's syndrome) with or without mental retardation. Here the clinical course is characterized by progressive regressions in all or some areas of development (motor, social-adaptive, and cognitive). In the early stages, these regressions may mimic symptoms indicative of autism but are distinguishable by their relatively specific times of onset, characteristic signs and symptoms on neurological, psychological, and cognitive testing, and unremitting deteriorating course.

IX. Predisposing factors: None known.

X. Family factors: None known. The syndrome has been identified in all parts of the world. Recent studies have revealed no correlation between autism and parental psychopathology.

XI. Operational criteria: A, B, C, D, and E are required.

A. Signs and symptoms present prior to 30 months of age.
B. Disturbances of developmental rate and/or sequences.
C. Disturbances of responsiveness to sensory stimuli.
D. Disturbances of speech, language, and cognitive capacities.
E. Disturbances in relating to people, events and objects.

APPENDIX B

A Short Definition of Autism

Autism is a severely incapacitating lifelong developmental disability which typically appears during the first three years of life. It occurs in approximately 5 out of every 10,000 births and is four times more common in boys than girls. It has been found throughout the world in families of all racial, ethnic, and social backgrounds. No known factors in the psychological environment of a child have been shown to cause autism.

The symptoms are caused by physical disorders of the brain. They must be documented by history or present on examination. They include:

(1) Disturbances in the rate of appearance of physical, social, and language skills.

(2) Abnormal responses to sensations. Any one or a combination of sight, hearing, touch, pain, balance, smell, taste, and the way a child holds his body are affected.

(3) Speech and language are absent or delayed, while specific thinking capabilities may be present. Immature rhythms of speech, limited understanding of ideas, and the use of words without attaching the usual meaning to them are common.

(4) Abnormal ways of relating to people, objects, and events. Typically, they do not respond appropriately to adults and other children. Objects and toys are not used as normally intended.

Autism occurs by itself or in association with other disorders which affect the function of the brain such as viral infections, metabolic disturbances, and epilepsy.

On IQ testing, approximately 60% have scores below 50, 20% between 50 and 70, and only 20% greater than 70. Most show wide variations of performance on different tests and at different times.

Autistic people live a normal life-span. Since symptoms change, and some may disappear with age, periodic reevaluations are necessary to respond to changing needs.

The severe form of the syndrome may include the most extreme forms of self-injurious, repetitive, highly unusual, and aggressive behaviors. Such behaviors may be persistent and highly resistant to change, often requiring unique management, treatment, or teaching strategies.

Special educational programs using behavioral methods and designed for specific individuals have proven most helpful.

Supportive counseling may be helpful for families with autistic members, as it is for families who have members with other severe lifelong disabilities. Medication to decrease specific symptoms may help certain autistic people live more satisfactory lives.

Notes to Appendices:

1. Adopted by the Board of Directors of the National Society for Autistic Children, Inc., June 27, 1977.

2. These are working definitions. They will be altered as indicated by the results of ongoing research.

REFERENCES

American Psychiatric Association: *Diagnostic and Statistical Manual of Mental Disorders (DSM) III,* draft version. Task Force on Nomenclature and Statistics, 1978.

Kanner, L.: Autistic disturbances of affective contact. *Nerv Child 2:*217-250, 1943.

Ornitz, E. M. and Ritvo, E. R.: The syndrome of autism: a critical review. *Am J Psychiatry, 133:*609-621, 1976

Ritvo, E. R.: Autism: From adjective to noun. In Ritvo, E. R. (Ed.): *Autism: Diagnosis, Current Research and Management.* New York, Spectrum 1976, pp. 3-7.

Chapter 2

THE SYNDROME OF AUTISM
A Critical Review of Diagnostic Systems, Follow-up Studies, and the Theoretical Background of the Behavior Observation Scale*

B. J. Freeman and Edward R. Ritvo

CRITICAL REVIEW OF PRIOR CLINICAL DIAGNOSTIC SYSTEMS

WHEN EARLY INFANTILE AUTISM was first described by Kanner (1943), he proposed the following diagnostic criteria: (1) onset before age two; (2) presence of selected age-appropriate intellectual abilities; (3) preference for extreme "self-isolation" or "aloneness"; and (4) obsessive insistence on the preservation of "sameness" in the environment. He further postulated (Kanner, 1943) that the primary disturbance of autism was an inability to relate to people and objects in the environment. Despite providing rich clinical descriptions, he never attempted to develop an objectively based diagnostic system and other investigators soon added their clinically based categorizations to the literature.

Rank (1955) describes an apparently similar group of children as having "atypical development." She notes that their outstanding symptoms were "withdrawal from people, retreat into a world of fantasy, mutism or the use of language for autistic purposes, bizarre posturing, seemingly meaningless stereotyped

Supported by MH29248 awarded to senior author and Maternal and Child Health Project #927 and MH30897 awarded to Peter Tanguay, M.D. for Clinical Resource Center for the study of childhood psychosis. Computing was done at the Health Sciences Computer Facility, UCLA.
* This chapter is also published in *Autism and Severe Childhood Psychopathology*, Karroly Steffen, Editor, N.Y., Gardner Press, 1981.

17

gestures, impassivity or violent outbursts of anxiety and rage, identification with objects or animals, and excessively inhibited or uninhibited expression of impulses. . . . (Other) features common to all are lack of contact with reality, little or no communication with others and lack of uniformity (fragmentation) of ego development" (Rank, 1955). She also includes extremes of activity and passivity, ritualistic mannerisms, and lack of eye contact.

Mahler (1952) coins the term *symbiotic psychosis* to categorize another group of children for whom she tested the following clinical criteria: (1) Deviant behavior may or may not be present in the first year of life. If it is present, it usually is manifested as a sleep disturbance. (2) At ages one and two, the child may have difficulty separating from mother. (3) By ages two through three and one-half, there is separation anxiety and affective panic reaction. (4) The child's body feels like it is denying boundaries and melting into one's own. (5) Child focuses on parts of his body excessively. (6) Child attempts restitution of oneness with the mother through delusions and hallucinatory behavior. (7) Child attempts to maintain and control presence of person he is attached to through the manipulation of sameness of the environment, tantrums, and anxiety. (8) They are impulse ridden. Mahler (1961) postulates that the major causal factor in infantile psychosis is a breakdown in communication between the mother and infant.

Bender (1942) also clinically describes a similar group of children, but labels them "childhood schizophrenics." She notes that they "revealed pathology at every level and in every field of integration within the functioning of the central nervous system, be this vegetative, motor, perceptive, intellectual, emotional or social" (pp. 138-140). She utilized for diagnosis the presence of primitive levels of CNS organization, immature cognitive abnormalities, and disorders of perception and body image. She also stresses that the age of onset is important and uses it to divide the syndrome into three groups: (1) The "pseudo-defective type" appearing within the first three years of childhood (this group is most similar to patients labeled autistic by others); (2) "pseudo-neurotic type" appearing in middle childhood; and (3) "pseudo-psychopathic type" commencing just prior to adolescence.

Bender's view of the relationship of schizophrenia and autism was not shared by Eisenberg and Kanner (1957) who postulate that they are distinctly separate syndromes. They argued that differing parental psychopathology, frequency of psychosis in parents, and the failure of most autistic children to develop typical schizophrenic symptoms in later life is evidence for this distinction.

Eisenberg and Kanner (1956) refined their diagnostic criteria for autism in 1956 to state that two symptoms must be present to indicate the diagnosis: extreme self-isolation and the obsessive insistence on the preservation of sameness. They felt that language disturbances were secondary to problems of relating and thus were not part of the necessary criteria. However, good intellectual potential and age of onset remain delineating criteria. The age at which symptoms could emerge was expanded to include the first two years and Eisenberg (1966) later specifically excludes from the diagnosis those children who demonstrate specific CNS pathology.

Anthony (1958), working within a psychoanalytic framework, delineates two types of autism — primary and secondary — each a subtype of childhood psychosis. He characterizes primary autism by an "early onset with little or no upheaval." On the other hand, he postulates that secondary autism is characterized by a withdrawal response to a "turbulent" event that occurred after a period of normal development. Anthony's primary groups were similar to those described by Kanner (1943) and did not exclude children with evidence of specific organic brain dysfunction.

Goldfarb (1961; 1964) uses the term *childhood schizophrenia* and identifies two categories, organic and nonorganic. His diagnostic criteria were not objectively defined but included the following: (1) impaired relationships; (2) disturbances in personal identity; (3) resistance to change; (4) marked anxiety; (5) perceptual difficulties; (6) communication problems; (7) bizarre motility; (8) unusual preoccupations; and (9) sometimes severe intellectual retardation. He does not specify which of these symptoms were necessary to receive the diagnosis; however, symptoms one, three, five, six, seven, eight, and nine are the ones often seen in children labeled autistic by other investigators.

Creak et al. (1961) summarize the conclusions of a meeting of the British Working Party (BWP). This was a group of pediatricians and psychiatrists trained to hopefully clarify the confusion then present amongst investigators. Their work resulted in a list of nine diagnostic points to be used to establish the diagnosis of "schizophrenic children." The points as abstracted by Werry (1971) follow: (1) gross and sustained impairment of relationships with people; (2) apparent unawareness of his own personal identity to a degree which is inappropriate for his age; (3) pathological preoccupations with particular objects or certain characteristics of them, without regard to their accepted functions; (4) sustained resistance to change in the environment and a striving to maintain or restore sameness; (5) abnormal perceptual experience (in the absence of discernible organic abnormality); (6) acute, excessive, and seemingly illogical anxiety as a frequent phenomenon; (7) speech either lost, or never acquired, or showing failure to develop beyond a level appropriate at an earlier age; (8) distortion of motility patterns; (9) a background of serious retardation in which islets of normal, near normal, or exceptional intellectual function or skill may appear.

Of these points, the first, impairment of relationships with people and the ninth, retardation with islands of normal functioning were considered the primary symptoms. They are consistent with the criteria Eisenberg and Kanner (1956) established for diagnosing autism.

The nine points developed by the British Working Party became increasingly accepted as a basis for diagnosis of "childhood psychosis" during the 1960s and were incorporated into the classification of childhood psychiatric disorders by the Group for the Advancement of Psychiatry (GAP) in 1966. This occurred despite the fact that the British Working Party adopted the term "schizophrenic syndromes of childhood," which was antithetical to then current thinking (Werry, 1971). The GAP classification also differentiates the psychosis of infancy and early childhood from psychosis of later childhood. The psychoses of infancy and early childhood are further subdivided into (1) early infantile autism, corresponding to Kanner's syndrome; (2) interactional psychosis, incorporating Mahler's symbiotic psychosis; and (3) other psychoses, in which were clinical syndromes that did not exactly fit the other subtypes. Psychoses of later childhood are divided into two groups: (1) schizophrenia and (2) other psychoses of later childhood. In contrast to the BWP point of view, but consistent with Eisenberg's (1966), the presence of chronic brain syndromes or mental retardation precluded the diagnosis of childhood psychosis.

In 1965, Rutter reviewed the BWP's nine points. He points out that, while clinicians differed in the emphasis placed on each point, there was at that time general agreement regarding the symptoms needed to establish a diagnosis of autism. He conceives of autism, or "child psychosis," as a relatively rare condition, present at birth or developing within the first few years of life, in which the most striking abnormality is a severe and lasting impairment of emotional relationships. In most, but not all children, there is a background of intellectual retardation, sometimes associated with so-called islets of normal intelligence. Nearly all of the children have severe communication abnormalities and about half never develop any useful speech. Morbid preoccupation with particular objects or activities, obsessional characteristics, a sustained resistance to change in the environment, hyperkinesis, and peculiar ritualistic mannerisms are also often a part of the clinical picture. Apparent failure to react to sounds and also hypersensitivity to sounds are noted. Aggressive and self-injurious behavior and eating and sleeping disturbances frequently occur. In addition, Rutter points out that "psychotic children" may or may not have evidence of specific organic brain pathology.

Rutter (1966) and Rutter and Lockyer (1967) criticized the nine points of the BWP as being highly inferential, having overlapping items, and failing to specify how many of the nine points were necessary to establish the diagnosis. They retrospectively compared case histories of sixty-three "psychotic" children to those of a group of children with emotional and behavioral problems. They used a checklist of symptoms covering the areas of relationships, speech, compulsions, motor phenomena, concentration, self-injury, response to pain, and behavior problems. Generally, these items were vague, undefined and global, and of apparent unchecked reliability (Werry, 1971). Even though the checklist differed somewhat from the nine points, all were covered. They concluded that twenty-two of thirty-four items significantly differentiated psychotic from nonpsychotic children, no symptom occurred exclusively in the psychotic group, and only two (abnormal relationships and speech retardation) occurred in all psychotic children. Methodological problems in Rutter's study include the fact that it was retrospective, it used records, there were questions as to the suitability of the control group, and unreliable definitions of symptoms were used. In spite of these problems, Rutter's study is important in that it represents one of the first attempts to establish objectively which symptoms are necessary to establish the diagnosis.

Another important series of studies were conducted by Menolascino (1965) and Eaton and Menolascino (1966). They reviewed, in detail, problems with diagnostic systems and reported a study of 616 children. The children ranged in age from infancy to eight years and had been referred for evaluation because of suspected mental retardation. Of these they noted that thirty-two (5.2%) displayed psychotic symptoms. Two could be diagnosed as autistic using the criteria of Kanner (1943); six as having childhood schizophrenia using the criteria of the BWP, Creak (1963), and Despert and Sherwin (1958); and twenty-four as having chronic brain syndromes with psychosis as defined by Ingram (1963) and Kucera (1961). These studies are particularly important because they clearly demonstrate the important and often confusing role diagnosis of mental retardation plays. Eaton and Menolascino (1966) also provide some guidelines for interpreting medical, psychiatric, psychological, and behavioral test results in relation to differentiating children with just mental retardation from those with childhood psychoses and mental retardation.

Eisenberg (1966) addresses issues that arise when the medical model of etiological classification is applied to childhood psychoses. He further subdivided the organic group according to cause, e.g. toxic or metabolic psychoses. The main problem with this classification system centered around the inadequacies of scientific methods available to determine whether or not tissue pathology actually existed.

In 1968, Ornitz and Ritvo (1968) reviewed the literature to date and summarized, from a developmental point of view, the symptoms that were used to describe autistic children. They conceive of autism as a specific syndrome of abnormal development that can be defined by observable behavior patterns that occurred as clusters of symptoms in the following areas: (1) perceptual integration, (2) motility patterns, (3) capacity to relate, (4) language, and (5) developmental rate. This work was a landmark in providing the basis for a developmentally based descriptive analysis of the syndrome. This approach to diagnosis was based on the assumption that many symptoms occurring together comprised the syndrome, and that no one symptom alone or list of symptoms occurring together comprised the syndrome, and that no one symptom or list of symptoms could define the disease. They also postulate that a perceptual abnormality due to faulty modulation of sensory inputs within the brain was primary. In spite of detailed listing of symptoms and clusters of symptoms, they provide no objective method for determining whether or not a symptom is present in any individual case.

In contrast to Ornitz and Ritvo (1968), Wing (1966) analyzes the visual and auditory abnormalities that occur in autism and concludes that disturbed language functions were primary. Later, Wing and Wing (1971) concluded that while language problems are prominent, the following abnormalities also occur in autism: (1) visual perceptual problems, including a tendency to use peripheral rather than central vision and a preference for exploring objects by means of touch, taste, and smell and engaging in stereotyped movements; (2) difficulties in copying skilled movements; (3) a paradoxical combination of hypersensitivity and hyposensitivity of auditory, visual, and tactile input. These investigators concluded, as did Ornitz and Ritvo (1968), that autistic children must be described in terms of cluster impairments.

In 1970, Ward reviewed the literature to date on diagnosis,

etiology, and treatment. He reached two conclusions: first, there was a general state of confusion in the literature; second, many subjects labeled *autistic* had significant amounts of organic pathology. He then proposed the following diagnostic criteria: (1) lack of object relations; (2) lack of use of speech for communication; (3) maintenance of sameness in stereotypic behavior; and (4) lack of neurologic dysfunction.

These criteria, ruling out children with apparent neurologic dysfunction, were consistent with those previously proposed by Eisenberg (1966), but not with those of some others, e.g. Creak et al., 1963; Ornitz and Ritvo, 1968. Thus, the question of whether or not children with known organic and/or neurologic dysfunction should be labeled autistic remained a point of controversy.

In 1971, Kolvin addressed the problems of establishing objective operational diagnostic criteria. After reviewing the literature, he suggests that three groups of psychoses in childhood could be distinguished by the ages of onset: under three years (IP — Infantile Psychosis), three to five years, and over five years (LOP — Late Onset Psychosis). He then proposes diagnostic criteria for the Infantile Psychosis and Late Onset Psychosis groups.

The criteria for Infantile Psychosis (IP) were based on the work of Kanner (1943) and Creak (1963). Specifically they were the following: (1) age of onset before the age of three years; (2) a self-isolating pattern of social behavior; and (3) at least one of the following: (a) catastrophic reactions to environmental changes, particularly of a topographical variety, (b) gross stereotypes either of a global class such as headbanging, pirouetting, or rocking, or of the idiosyncratic type, such as finger flicking, specific motor patterns, and self-stimulation.

The criteria of Late Onset Psychosis (LOP) were based on those established for adult schizophrenia. Specifically, they were the following: (1) onset during the main school period of five to fifteen; (2) adult schizophrenic symptoms of the first rank (Schneider, 1942); and (3) other adult schizophrenic symptoms in the areas of affect, motility, and volition. Kolvin pointed out that in making the diagnosis of LOP, allowances have to be made for language limitation or limited ability for complex abstractions.

Kolvin, Ounstead, Humphrey, and McNay (1971) describe the clinical picture of the two above mentioned groups of children and report that the two syndromes have different courses. Furthermore, if examined in detail, factors other than age of onset could be used to discriminate between the two groups. Kolvin and his associates did not characterize psychotic children with onsets between three and five years because of this low incidence.

Kanner (1971a) reviews briefly the history of the syndrome of autism. While he notes that there was still much confusion over terminology, he offers no new guidelines for diagnosis.

In 1971, Rutter published an important theoretical paper entitled "Childhood Schizophrenia Reconsidered." In it he lucidly describes the problems that exist regarding diagnosis and confusion over the terms *childhood schizophrenia* and *autism*. He proposes that the term *childhood schizophrenia* has outlived its usefulness. Since children with schizophrenia have many of the same symptoms as adults with schizophrenia, they should simply be labeled as *schizophrenics*. In addition, he proposes two other subgroups of Childhood Psychosis — Autism and Psychosis, Other.

Rutter objects to the use of just an etiological model to classify psychotic children. Rather, he suggests a multiaxial approach. Earlier, Rutter, Lebovici, Eisenberg, Sneznovski, Sadoun, Brooke, and Lin (1969) reported the results of the World Health Organization (WHO) Seminar on Psychiatric Disorders in the age group three to twelve years. This WHO Seminar proposed a four axes approach. The first axis was the clinical psychiatric syndrome; the second, intellectual level; the third, etiological or biological factors; and the fourth, associated or etiological psychosocial factors. Rutter, Shaffer, and Sheperd (1973) applied the schema in a clinical setting and found a clear preference for it expressed by clinicians. In spite of the potential usefulness of a multiaxial approach in classifying psychoses, it is not by itself an objective diagnostic tool, and no guidelines for how subdivisions along each axis are to be made have been provided. However, it does provide much useful clinical information and takes into account the important problems of age of onset and presence or absence of known organic brain syndrome.

Eisenberg addressed again the issue of classification in 1972. While agreeing with Rutter that a multiaxial approach to the problem was the best solution, he disagreed concerning the need for an etiologically based classification. He also reiterated his position that the diagnosis of infantile autism should not be given to children with clearly identifiable cerebral pathology.

Chess (1972), in an editorial for the *Journal of Autism and Childhood Schizophrenia,* discusses the problem of differential diagnosis of the childhood psychopathologies. She points out, as did Rutter and Eisenberg, that it is unlikely that a one-to-one relationship between a syndrome and a single etiologic agent exists. Rather, at this state of its development, child psychiatry and psychology face a two-fold challenge: (1) to develop data and techniques of analysis that can separate etiologies that produce similar symptoms and, (2) to develop ways of relating apparently dissimilar symptoms to a common etiology in certain disorders. In the case of autism, this challenge cannot be met until an objective schema for describing the syndrome is developed.

Call (1974) also discusses the problem of differential diagnosis in young children. He is particularly concerned with early symptom formation (under two years) and how it contrasts with normal development. He presents a detailed table of the differential diagnosis of developmental disabilities in infancy. He then reviews developmentally the symptoms of autism one should look for from birth until age two years. While not concerned with providing objective criteria for diagnosis, his work is extremely important because he points out the importance of diagnosing within a developmental framework. What is needed is an objective descriptive schema that can be applied within the developmental framework to the problem of the differential diagnosis of autism and other severe psychopathologies of childhood.

Ornitz and Ritvo (1976) recently reviewed the clinical features and behavioral characteristics of autism, problems of differential diagnosis of the syndrome, clinical, neurophysiological and biochemical research, and the medical management and treatment of the syndrome. These authors present a particularly lucid review of the problem of differential diagnosis and the confusion that exists over terminology. They define autism much as they did in their earlier work (Ornitz and Ritvo, 1968) and still consider it to be a behaviorally based syndrome. While providing detailed descriptions of symptoms and many references to the clinical literature, as in their earlier work, they failed to provide objective means by which to establish the diagnosis.

In 1977, the National Society for Autistic Citizens adopted a formal "Definition of the Syndrome of Autism" (Ritvo and Freeman 1978a, b, c). This definition provides a detailed clinical description of the syndrome and establishes the following necessary criteria as sufficient and necessary for making the diagnosis: (a) signs and symptoms present prior to thirty months of age; (b) characteristic disturbances of developmental rate and/or sequences; (c) characteristic disturbances of responsiveness to sensory stimuli; (d) disturbances of speech, language, and cognitive capacities; and (e) characteristic disturbance of relating to people, events, and objects.

Accompanying this definition is a discussion of the problem of differential diagnosis. The authors stress that autism may coexist with other developmental disabilities — e.g. mental retardation, major sensory deficits, congenital developmental and acquired disorders of the central processing of language, epilepsy, sequelae of physical and psychological trauma — and that the diagnosis is not meant to be mutually exclusive of other conditions.

CRITICAL REVIEW OF PRIOR BEHAVIOR CHECKLISTS AND RATING SCALES

A first attempt at establishing a checklist was made by Polan and Spencer (1959). They described five case histories of autistics and abstracted a checklist of symptoms. The symptoms were grouped as follows: (1) language distortion; (2) social withdrawal; (3) lack of integration; (4) obsessiveness, and (5) family characteristics. Objective definitions were not provided, nor were criteria for determining which symptoms were necessary and sufficient for establishing the diagnosis. In reality, what was presented as a checklist was but a detailed clinical description of the syndrome similar to that provided by Creak et al. (1961).

In a series of papers, Barbara Fish (Fish, 1957; 1960; Fish & Shapiro, 1965; Fish, Shapiro, Campbell & Wile, 1968) attempts to objectify Bender's diagnostic criteria. She employs a standard psychiatric examination of apparently adequate interobserver reliability that focuses on (1) relationship to examiner, peers, and environment; (2) speech; (3) affect; (4) motility; and (5) adaptive functioning. Of special interest were irregularities in development. In her classification, Fish employs a two-dimensional system. The first dimension, a qualitative one, is clinically similar to Bender's three categories of pseudodefective, pseudoneurotic, and pseudopsychopathic. The second dimension is quantitative and includes rating scales for severity. These scales are important in the history of describing childhood schizophrenia because she addresses herself to the question of severity. However, she fails to provide adequate objective definitions of symptoms and how they are to be rated.

Wolf and Chess (1964) also address the issue of providing a means of assessing the severity of the syndrome. However, they offer no concrete solutions.

In 1964, Rimland published a diagnostic questionnaire (Form E-1) that included seventy-six questions on such topics as the child's birth history, speech characteristics, and age of onset of symptoms. It was designed to be answered by the parents and was intended for children up to about seven years of age. However, replies from parents indicate that the most profound behavioral changes occurred prior to five-and-one-half years of age and Form E-2 was developed to collect data prior to age five-and-one-half. Form E-2 consists of eighty questions that request information on social interactions, affect, speech, manipulative ability, intelligence, reaction to sensory stimuli, family characteritics, illness, development, and physiological data.

A score was obtained on Form E-2 by allowing one plus point for each question defined to be characteristic of autism and one minus point for each question answered as defined to be non-autistic. The child's total score is the mathematical sum of his autism (+) and non-autism (−) scores. A cutoff score of + 20 was proposed for establishing the diagnosis of autism.

Rimland (1971) reports data on 2,218 questionnaires. The checklist shows 9.7 percent of the children to have autism, i.e. scores of + 20 or better. He takes this as confirmation of Kanner's (1962) estimate that only 10 percent of patients called autistic by others were correctly diagnosed.

Rimland's diagnostic checklist suffers from several methodological problems. First, it relies on parental report of symptoms and does not incorporate observations of the children. Second, it does not provide objective definitions of behaviors the parents rate. Third, the scoring key that would allow other investigators to use it scientifically has not been published. Fourth, it only differentiates autistic from nonautistic children and does not really provide a precise description of the non-autistic children. Finally, and most importantly, it begins with a priori definition of the syndrome rather than letting the data divide the children into different categories. Master and Miller (1970) provide a detailed critique of these methodological problems.

In 1975, Prior, Boullin, Gajzago, and Perry attempted to devise a rating system based on amount and type of symptomatology reported. These investigators applied multivariant analysis techniques to derive a numerical taxonomy based on responses to items on Form E-2. Data on 162 children ranging in age from three-and-one-half to thirteen years were analyzed. Inclusion in their sample was based on the following criteria: (1) an independent diagnostic label of any of the childhood psychoses or referral to an institution or therapy milieu specifically designed for treatment of these children; (2) no definite evidence of gross neurological signs on history; (3) no evidence of major sensory handicaps; (4) maximum age of thirteen years at the time of referral; and (5) satisfactory completion of diagnostic checklist by parents.

The authors made two modifications in the eighty-item checklist. First, twelve items were eliminated entirely from the data analysis on one or more of the following grounds: (1) the responses were not relevant to diagnosis, e.g. age or sex of child, or (2) reliability was extremely doubtful, or (3) the item had no known relevance to a diagnosis of childhood psychosis, e.g. reports of whether child was "attractive" or "looked intelligent."

These investigators report that their taxonomic analysis distinguished two classes of children in terms of age of onset. The more severely impaired had an onset before two years (Class 1) and had a homogeneous set of symptoms. In Class 2, there were wider variations in symptomatology and in the majority of cases some "normal" development was reported prior to the onset of the disorder. Class 1 included all children diagnosed as autistic on the E-2 plus others with similar symptoms that would fall outside of "pure Kanner's Syndrome" as defined by the Rimland method. The authors conclude that their data would tend to support a system of classification in childhood psychoses based on age of onset. However, they point out that the data do not preclude classification on the basis of other variables as well, e.g. organic signs.

This study is important in examining the problem of differential diagnosis because it makes use of highly sophisticated statistical techniques. However, the results of the study must be viewed as tentative since the E-2, with all of its accompanying methodological problems, served as the source of raw data. It is not surprising that the diagnostic groups did not entirely correlate with those predicted from the E-2, since the investigators eliminated and/or modified some of the terms. In fact, this supports the criticism mentioned above that the E-2 is not really an objective assessment tool since it cannot be separated from Rimland's theoretical model. Furthermore, the authors may have eliminated questions that are in fact relevant to differential diagnosis and if left in, the analysis would have resulted in a better classification scheme.

In spite of these many problems, the statistical methodology described holds great promise for developing an objective classification system. Application of these techniques to data obtained by observing children directly and coding their behaviors objectively is needed.

Wing (1969) also uses a questionnaire that parents complete in order to compare the behavior of autistic children to that of children with disorders of sensory, perceptual, and executive functions. The results of this study showed that autistic children were multi-handicapped. They combined problems of comprehension and use of speech, hand right-left, up-down, and back-front disorientation similar to those found in the congenital aphasic syndromes, had abnormalities in the use of vision, difficulty in understanding gestures, abnormal bodily movements, and preference for the proximal senses as in congenitally deaf/blind children. These data have often been misinterpreted to mean that autistic children are similar to deaf/blind children. However, it has been shown that there is a high incidence of autism in children who are congenitally deaf and blind because of either rubella (Chess, 1971) or retrolental fibroplasia (Keeler, 1958). Thus, there is a high probability that at least some of the congenitally deaf/blind children in Wing's study also had autism. Wing's study is important in that she attempts to separate autistic symptoms from those of other developmental disabilities. However, as with Rimland's (1971) questionnaire, she relied on parents' reports and retrospective data and did not attempt to obtain information on the children's current clinical status.

Rendle-Short (1969) developed still another parental questionnaire. He subdivided the nine diagnostic points proposed by Creak et al. (1961) into fifty-four items that could be answered on a yes/no basis by parents. He then had parents of thirty-two normal children, twenty-five subnormal children, twenty-five deaf children, fifteen children with cerebral palsy and twenty-five autistic children complete the questionnaires. He states that the autistic children were diagnosed by "the criteria current at that time," but fails to describe this diagnosis further. The data were analyzed using numerical taxonomy methods and fourteen items of behavior were found to discriminate the autistic group from the other groups. In addition, the autistic group differed significantly from the non-autistic groups on these behaviors. The author proposed that if a child shows more than half of the behaviors, then the diagnosis of autism must be seriously considered. He points out, however, that additional data from a thorough clinical history and examination, careful assessment of family interpersonal relationships, psychological assessment using all relevant tests, EEG and urine amino acid tests would be necessary to confirm the diagnosis.

Rendle-Short also suggests a classification for autism. He proposes three groups: Group 1(a) is equivalent to the classic Kanner's Syndrome; 1(b) is made up of children whose symptoms appear in the first three years of life, after an "acute event"; Group 2 consists of children who show autistic symptoms secondary to gross mental retardation or in association with handicaps arising from an organic brain lesion; and Group 3 consists of children who present clinically as autistic, but whose behavior is related to specific psychological trauma without preceding abnormal behavior.

While Rendle-Short's classification system is open to the same criticism as those based on other parental questionnaires, his study is important because, as did Wing (1969), he recognized that behaviors considered to be unique to the syndrome of autism often resemble and may overlap with those found in other developmental disabilities. Furthermore, he recognized that a list of behaviors alone is not sufficient to make the diagnosis. Often, other information is needed. In our opinion, if this additional clinical, psychological, and family data were collected in a systematic manner and combined with direct objective observations of the child, then sophisticated computer analysis could be applied to all the data and diagnostic profiles generated. This technique could lead to objective differential diagnoses of the childhood psychoses.

DeMyer, Bryson and Churchill (1973) employed a semistructured parental interview to compare symptoms present during infancy to those of childhood. Their subjects were divided into four groups: (1) thirty-two normal children; (2) thirty-six emotionally "immature" children; (3) twenty-four childhood schizophrenics and (4) seventy autistics diagnosed using the criteria of DeMyer and Churchill. The parental interviews were taped, transcribed, and a symptom checklist devised. Symptoms were divided into the following areas: (1) relations to people and emotional expression; (2) response to sensory stimulation; (3) body use and motor development; (4) physiological problems; (5) intelligence; and (6) speech.

The following were the primary goals of the study: (1) to identify infantile symptoms that would predict childhood symptoms or symptom complexes; (2) to determine whether symptoms cited as diagnostic criteria would differentiate psychiatric and neurological groups; and (3) to determine whether clusters of children based on similar symptom patterns would provide more adequate diagnostic groupings.

The results could be summarized as follows: (1) within the autistic group, there were no differences between those with and without obvious brain damage. (2) The four groups were on a continuum of severity with normal infants and children exhibiting the fewest symptoms, followed by the emotionally immature, schizophrenic, and autistic children. (3) The chief qualitative differences among the four groups in childhood were the interpersonal relatedness and communication. (4) The two psychotic groups were more likely to be upset by environmental change and to exhibit more restricted interests than the two nonpsychotic groups. (5) The three pathological groups resembled each other most in having repetitive body uses, slow and awkward motor development, and lowered intelligence, the latter two of which were considered to be symptomatic of neurological dysfunction. (6) Some symptoms, including cuddliness, overplacidity, unusual response to sensory stimulation, repetitive body use and anxiety to environmental change, which had previously been used to differentiate autism from other groups, were found to be less useful than expected. (7) No infantile symptoms predicted the development of a specific childhood abnormality including autism. However, infantile symptoms could be used to predict normal or abnormal behavior in childhood. Further, an individual infantile symptom was more likely to continue into childhood than it was to cease. (8) Finally, while the cluster analysis of cases based on symptom frequency for infancy and childhood did yield six cluster groups, symptom overlap hindered clear definition of subgroups.

This study by DeMyer et al. has been reviewed in detail because it represents one of the first attempts to differentiate autistic children by using a diagnostic profile that covers several areas of development and should serve as a model for future studies. However, two methodological problems limit its usefulness. First, as the authors point out, retrospective data obtained from parents is not entirely reliable. Second, another control group of mentally retarded children is needed for comparison purposes.

In spite of these methodological problems, two of their results warrant further detailed investigation. First, the finding that no infant behaviors were found to be unique to psychosis is intriguing. Secondly, the symptomatic picture for autism may begin to change earlier than the often cited five years of age (Rimland, 1964). DeMyer et al. report changes in the symptoms of 69 percent of their sample, all of whom were under five-and-one-half years of age at the time of evaluation.

Recently, Ornitz, Guthrie, and Farley (1977) compared parental responses to questions on development in autistic and normal children. A detailed questionnaire containing highly specific responses about the early motor, speech, language, and perceptual development of their children was completed by the parents of seventy-four autistic and thirty-eight normal children. The mean age was less than four years of age. The autistic children were diagnosed according to the criteria of Ornitz and Ritvo (1968; 1976). The data indicate that the autistic children are reported to have had significant delays in the development of motor abilities, speech, comprehension and, to a lesser extent, perception during their first two years of life.

This study is subject to the same criticisms as all others that rely primarily on retrospective parental questionnaire data. As with the majority of other studies, these investigators also failed to utilize adequate comparison groups of other developmentally delayed children. However, this questionnaire has several advantages over those of other investigators. First, some of the questions are designed to elicit specific information in terms of the specific age at which certain behaviors occurred. This permits comparison to other developmental norms. Of course, as with other questionnaires, requests for parents to rate behaviors along continua remains a problem.

In our opinion, a developmental questionnaire that defines such terms as *rarely* and *frequently* for parent raters is also needed. This could be accomplished by developing a numerical scale for these terms. For example, in its current form, rarely could be interpreted to mean once a day by some parents and once a week by others. Redefining this type of terminology numerically, i.e. rarely could mean no more than once a week, for each question should increase the accuracy of parental report.

In 1973, Makita and Umezu described the Checklist for Autistic Children (CLAC) they developed in Japan. CLAC is not a diagnostic tool as such, but was designed to measure a child's progress during behavior therapy treatment. It is composed of a total of twenty-eight items and covers eleven areas of behavior, e.g. eating, elimination, sleeping, activities of daily living, play, interpersonal relationship, speech and language, expressing behaviors, manipulation of hands and fingers, autonomy of behaviors and emotional expression. CLAC is completed by the parents with the aid of the evaluator and responses are then placed on a diagram. Changes in the shape of the diagram reflect response to treatment. In addition to autistic children, the authors also report that they have collected data on a control population of eighty-six normal children (all under four years).

The CLAC system has several serious methodological problems. First, objective definitions of behaviors are not provided, and reliability data are not reported. Second, only normal children under four years of age have been used as controls and thus limits comparison of levels of development. What is needed are data on mentally retarded children of the same chronological and mental ages as the autistic group and two groups of normal children, one matched to the autistic group on the basis of chronological age and the other on the basis of mental age. These groups would permit the evaluation of how developmental changes affect autistic behaviors. This type of comparison is essential especially when attempting to describe response to treatment and outcome.

Ruttenberg, Kalish, Wenar, and Wolf (1974) have published a detailed Behavior Rating Instrument for Autistic and other Atypical Children (BRIAAC). The BRIAAC consists of eight scales, each which delineates a specific category of behavior: (1) relationship, (2) communication, (3) drive for mastery, (4) vocalization and expressive speech, (5) sound and speech reception,

(6) social functioning, (7) body movement, and (8) psycho-sexual development. Each scale is graded into ten descriptive levels. Only observed behavior is scored. The rater has ten points that he must distribute among ten levels of each scale. Generally, the lower the rating relative to the chronological age, the more severe the child's overall disturbance. All scales are used to obtain a cumulative rating and an interscale profile.

The basic data gathering approach of the BRIAAC, observing the children and rating their behavior, is commendable. However, the developers failed to objectively define behaviors to be rated and scoring criteria are extremely vague and complicated.

In 1971, DeMyer, Churchill, Pontius, and Gilkey compared five diagnostic systems designed to differentiate autism and early childhood schizophrenia. They report that, while the autistic scales devised by Rimland (1968), Polan and Spencer (1959), Lotter (1966), and the British Working Party (Creak et al., 1961) correlate significantly, the degrees of correspondence (35%) indicate that some children obtain high autistic scores in one system and low scores in another. Further, they describe their own criteria: to be autistic a child must show (1) emotional withdrawal from people before the age of three; (2) lack of speech for communication; (3) nonfunctional repetitive use of objects; and (4) failure to engage in role play alone or with other children. If the child has near normal perceptual-motor performance, he is said to have primary autism: if his perceptual-motor performance curve is flat, he is said to have secondary autism. These investigators also delineate other subgroups of psychotic children. They note that their category of "primary autism" most resembles Rimland's "true autism" as measured on the E-1 scale.

DeMyer et al. (1971) summarize the problems of differential diagnosis as follows: "Good agreement on diagnosis, even concerning subcategories of psychotic conditions in children, is common among people working in close collaboration. . . . However, this agreement lessens considerably when diagnosticians without constant feedback compare diagnosis, even when relatively structured and standardized diagnostic systems are in use" (p. 188). A necessary remedy for the problems inherent in

DeMyer's conclusion is the establishment of an objectively based diagnostic system. One goal of such a systematic quantitative method would be to design it in such a way that it could be readily applied by diagnosticians who do not work in close collaboration.

CRITICAL REVIEW OF PRIOR STRUCTURED OBSERVATIONAL STUDIES

At the present time, these are but a few studies of structured evaluations. The earliest reports are of interactions with children in playroom followed by written summaries, e.g. Wright, 1960. Easton (1962) and Gellner (1959) suggest making home visits and nursery school observations to study styles of social interaction, responses to learning opportunities and patterns of play. Call (1965) compares the parent-child interactions of schizophrenic and normal children by recording the observational data on audio tape and kymograph. Wolff and Chess (1964) compare detailed descriptions of autistic children obtained from their mothers with data obtained from direct observations of children at home and in the classroom. Prall (1960) utilizes motion picture films for the study of "motility disturbances" in psychotic children. He emphasizes both the quantitative and qualitative variations of these behaviors and outlined the activities according to the parts of the body involved.

Ritvo, Ornitz, and LaFranchi (1968) also utilize motion pictures to assess the frequency of repetitive movements and to demonstrate a high degree of stability and consistency of roles between and among six carefully diagnosed autistics. They postulate that behaviors such as handflapping are evidence of a neuropathophysiological process, rather than expressive of psychopathology as had been suggested by others.

Simmons, Leiken, Lovaas, Schaeffer, and Perloff (1966) studied the effects of LSD-25 on the behavior of a pair of identical autistic twins by utilizing a series of standard test situations, including a 20 minute period of social isolation. Behaviors were observed through a one-way screen and recorded on a pushbutton console connected to an event recorder. A decrease in "self-stimulation" behaviors was observed after LSD-25.

Hutt, Hutt, and Ounsted (1963) and Hutt, Hutt, Lee, and

Ounsted (1965) utilized a one-way mirror while narrating behavior and changes in location on a two channel audio tape. Autistic children were observed for 3 minute periods in four environments of "increasing complexity": an empty room; the same room with toy blocks present; the same room with the blocks plus an inactive adult; and the same room with an adult attempting to engage the child in playing with the blocks. Activities were found to occur more frequently as the environment was made more complex, but the results are not significant due to the limited duration of the observation periods.

Sorosky, Ornitz, Brown, and Ritvo (1968) recorded the behaviors of six autistic children and one child with Down's syndrome. Observation sessions lasted over six hours under conditions of social isolation in a sound-attenuated room and the frequency and duration of occurrence of behaviors were recorded on multiple event recorders. Peaks of activity were found to occur at random intervals and there was no evidence of periodic or cyclic patterning. The major finding of their work was the demonstrated persistence of autistic behaviors under conditions of prolonged observations with control of environmental variables.

Ornitz, Brown, Sorosky, Ritvo, and Dietrich (1970) introduced controlled human and inanimate stimuli while observing motility patterns. These patterns were not significantly influenced by presentation of spinning objects. The reaction to human intervention was highly variable. Visual input restriction (total darkness) reduced the autistic behavior in one child, and induced the substitution of tactile self-stimulation. Their results were consistent with the hypothesis that autistic motility disturbances are largely independent of environmental influence, but may provide sensory input to the autistic child.

DeMyer, Norton, and Barton (1971) conducted structured psychiatric interviews with 101 children encompassing a broad clinical diagnostic spectrum from normalcy through psychoses, mental retardation, and brain damage. Their results were as follows: (1) mean rater reliability was 85.7; (2) validity measures with Alpern infant test scores (Alpern, 1967) were 0.65, with Vineland Social Maturity Scales (Doll, 1953) 0.72 and with a group of items from other standardized tests 0.85 (p for all correlations less than 0.01); (3) nine distinct groups were identified by factor analysis of the behavior traits. From inspection of the correlation matrices, the authors identified these nine groups without reference to prior clinical diagnoses. Social behavior trait and adaptive task performance scores ranged on a continuum over the nine groups from highest normalcy and lowest pathology scores in Group 1 to highest pathology scores and lowest normalcy scores in Group IX. High adaptive task performance scores were found in the group with high social normalcy. Lower adaptive scores were accompanied by low social normalcy scores and by high social pathology scores. A main shortcoming of this study was that while close attention was paid to social and adaptive behaviors, the task of assessing the frequency and duration of abnormal behaviors was not addressed.

In 1971, Reichler and Schopler reported a study entitled "Nature of Human Relatedness." A fourteen point diagnostic scale based on Creak's (1961) criteria was used to evaluate fifty-five boys and thirteen girls referred with a diagnosis of childhood psychosis. Each of the fourteen variables were rated by trained observers on a scale of one to four. The authors hypothesized that human relatedness was a multidimensional complex construct that could be analyzed in terms of simpler, more basic functions. They overcame many of the methodological obstacles present in other studies by observing children to quantify behaviors and using adequately trained observers. However, they focused on only one aspect of the syndrome, relatedness, and their rating scale emphasized items relating to perceptual functioning.

Black, Freeman, and Montgomery (1975) report a study of the quantification of play behavior in four environments. Five autistic children were observed and rated individually on a 0 to +3 scale for the occurrence of behaviors including touching another child, aggression, talking or playing, ignoring objects, perseverative or negative use of objects, and appropriate use of objects. Behaviors were all objectively defined and high interrater agreement was obtained. The results documented the following: (1) with some autistic children, environmental factors have little or no effect on play behaviors; (2) when presented choices, autistics frequently related to objects rather than to peers; (3) object play frequently involved solitary repetitive behavior; and (4) within a confined space designed to facilitate a movement flow (thera-play), autistics modeled, imitated, and engaged in gross motor play together.

Lichstein and Whaler (1976) describe in detail the application of naturalistic observation methods to the behavior of an autistic child. Observations were made in three settings over a period of six months. Sixteen behaviors of the child and six behaviors of adults and peers were scored. Cluster analyses were performed to identify response classes within the behavioral structure of the child and to see if correlations exist between response and stimulus events. In order to examine intra- and intersetting changes, Spearman rank correlations and t-tests were also computed. The authors report that the child exhibited a diversity of behavior over time in a given setting and across settings and no behavioral predictions could be made on a statistical basis.

While this study represents an important methodological contribution to the literature, interpretation of the results are difficult. First, only one child was examined. This makes generalizations almost meaningless since it is well documented that autistic children function at varying cognitive levels and demonstrate changing symptoms over time. Second, the behaviors coded may or may not have been significant to autism. No normative data are presented nor are data on other behaviors in which the child may have engaged. Regarding several studies discussed earlier, the author's theoretical bias led to his selection of behaviors to be studied. This, of course, is an unavoidable problem if only one set of behaviors and not all behaviors that comprise the syndrome are studied. Applying systematic objective observation techniques to as many of the behaviors as possible that have been associated with autism is the only way to mitigate bias concerning the importance of any one set of symptoms.

Summary

In summary, much confusion exists in the literature not only regarding the necessary and sufficient conditions to establish the diagnosis, but also over the term *autism*. One solution to the problem is to develop an *objective diagnostic schema*. Such a tool would not only shed light on the perplexing clinical problem of diagnosis, but might also aid in answering other questions.

CRITICAL REVIEW OF FOLLOW-UP STUDIES

A careful review of the literature reveals that the majority of follow-up studies have been aimed at clarifying the etiology and/or prognosis of the syndrome. Cross-comparison among studies has been seriously limited because of several methodological problems. These include the following: (1) retrospective nature of most studies; (2) lack of initial diagnostic specificity; (3) variations in initial ages of children; (4) variations in intervals of follow-up; (5) variations in criteria for outcome; (6) failures to actually reevaluate children at follow-up (most studies present either anecdotal or data obtained from records); (7) failures to provide serial follow-up data on the same sample of children and/or parameters; (8) failures to carefully document types of treatment programs; (9) failures to examine changes in the family and/or living situation that could affect outcome; and (10) failures to employ adequate control groups.

The first carefully conducted prospective follow-up study of children specifically diagnosed as autistic was conducted in England by Rutter and his colleagues (Lockyer & Rutter, 1969; 1970; Rutter, 1966; 1969; Rutter, Greenfield & Lockyer, 1967; Rutter and Lockyer, 1967). Prior to this, only anecdotal and clinically descriptive data of adolescents who had been diagnosed as autistic in childhood either by the criteria of Kanner (Eisenberg, 1956; Eisenberg & Kanner, 1956; Kanner, 1943; Kanner & Eisenberg, 1956; Kanner & Lesser, 1958) or Creak (1961; 1962; 1963) had been reported. In addition, several other studies had been reported prior to those of Rutter that did not provide as clear-cut diagnostic criteria for inclusion of a child in the study. Thus, their populations were very heterogeneous (Annel, 1963; Bettleheim, 1967; Bender, 1955; 1956; 1961; 1963; Brown, 1960; 1963; 1969; Davids, Ryan & Salvatore, 1968; Miller, Gillies & Jukes, 1966; Reiser & Brown, 1964).

In addition, some investigators had reported only single case examples (Bruch, 1958; Darr & Warden, 1951; Schacter, 1968). Thus, while follow-up studies reported prior to those of Rutter and his colleagues provide some indication of what autistic children might be like in adolescence, they were not carefully conducted, which made it difficult to make generalizations and conclusions.

The series of studies conducted by Rutter and his colleagues at the Maudsley Hospital provided careful clinical descriptions. It was primarily retrospective and relied on hospital records for the initial descriptions of patients. Sixty-three psychotic children from the Maudsley Hospital (1950-1958) who met criteria described by Cameron (1958) and Anthony (1958) for the diagnosis of childhood psychosis were identified: for each psychotic child another nonpsychotic comparison case of the same sex who had been seen at the hospital during the same year was selected. The children were also matched as closely as possible on age and IQ. The mean age when initially identified was five years, eleven months.

The children in both groups were then seen individually at follow-up (in 1963, 1964) and given neurological, psychiatric, and psychological examinations. The mean age at follow-up was fifteen years, seven months and the mean duration of follow-up was nine years, eight months. Their striking findings were that those children with the lowest IQs had the poorest prognosis; also that low IQ and absence of speech prior to five years of age were the best prognostic indicators; finally, that upon follow-up, ten of the sixty-four children had developed seizures.

The primary methodological problem of the Maudsley studies centers around definition of the initial sample, the wide disparity in age range, and in the number of years to follow-up. The strong point of this series of studies is that the investigators actually saw the children initially and then reevaluated them.

Menolascino and Eaton (1967) reported a retrospective five year follow-up study of twenty-nine children diagnosed as psychotic. The sample was selected from a larger group of mentally retarded children with an average initial age of four years, ten months. Three diagnostic categories were used: (1) chronic brain syndrome with psychosis (after Ingram, 1963, and Kucera,

1960); (2) childhood schizophrenia (after Creak, 1963; Despert & Sherwin, 1958), and (3) early infantile autism (after Kanner, 1943, & Rimland, 1964). Five year follow-up consisted of an interim history, physical and neurological studies, behavioral observations and psychological tests. Three levels of treatment were also identified for comparison: intensive, moderate, and no treatment. They did not specify what other services the no treatment group received.

The authors report finding no correlation between treatment and prognosis and further cautioned that psychological tests may not be an adequate indicator of outcome. This last finding may have resulted from sampling difficulties. As the authors themselves pointed out, their sample consisted entirely of children who were initially referred for an evaluation of mental retardation and they were dealing with a special subgroup of children labeled as psychotic, e.g., five cases of childhood schizophrenia and two of autism. No specific definition of outcome was provided and no cross-correlation of results from the several evaluations was performed. In general, these methodological problems coupled with the heterogeneous definitions of psychosis and small sample sizes makes interpretation of the results very difficult.

In 1968, Havelkova reported a clinical follow-up study of seventy-one psychotic children (forty-two treated and twenty-nine untreated). All were initially assessed during preschool years and followed prospectively for four to twelve years so that ages at follow-up were between eight to seventeen. The diagnostic criteria included Kanner's for infantile autism, Bender's descriptions of childhood schizophrenia, and those of the British Working Party. Initial evaluations included psychiatric, neurological, EEG, hearing and speech, psychological, and family assessments, and children were classified as severely (seventeen children), moderately (twenty-nine children), or mildly (twenty-five children) affected. Severely affected children were not admitted to treatment.

The author concludes that childhood psychosis produced severe intellectual impairment that was only partially modified by treatment. There are several sampling problems that limit interpretation of their conclusions. These include lack of diagnostic specificity, lack of an objective definition of the severely, moderately, and mildly affected groups, and sampling biases in assigning children to treatment. However, on the positive side, the study was prospective in nature and did attempt to evaluate specific therapeutic interventions.

Rutter, in 1970, reported an extension of the original Maudsley study. He sent out a postal questionnaire to parents and obtained reports from hospitals and clinics. At this time the children were ages fifteen to twenty-nine years with a mean age of twenty-one years, eight months. Rutter further divided the original sample of psychotic children in terms of his specific diagnostic criteria for autism. This produced a sample of fifty-six "truly" autistic children. The results confirmed those of the earlier report, namely that IQ remained the best prognostic indicator. Interestingly, by this time, 28 percent of the sample had developed seizure disorders and the amount of schooling experienced seemed to be related to outcome. This was extremely hard to evaluate because of the variability in what was defined as schooling. While this study is the longest reported follow-up to date, it suffers from many of the methodological problems discussed earlier as well as those associated with obtaining adequately valid and reliable data from parental questionnaires.

In 1971(b), Kanner presented an interesting anecdotal report on eleven autistic children he first saw in 1943. The initial age of the children had been between two and eight years and the follow-up interval was twenty-eight years. Information was obtained by having a social worker locate the children and review hospital records. The data were presented in an anecdotal manner that did not permit statistical or other objective analyses.

Kanner, Rodriquez, and Ashenden (1972) report case histories of an additional nine autistic children who had made "some type of social adjustment." Kanner notes retrospectively that the one thing these children had in common was speech prior to five years of age and none had been institutionalized. While the reports of Kanner and his colleagues provide rich clinical material on a well-defined, but small, population, they fall short of providing useful information regarding what variables affect prognosis and response to treatment. Such information will only be obtained from systematically designed prospective follow-up studies.

In 1972, Bender and Faretra reported follow-up data on a large sample of childhood schizophrenics seen at Bellevue Hospital from 1935 to 1952. According to the authors, these cases were selected because they had the best hospitalization information and adequate data into adulthood. This built a sampling bias into the study at the outset. The follow-up data obtained in 1968-1969 was primarily from correspondence with other facilities, in some cases by personal interview of these subjects with whom the authors had contact, or by reports from other staff members who had current information about the patient. The study is divided into two parts. In Part *I*, fifty patients were diagnosed as autistic by Bender's criteria. Initial ages were from two-and-one-half to thirteen years. Age at follow-up ranged from twenty-two to forty-five years. This group was further subdivided by age of reported onset and demographic variables. In Part *II*, fifty-seven children, only fourteen of whom were autistic, were followed up. Their initial ages ranged from six to fifteen years and age at follow-up was from 18 to twenty-seven years. The authors observed that, of all the children studied, those who had received the diagnosis of autism had the worst prognosis. They further noted that this group of children had the greatest number of intact, concerned, and financially independent families and the majority resided in institutions or hospitals at the time of follow-up despite early treatments.

The study of Bender and Daretra contains almost all the methodological problems described earlier. However, it is significant that these investigators realized the importance of examining family factors and attempted to relate them to outcome. However, they did not go beyond providing descriptive data and examining how major changes in a family might affect outcome, particularly hospitalization for any given autistic child.

DeMyer, Barton, DeMyer, Norton, Allen, and Steele (1973) reported a detailed twelve year follow-up study of 126 autistic children who had been referred to the Clinical Research Center for Early Childhood Schizophrenia between 1954-1969. Thirty-six mentally retarded children also referred to the center served as controls. Diagnostic criteria for autism were those reported earlier by this group (DeMyer, Churchill, Pontius, and Gilkey, 1971). All subjects were divided into high, middle, and low autism groups. We have reviewed elsewhere the problems with this diagnostic schema. The initial mean age of the children was five years, six months and the mean follow-up interval was 6.1 years (range two to sixteen years).

All subjects received the same evaluations at follow-up that they had received initially. These included two psychiatric examinations, language and psychological testing, physical and neurological examinations, and several laboratory studies. Parents were also interviewed to obtain descriptions of the child as well as current home conditions and family relationships. The conclusions confirmed earlier reports that most autistics remained intellectually retarded and 42 percent were institutionalized at follow-up. The best predictor of later work/school adjustment was intaking rating of severity of autism (i.e. high, middle or low) and IQ was the next best predictor.

This study of DeMyer et al. is the most comprehensive and best designed of those we have reviewed. However, it has several methodological limitations such as a lack of initial objective diagnostic data, a lack of objective rating of parental functioning, variation in follow-up interval, and the need for longer follow-up periods. They report data on children were initially an average of five years, six months old and a minimum follow-up period of two years. Younger children may need more frequent reevaluation as their symptom patterns may change more rapidly than those of older children (Ornitz and Ritvo, 1968, 1976). Furthermore, no data is given on the types of treatments (other than special education) that the children received. The discrepancy between reported improvements in social adjustment and speech, and the lack of improvement in work/school ratings might be accounted for by the initial nonreliable measures of severity. In addition, since the data are based on heterogeneous age groups, reported changes or nonchanges in clinical state may be an artifact of either initial age, age at follow-up, follow-up interval, or a combination of these variables. Also, obviously, these variables must be examined in a sequential study before definitive information as to the prognosis of the syndrome of autism can be ascertained.

In 1973, Piggot and Gottlieb summarized diagnostic criteria and follow-up findings on groups of children diagnosed by various investigators as childhood schizophrenic, autistic, or atypical and discussed some methodological problems that limit comparisons of studies. They stressed in particular the "diagnostic heterogeneity" that exists in the literature.

Also in 1973, two studies that evaluated the effects of specific treatment programs on outcome were reported (Lovaas, Koegel, Simmons, and Long, 1973; Treffert, McAndrew, and Dreifuerst, 1973). The goal of both of these studies was to evaluate treatment programs and not follow individual children and, hence, it is difficult to compare them to other studies in this review.

Lovaas et al. (1973) examine the generalization effects of intensive inpatient behavior modification treatment on twenty autistic children. The criteria for diagnosis are their own, and measures of improvement are related to specifically defined behaviors. The authors report that improvement on follow-up (number of specific behaviors present) one to four years after treatment depends primarily on the post treatment environment that the child was living in.

Treffert et al. (1973) also report the affects of an inpatient treatment program on fifty-seven "autistic and schizophrenic" children, using their diagnostic criteria. The treatment program included inpatient psychiatric hospitalization, a specialized sequential school with task defined curriculum. The sole outcome measure was discharged to the home. They observed that the rate of discharge was positively correlated with late onset of the syndrome, development of speech by age five, and completion of bowel and bladder training by the time of admission to the hospital. The thirty-three patients diagnosed as autistic had the most notable tendency to remain chronically hospitalized.

Both the Lovaas et al. and Treffert et al. studies address themselves to outcome, and neither provided prospective data on how their patients changed over time. Lovaas et al. attempt to define very specific outcome measures, but in doing so they fail to provide an overall clinical picture of the children. Treffert et al. also attempt to assess a very specific outcome, but the many factors that could influence discharge from a state hospital were not examined. Before studies of treatment effects can be evaluated meaningfully, careful prospective follow-up studies to determine natural history of the syndrome of autism must be conducted. Such data are critical since treatment effects can only be evaluated in relationship to developmental parameters.

In 1974, Goldfarb reported a systematic prospective longitudinal study of children he diagnosed as having childhood schizophrenia. He used criteria that included children other investigators usually label autistic. He studied forty children within a three year age range (mean age 6.9 years) who were receiving treatment at the Ittleson Center (mean treatment duration 4.2 years). Normal children in public schools served as comparison subjects. Children were evaluated annually while inpatients and bi-annually after discharge to intact families and received the same initial and follow-up tests. There were forty separate measures including neurological status, demographic family information, Wechsler Intelligence Scale for Children, educational achievement tests, self-care and social competence ratings, and psychiatric evaluation of clinical progress.

Goldfarb concludes that schizophrenic children made significant improvement in structured educational settings, and those with the higher initial IQs made the most progress. Furthermore, he notes that response to treatment or environmental enrichment cannot be considered automatic and suggests that some changes probably resulted from general maturation of the nervous system.

Goldfarb's study can serve as a methodological model for other prospective longitudinal studies. However, it is difficult to generalize his results beyond this sample and educational setting. As he himself notes, children in the seven to ten age range do not change as rapidly as younger children, and thus improvements noted may not reflect accurately what should be expected of children in other ages and in other settings. Also, we must note that the majority of children (60%) had WISC IQs greater than 70, which indicates the presence of good language skills. Rutter (1970) reported 50 percent of his sample were nonverbal and thus his data may also reflect a sampling bias. In addition, evaluating only children who had intact families may have added a further sampling bias since it remains to be demonstrated objectively whether schizophrenic children with intact families get earlier diagnoses, better services, or are more likely to remain in the home.

Lotter (1974) reports an interesting eight year follow-up study of thirty-two autistic children identified during an epidemiological survey in England. The initial age was eight to ten years. When followed up, Lotter observed that overall initial speech and IQ together correlated most highly with eventual outcome. However, subgroups of children had different outcomes, and he discusses the need for better classifications of autistic children and the critical issue of an initial well-defined population for obtaining meaningful longitudinal follow-up data. He states, ". . . since prognosis is clearly different for different subgroups of autistic children, the exploration of factors associated with outcome might be more fruitfully pursued by an explicitly comparative appoach, based on subcategories defined within groups of autistic children" (p. 276).

Rees and Taylor (1975) report a study of fifty-nine children (seen between 1956 and 1962) diagnosed as autistic by Cameron's criteria. On initial evaluation, ages ranged from 18 months to five years (mean three years, nine months) and follow-up data were obtained at least ten years later (mean thirteen years, six months). Initial data came from files and follow-up data from contacts with families, schools, and institutions. The children themselves were not directly re-evaluated and the authors attempted retrospectively to establish criteria for successful and unsuccessful outcomes. They report that a cluster of twenty-three items differentiated the groups. Since these criteria were not objectively defined, interpretation is difficult. In spite of this, as the authors and others have observed, initial IQ, and not treatment per se, was the most important prognostic factor.

Although this study suffers from most of the methodological limitations described initially, it is unique in that the authors focused on a younger population than have others. It is critical for follow-up studies to examine young children and follow them longitudinally. However, it must be recognized that when examining young children, one must give special attention to developmental parameters per se. This results in the need for a careful look at normal development and comparisons to groups of carefully described normal children.

Piggot and Simpson (1975) report the case findings of children originally diagnosed as psychotic in the 1950s and 1960s. In 1973, the authors rediagnosed each case separately using the criteria of DeMyer and Churchill. They found that only one-third of the total group met the newer and stricter criteria for childhood psychosis. This study is important because it clearly highlights the problem of taking at face value data that lacks initial diagnostic specificity.

Knobloch and Passamanick (1975) report a study of fifty children (diagnosed as autistic by Kanner's criteria) who were referred to a pediatric developmental service. The median age of the sample was eighteen months. All had evidence of organic brain disease and three-fourths had "mental deficiency" in varying degrees. Follow-up examinations and reports of forty of the forty-five survivors (mean follow-up period of five years and median age at follow-up was seven years) showed that none of the patients had received treatment specifically for their psychiatric symptoms. However, the authors reported that three-fourths had established social responses appropriate to their level of cognitive functioning. Those who did not were generally over three years of age at the time of their first examination or had initial developmental quotients of thirty-five or less. The degree of mental deficiency was as great or greater at follow-up as it was initially.

Knobloch and Passamanick's follow-up study is noteworthy because they observed that three-fourths of their sample showed a decrease in psychosomatic symptoms. The authors discuss this finding in relation to other follow-up studies, particularly those of Rutter, his colleagues, and Eisenberg and Kanner. They point out three major differences between their study and those of others. First, their population was drawn from patients referred for pediatric — not psychiatric — evaluation.

Therefore, the population tended to have more children with neuromuscular disorders and other specifically diagnosable diseases. These children are rarely referred for psychiatric examination even when older.

The second difference was the age of the initial sample. Three-fourths of the children they studied were under two years of age at the time of the initial evaluation. The third difference had to do with severity and persistence of the autistic symptoms. The authors concluded that autistic symptoms present in very young children may disappear with age. As such children got older they tended to receive diagnoses of mental retardation and not psychoses. Further, since in the other follow-up studies the children were older, they may also have had more severe cases of psychoses. In spite of these differences, one main observation agreed with that of others, i.e. IQ was the best prognostic indicator. While it is not clear exactly how the diagnosis of autism was made by Knobloch and Passamanick, the results are intriguing and again point out the need for a prospective longitudinal follow-up study of very young autistic children.

Dahl (1976) reports a twenty year follow-up study based upon a survey of the records of 322 children admitted to child psychiatric hospitals in Denmark from 1949 to 1951. The criteria for initial diagnosis of "psychosis infantilis" were unique to their study, but Dahl attempts to make them consistent with those of Kolvin (1971). Out of the total of twenty-three patients, seventeen were labeled as psychotic and six as borderline, and initial ages ranged from two years, nine months to fourteen years. Both initial and twenty year follow-up data were obtained from records. The results were consistent with those from other countries. Fourteen of the seventeen patients initially diagnosed as psychotic had been admitted to psychiatric hospitals during the follow-up period and one was residing in a home for the mentally retarded. Four of the remaining six borderline children were chronic inpatients and two were chronic outpatients and the inpatients had lower IQs. Dahl concludes that these

results are consistent with the hypothesis that childhood psychosis can lead to adult schizophrenia and may not be a separate
disease, a position taken by other investigators (Kolvin, 1971;
Rutter, 1970).

Even though Dahl's study has many of the same methodological problems already described, it is important for two reasons.
First, it supports the findings of investigators in other countries
that childhood psychosis is a lifelong chronic condition and that
initial level of functioning is critical to prognosis. Second, it
addresses the question of whether autism and childhood schizophrenia are the same or different syndromes (Rutter, 1972;
Fish and Ritvo, 1977; Ornitz and Ritvo, 1976). This issue may
well be a semantic one that results from different initial diagnostic criteria and/or different conceptions of schizophrenia in
Europe and America. Whether there are one or two syndromes
is a question that can only be answered by the systematic prospective longitudinal study that begins with an objectively defined
group of young children and traces their development over
time.

In 1976, Bartak and Rutter reported a careful study examining the relationship of IQ to outcome. This sample was pooled
from previous studies (Bartak and Rutter, 1973; Rutter and
Bartak, 1973; Bartak, Rutter and Cox, 1975; Cox, Rutter, Newman, and Bartak, 1975) and restricted to boys less than eleven
years of age who met Rutter's criteria for autism. The sample was
further divided into those with nonverbal IQs 69 or less (autistic-
mentally retarded group, N = 17) and those with IQs above 69
(autistic-normally intelligent group, N = 19). Information about
each child was obtained from parents and by direct observations
of the child. The authors reported that the two groups differed
in patterning of symptoms, were similar in terms of the main
clinical phenomena associated with autism, and yet outcome was
markedly different. All children were followed until at least
seventeen years of age. One-third with IQs below 70 developed
seizures in adolescence, whereas very few of those with normal
intelligence did so. Very few of the mentally retarded autistic
children had obtained paid employment, but roughly half of
those with an IQ of 70 or more were gainfully employed.

While Bartak and Rutter's study was carefully conducted, it does not meet all the criteria of the carefully constructed prospective longitudinal study described previously. Unfortunately, while the authors describe the detailed symptom picture of each subject, these symptoms were not observed directly nor is there a report of serial evaluation data.

In 1977, Campbell, Hardesty, Breuer, and Polevoy published a pilot study of ten children reevaluated after three and one-half to ten years. The sample was randomly selected from a population of fifty-eight former patients at their therapeutic nursery school who had been initially seen at the ages of two years, one month to six years, eight months. They all met Creak's (1963) criteria for childhood psychosis. Detailed initial work-ups were obtained from the children's records. At follow-up, all interim records were obtained, parents interviewed, and assessments of current status and adjustment obtained as well as detailed examination of the children. The latter included physical and neurological examinations, clinical psychiatric assessments, psychological tests, and other semiobjective behavioral ratings.

At the time of follow-up, the children's ages ranged from nine years, five months to nineteen years, one month (mean of fourteen years). The results indicate that those children who initially had some verbal skills and thus higher IQs had a better prognosis. The authors observed no relationship between outcome and type of treatment, but emphasized that the meaning of this finding is still unclear. While this study contains methodologic improvements, the measures of outcome need to be made more specific and objective to be extended to larger groups of children.

The final study to be reviewed here was reported by Chess (1977). She conducted a longitudinal study of 242 children with congenital rubella: she noted that eighteen of these children also had symptoms indicative of autism. She follows this subgroup up at eight to nine years of age. Her results confirmed those of other investigators in that the initial degree of mental retardation was correlated with outcome. While this study was primarily concerned with the association between rubella and autism, it is included here because of its longitudinal nature. Since it is subject to most of the methodological criticisms discussed above, it adds little to previously reported follow-up studies which do not provide objective definitions of initial symptoms or measures.

THEORETICAL BACKGROUND FOR THE BEHAVIORAL OBSERVATION SCALE (BOS)

An overview of the preceding critical review sections reveals that the previously proposed diagnostic systems have serious theoretical and methodological limitations. Hence, none have gained widespread acceptance nor been applied outside of the research center of their origin. Analysis of these limitations reveals that they are of three types: first, failure to provide objectively defined behaviorally based scale items which would permit high interrater reliability; second, failure to adequately assess developmental influences on scale items; and third, failure to develop objective profiles of "normal" and "pathological" states. In this regard, most also failed to establish parameters of normal and pathological development independent of theoretical notions of specific diseases and their presumed causes.

With these considerations in mind, we recently decided to develop an objectively based behavior rating and diagnostic system. It is called the Behavioral Observation Scale (BOS) and has the following goals:

(1) To differentiate, on the basis of computer-generated profiles, normal children from those with the syndrome of autism, mental retardation, and other developmental disabilities.
(2) To differentiate on the basis of computer generated profiles, subgroups of autistic children according to clusters of symptoms for correlation with historical, biomedical, and treatment factors.
(3) To generate computer based continua of severity within the subgroup of autistic children.
(4) To generate computer based profiles of the natural course of autism based upon multiple observations of patients over a number of years.

Once these goals for the BOS were agreed upon we turned our attention to compiling scale items. Each item had to be objectively defined in behaviorally based terms. This was necessary so that notions as to causes of the observed behaviors could be eliminated from the outset. For example, such terms as *avoids eye contact* or *self-stimulating* contains notions of why the child does or does not do what is being described — hence could prejudice an observer. More suitable behaviorally based terms such as *looks at examiner – present or absent* and *hits self – present or absent* are simply descriptive and can be scored without reference as to what might or might not be the purpose, goal, or meaning of the action.

Each scale item also had to be simply as well as clearly defined so that observers could be trained quickly to apply the Scale. Simplicity also was an important factor if we were to achieve high interrater agreement and reliability for the Scale. Since a lack of reliability proved the nemesis of several prior scales, particular efforts were expended in the design states of each Scale item to enhance reliability. For example, test runs were made and items rejected that were not easily taught and highly reliable.

Finally, each Scale item was designed to be scorable on all subjects regardless of age and diagnosis. To accomplish this, definitions of Scale items had to be free from theoretical notions. Items like neuroticism, psychotic ideation, and regressed ego functioning were rejected because they obviously are based on psychoanalytic theory and because they could not be scored in all subjects, i.e. mute or severely mentally retarded children.

Once the preliminary group of Scale items had been assembled, we tackled the most interesting theoretical issue raised in the entire project, namely, how to assess developmental factors. Our historical survey clearly revealed that this was the most poorly understood and inadquately assessed factor in the diagnostic systems reviewed. Indeed, many previous investigators simply had not attended to developmental factors at all. In direct contrast to this, we began with the posture that it was crucial to determine developmental parameters for each Scale item, for the clusters of behaviors, and for the normative and diagnostic profiles.

The necessity for assessing developmental aspects for Scale items becomes further apparent when one considers the fact that autism and other developmental disabilities often coexist, and their relative degrees of severity can compound the diagnostic process. Furthermore, clinical observation documents that certain behaviors occur at specific chronological ages independent of, and not indicative of, pathology. However, when these same behaviors occur at other chronological ages, they are indicative of, or pathognomonic of, specific diseases. Thus, one must enter developmental parameters into the diagnostic equation and accept that they make the formula very dynamic and very complex.

An initial classification of developmental factors requires a minimum of five categories relating to chronological age of appearance and persistence.

First: Behaviors present at birth and which persist with increasing chronological age (CA).

Second: Behaviors present at birth but disappearing with increasing CA.

Third: Behaviors not present at birth but that appear at specific chronological ages and then persist, e.g. walking, speech.

Fourth: Behaviors not present at birth and seen only during specific chronological ages, e.g. hand flapping, echolalia, intermittent enuresis, monster dreams.

Fifth: Behaviors not related to CA and only seen in association with specific pathological states, e.g. seizures, spasticity.

A first step in generating diagnostic profiles would be to determine the developmental relationships of Scale items in terms of their expected appearance by chronological age and persistence or disappearance by observing "normally developing" children. The logical second step would then be to generate profiles to objectively define "normality" at given chronological ages. The next logical step would be to generate profiles of CA groups from serial observations of children with known developmental disabilities such as autism and mental retardation. Such profiles would yield the ratings of individual Scale items as deviations from normal and automatically take into account the factor of CA. Finally, with such data, computer generated profiles could be constructed for CA groups to discriminate "normals" from those with specific behaviors (symptoms) and from those with clusters of behaviors diagnostic of syndromes.

In summary, to achieve the diagnostic objectivity, reliability, and validity that were the original goals for the BOS, the Scale must account for the effects of developmental factors on each item and cluster of items. "Normality" can then be defined along developmental parameters and contrasted with pathological states. It is indeed a curious fact that our extensive review of the literature revealed that this developmentally oriented task has not been accomplished to date.

REFERENCES

Alpern, G. D. and Boll, T. J.: *Developmental Profile*. Indianapolis, Psychological Development Publications, 1972.

Annell, A.: The prognosis of psychotic syndromes in children: a follow-up study of 115 cases. *Acta Psychiatr Scand, 39:*235-297, 1963.

Anthony, E. J.: An experimental approach to the psychopathology of childhood. *Br J Med Psychol, 31:*211-223, 1958.

Bartak, L. and Rutter, M.: Differences between mentally retarded and normally intelligent autistic children. *J Autism Child Schizophr, 6:*109-120, 1976.

Bartak, L., Rutter, M. and Cox, A.: A comparative study of infantile autism and specific developmental receptive language disorder. I. The children. *Br J Psychiatry, 126:*127-145, 1975.

Bender, L.: Schizophrenia in childhood. *Nerv Child, 1:*138-140, 1942.

Bender, L.: Childhood schizophrenia. *Psychiat Q, 27:*663-681, 1953.

Bender, L.: Twenty years of clinical research in schizophrenic children with special reference to those under six years of age. In Caplan, G. (Ed.): *Emotional Problems of Early Childhood*. London, Tavistock, 1955, pp. 503-515.

Bender, L.: Childhood schizophrenia. II. Schizophrenia in childhood — its recognition, description, and treatment. *Am J Orthopsychiatry, 26:*499-506, 1956.

Bender, L.: Childhood schizophrenia and convulsive states. In Wortis, J. (Ed.): *Recent Advances in Biological Psychiatry*, vol. 3. New York, Plenum, 1961, pp. 96-103.

Bender, L.: The origin and evolution of the gestalt function, the body image and delusional thought in schizophrenia. In Wortis, J. (Ed.): *Recent Advances in Biological Psychiatry*. New York, Plenum, 1963, pp. 38-62.

Bender, L. and Faretra, G.: The relationship between childhood schizophrenia and adult schizophrenia. In Kaplan, A. (Ed.): *Genetic Factors in Schizophrenia*. Springfield, Ill, Thomas, 1972.

Bettleheim, B.: *The Empty Fortress: Infantile Autism and the Birth of the Self*. New York, MacMillan, 1967.

Black, M., Freeman, B. J. and Montgomery, J.: Systematic observation of play behavior in autistic children. *J Autism Child Schizophr, 5:*363-371, 1975.

Brown, J. L.: Prognosis from presenting symptoms of pre-school children with atypical development. *Am J Orthopsychiatry, 30:*382-390, 1960.

Brown, J. L.: Follow-up of children with atypical development (infantile psychosis). *Am J Orthopsychiatry, 33:*355-361, 1963.

Brown, J. L.: Adolescent development of children with infantile psychosis. *Semin Psychiatry, 1:*79-89, 1969.

Bruch, H.: The various developments in the approach to childhood schizophrenia. *Acta Psychiatr Scand, 34:*1-48, 1958.

Call, J. D.: *A Comparison of Normal and Disturbed Three to Four Year Old Boys in Interaction with the Parents.* Read before 1965 meeting of the American Orthopsychiatric Association, New York, March 17-20, 1965.

Call, J. D.: Autistic behavior in infants and young children. *Practice of Pediatrics, 1:*1-9, 1974.

Cameron, K.: A group of 25 psychotic children. *Rev Psychiatry, 25:*117-122, 1958.

Campbell, M., Hardesty, A. S., Breuer, H. and Palevoy, N.: Childhood psychosis in perspective: a follow-up of ten children. *J Am Acad Child Psychiatry, 17:*14-28, 1978.

Chess, S.: Autism in children with congenital rubella. *J Autism Child Schizophr, 1:*33-47, 1971.

Chess, S.: Childhood psychopathologies: a search for differentiation. *J Autism Child Schizophr, 2:*111-113, 1972.

Chess, S.: Follow-up report on autism in congenital rubella. *J Autism Child Schizophr, 7:*69-81, 1977.

Cohen, D. J.: The diagnostic process in child psychiatry. *Psychiatric Annals, 6:*404-416, 1976.

Cox, A., Rutter, M., Newman, S. and Bartak, L.: A comparative study of infantile autism and specific developmental receptive language disorder. II. Parental characteristics. *Br J Psychiatry, 126:*146-159, 1975.

Creak, M.: Schizophrenia syndrome in childhood. *Br Med J, 2:*890, 1961.

Creak, M.: Juvenile psychosis and mental deficiency. In Richards, B. W. (Ed.): *Proceedings, London Conference of Scientific Studies of Mental Deficiencies.* Vol. 2. Dangenham, Eng.: May and Baker, 1962.

Creak, M.: Childhood psychosis: A review of 100 cases. *Br J Psychiatry, 109:*84-89, 1963.

Dahl, V.: A follow-up study of a child psychiatric clientele with special regard to the diagnosis of psychosis. *Acta Psychiatr Scand, 54:*106-112, 1976.

Darr, G. C. and Worden, G. G.: Case report 28 years after an infantile autistic disorder. *Am J Orthopsychiatry, 21:*559-570, 1951.

Davids, A., Ryna, R. and Salvatore: Effectiveness of residential treatment for psychotic and other disturbed children. *Am J Orthopsychiatry, 38:*469-475, 1968.

DeMyer, M. K., Barton, S., DeMyer, W. E., Norton, J. A., Allen, J. and Steele,

R.: Prognosis in autism: a follow-up study. *J Autism Child Schizophr, 3:*199-246, 1973.

DeMyer, M. K., Bryson, C. Q. and Churchill, D. W.: The earliest indicators of pathological development: comparison of symptoms during infancy and early childhood in normal, subnormal, schizophrenic and autistic children. *Biological and Environmental Determinants of Early Development.* Research Publication 51, Association for Research in Nervous Mental Disease, 1973, pp. 298-332.

DeMyer, M. K., Churchill, D. W., Pontius, W. and Gilkey, K. M.: A comparison of five diagnostic systems for childhood schizophrenia and infantile autism. *J Autism Child Schizophr, 1:*175-180, 1971.

DeMyer, M. K., Norton, J. and Barton, S.: Social and adaptive behaviors of autistic children as measured in a structured psychiatric interview. In Churchill, D. W., Alpern, G. D. and DeMyer, M. (Edsl): *Infantile Autism.* Springfield, Ill: Thomas, 1971.

Despert, J. L. and Scherwin, A. C.: Further examination of diagnostic criteria in schizophrenic illness and psychoses of infancy and early childhood. *Am J Psychiatry, 114:*784-790, 1958.

Doll, E. A.: *Vineland Social Maturity Scale of Directions.* Minneapolis: Educational Testing Bureau, 1967.

Easton, K.: Considerations on autism in infancy and childhood. *NY J Med, 62:*3628-3633, 1962.

Eaton, L. and Menolascino, F. J.: Psychotic reactions of childhood: experiences of a mental retardation pilot project. *J Nerv Ment Dis, 143:*55-67, 1966.

Eisenberg, L.: The autistic child in adolescence. *Am J Psychiatry, 112:*607-612, 1956.

Eisenberg, L.: The classification of psychotic disorders in childhood. In Eron, L. D. (Ed.): *The Classification of Behavior Disorders.* Chicago, Aldine, 1966.

Eisenberg, L.: The classification of childhood psychosis reconsidered. *J Autism Child Schizophr, 2:*338-342, 1972.

Fish, B.: The detection of schizophrenia in infancy. *J Nerv Ment Dis, 125:*1-24, 1957.

Fish, B.: Drug therapy in child psychiatry: pharmacological aspects. *Compr Psychiatry, 1:*212-227, 1960.

Fish, B. and Shapiro, T.: A typology of children's psychiatric disorders: I. Its application to a controlled evaluation of treatment. *J Am Acad Child Psychiatry, 4:*426, 1965.

Fish, B., Shapiro, T., Campbell, M. and Wile, R.: A classification of schizophrenic children under five years. *Am J Psychiatry, 124:*1415-1423, 1968.

Gellner, L.: *A Neurophysiological Concept of Mental Retardation and its Educational Implications.* Chicago, J. D. Levinson Research Fdn., 1959.

Goldfarb, W.: *Childhood Schizophrenia.* Cambridge, Mass., Harvard U Pr, 1961.

Goldfarb, W.: An investigation of childhood schizophrenia. *Arch Gen Psychiatry, 11:*621-634, 1964.

Goldfarb, W.: *Growth and Change of Schizophrenic Children: A Longitudinal Study.*

Washington, V. H. Winston, 1974.

Group for the Advancement of Psychiatry: *Psychopathological Disorders in Childhood: Theoretical Considerations and a Proposed Classification.* New York, Author, 1966, pp. 251-258.

Havelkova, M.: Follow-up study of 71 children diagnosed as psychotic in preschool age. *Am J Orthopsychiatry, 38:*846-857, 1968.

Hutt, C., Hutt, S. J. and Ounsted, C.: A method for the study of children's behavior. *Dev Med Child Neurol, 5:*233-245, 1963.

Hutt, S., Hutt, C., Lee, D. and Ounsted, C.: A behavioral and electronencephalographic study of autistic children. *J Psychiatry Res, 3:*181-197, 1965.

Ingram, T.: Chronic brain syndromes in childhood other than cerebral palsy, epilepsy, and mental defect. In Box, W. and MacKeith, R. (Eds.): *Minimal Cerebral Dysfunction.* London, Heineman, 1963, pp. 10-17.

Kanner, L.: Autistic disturbances of affective contact. *Nerv Child, 2:*217-250, 1943.

Kanner, L.: Follow-up study of 11 autistic children originally reported in 1943. *J Autism Child Schizophr, 1:*119-145, 1971(a).

Kanner, L.: Childhood psychosis: an historical overview. *J Autism Child Schizophr, 1:*14-19, 1971(b).

Kanner, L. and Eisenberg, L.: Notes on the follow-up of autistic children. In Hoch, P. H. and Zubin, J. (Eds.): *Psychopathology of Childhood.* New York, Grune, 1956, pp. 227-239.

Kanner, L. and Lesser, J.: Early infantile autism. *Pediatr Clin North Am, 5:*711-730, 1958.

Kanner, L., Rodriquez, A. and Ashenden, B.: How far can autistic children go in matters of social adaptation. *J Autism Child Schizophr, 2:*9-33, 1972.

Keeler, W. R.: Autistic patterns and defective communication in blind children with retrolental fibroplasia. In Hoch, P. H. and Zubin, J. (Eds.): *Psychopathology of Communication.* New York, Grune, 1958.

Knobloch, H. and Pasamanick, B.: Some etiologies and prognostic factors in early infantile autism and psychosis. *Pediatrics, 55:*182-191, 1975.

Kolvin, I.: Psychoses in childhood: a comparative study. In Rutter, M. (Ed.): *Infantile Autism: Concepts, Characteristics and Treatment.* London, Churchill, 1971.

Kolvin, I.: Studies in the childhood psychoses. I. Diagnostic criteria and classification. *Br J Psychiatry, 118:*381-384, 1971.

Kolvin, I., Ounsted, C., Humphrey, M. and McNay, A.: II. The phenomenology of childhood psychosis. *Br J Psychiatry, 118:*385-395, 1971.

Kučěra, O. and Kalektiv: Psychopathologické projerýpři lehkých detskych encefalopatiích (Psychopathologic manifestation in children with mild encephalopathy). Prague, Statni Zdravotnicke Naklodetelství, 1961, pp. 235-247 (cited here in English).

Lichstein, K. and Wahler, R. G.: The ecological assessment of an autistic child. *J Abnorm Child Psychol, 4:*31-54, 1976.

Lockyer, L. and Rutter, M.: A five to fifteen year follow-up study of infantile psychosis. III. Psychological aspects. *Br J Psychiatry, 115:*865-882, 1969.

Lockyer, L. and Rutter, M.: A five to fifteen year follow-up study of infantile psychosis. IV. Patterns of ability. *Br J Soc Clin Psychol, 9:*152-163, 1970.

Lotter, V.: Epidemiology of autistic conditions in young children. II. Some characteristics of the parents and children. *Soc Psychiatry, 1:*163-173, 1966.

Lotter, V.: Factors related to outcome in autistic children. *J Autism Child Schizophr, 4:*263-277, 1974.

Lovaas, O. I., Koegel, R., Simmons, J. Q. and Long, J. S.: Some generalizations and follow-up measures of autistic children in behavior therapy. *J Appl Behav Anal, 6:*131-166, 1973.

Mahler, M. S.: On sadness and grief in infancy and childhood. In Freud, A. (Ed.): *Psychoanalytic Study of the Child.* New York, Int Univ Pr, pp. 33-51.

Makita, K. and Umezu, K.: An objective evaluation technique for autistic children. An introduction of CLAC scheme. *Acta Paedopsychiatr, 39:*237-253, 1973.

Masters, J. C. and Miller, D. E.: Early infantile autism: a methodological critique. *J Abnorm Psychol, 75:*342-343, 1970.

Menolascino, F.: Psychosis of childhood: experiences of a mental retardation pilot project. *Am J Ment Defic, 70:*83-92, 1965.

Menolascino, F. J. and Eaton, L.: Psychosis of childhood: a five year follow-up study of experiences in a mental retardation clinic. *Am J Ment Defic, 72:*370-380, 1967.

Mittler, P., Gillies, S. and Jukes, E.: Prognosis of psychotic children: report of a follow-up study. *J Ment Defic Res, 7:*207-299, 1977.

Ornitz, E. M. and Brown, M. B., Sorosky, A. D., Ritvo, E. R. and Dietrich, L.: Environmental modification of autistic behavior. *Arch Gen Psychiatry, 22:*560-565, 1970.

Ornitz, E. M., Guthrie, D. and Farley, A. J.: The early development of autistic children. *J Autism Child Schizophr, 7:*207-229, 1977.

Ornitz, E. M. and Ritvo, E. R.: Perceptual inconstancy in early infantile autism. *Arch Gen Psychiatry, 18:*79-98, 1968.

Ornitz, E. M. and Ritvo, E. R.: The medical diagnosis. In Ritvo, E. R., Freeman, B. J., Ornitz, E. M., and Tanguay, P. E. (Eds.): *Autism: Diagnosis, Current Research and Management.* New York, Spectrum, 1976.

Piggott, L. and Gottlieb, J.: Childhood schizophrenia — what is it? *J Autism Child Schizophr, 3:*96-105, 1973.

Piggott, L. R. and Simson, C. B.: Changing diagnosis of childhood psychosis. *J Autism Child Schizophr, 5:*239-246, 1975.

Polan, C. and Spencer, B.: Check list of symptoms of autism in early life. *W V Med J, 55:*198-204, 1959.

Pral, R. C.: *Motility Disturbances in Childhood Psychosis: A Report of Film Research.* Read before the Pan-American Congress, Mexico City, 1960.

Prior, M., Boulton, D., Gajzago, C. and Pury, D.: The classification of childhood psychoses by numerical taxonomy. *J Child Psychol Psychiatry, 16:*321-330, 1975.

Rank, B.: Intensive study and treatment of preschool children who show marked personality deviations or "atypical development" and their parents. In Caplan, G. (Ed.): *Emotional Problems of Early Childhood.* New York, Basic, 1955.

Rees, S. C. and Taylor, A.: Prognostic antecedents and outcome in a follow-up study of children with a diagnosis of childhood psychosis. *J Autism Child Schizophr, 4:*309-322, 1975.

Reichler, R. and Schopler, E.: Observations on the nature of human relatedness. *J Autism Child Schizophr, 1:*283-296, 1971.

Reiser, D.: Psychosis of infancy and early childhood. *N Engl J Med, 269:*790-798, 844-850, 1963.

Reiser, D. E. and Brown, J.: Patterns of later development in children with infantile psychosis. *J Am Acad Child Psychiatry, 3:*650-667, 1964.

Rendle-Short, J.: Infantile autism in Australia. *Med J Aust, 2:*245-249, 1969.

Rimland, B.: The differentiation of childhood psychosis: an anlysis of checklists for 2,218 psychotic children. *J Autism Child Schizophr, 1:*161-174, 1971.

Rimland, B.: *Infantile Autism.* New York, Appleton-Century-Crofts, P. H., 1964.

Ritvo, E. R., Cantwell, D., Johnson, E., Clements, M., Benbrook, F., Slagle, S., Kelly, P. and Ritz, M.: Social class factors in autism. *J Autism Child Schizophr, 1:*297-310, 1971.

Ritvo, E. R. and Freeman, B. J.: National society for autistic children: definition of autism. *J Pediatr Psychol, 4:*146-148, 1977(a).

Ritvo, E. R. and Freeman, B. J.: Definition of the syndrome of autism. *J Autism Child Schizophr, 8:*162-167, 1978(b).

Ritvo, E. R. and Freeman, B. J.: National Society for Autistic Children definition of the syndrome of autism. *J Am Acad Child Psychiatry, 17:*565-575, 1978(c).

Ritvo, E. R., Ornitz, E. M. and LaFranchi, S.: Frequency of repetitive behaviors in early infantile autism and its variants. *Arch Gen Psychiatry, 19:*341-347, 1968.

Ruttenberg, B. A., Kalish, B. I., Wenar, C. and Wolfe, E. G.: *Behavior Rating Instrument for Autistic and Other Atypical Children.* Philadelphia, Developmental Center for Autistic Children, 1974.

Rutter, M.: The influence of organic and emotional factors in the origins, nature and outcome of child psychosis. *Dev Med Child Neurol, 7:*518-528, 1965.

Rutter, M.: Behavior and cognitive characteristics. In Wing, J. (Ed.): *Early Childhood Autism.* Oxford, Pergamon Pr, 1966, pp. 61-81.

Rutter, M.: Autistic children: infancy to adulthood. *Semin Psychiatry, 3:*435-450, 1970.

Rutter, M.: Childhood schizophrenia reconsidered. *J Autism Child Schizophr, 2:*315-337, 1972.

Rutter, M., Greenfield, D. and Lockyer, L.: A five to fifteen year follow-up study of infantile psychosis. II. Social and behavioral outcome. *Br J Psychiatry, 113:*1183-1199, 1967.

Rutter, M., Lebovici, S., Eisenberg, L., Sneznovski, A. V., Sadoun, R., Brook, E. and Lin: A tri-axial classification of mental disorders in childhood. *J Child Psychol Psychiatry, 10:*41-61, 1969.

Rutter, M., and Lockyer, L.: A five to fifteen year follow-up study of infantile psychoses. I. Description of the sample. *Br J Psychiatry, 113:*1169-1182, 1967.

Rutter, M., Shaffer, D. and Sheperd, M.: An evaluation of the proposal for a multi-axial classification of child psychiatric disorders: preliminary communication. *Psychol Med, 3:*244-250, 1973.

Rutter, M. and Sussenwein, F.: A developmental and behavioral approach to the treatment of preschool autistic children. *J Autism Child Schizophr, 1:*376-397, 1971.

Schachter, M.: Evolution et prognostic de l'autisme infantile pre coce: Etude catamnestique d'un cas suivi de 4 a 17 ans. *Acta Paedopsychiatrie, 35:*188-199, 1968.

Schneider, K.: *Mental Symptoms and Psychiatric Diagnosis.* Leipzig:Thieme, 1942.

Simmons, J. Q., Leiken, S., Lovaas, O. I., Schaeffer, B. and Perloff, B.: Modification of autistic behavior with LSD-25. *Am J Psychiatry, 122:*1201-1211, 1966.

Sorosky, A., Ornitz, E., Brown, M. and Ritvo, E.: Systematic observations of autistic behavior. *Arch Gen Psychiatry, 18:*439-448, 1968.

Treffert, D. A., McAndrew, J. B. and Dreifurst, P.: An inpatient treatment program and outcome for 57 autistic and schizophrenic children. *J Autism Child Schizophr, 3:*138-153, 1973.

Ward, A. J.: Early infantile autism: diagnosis, etiology and treatment. *Psychol Bull, 5:*350-362, 1970.

Wenar, C.: The reliability of developmental histories. *Psychosom Med, 25:*505-509, 1963.

Weery, J. A.: Childhood psychosis. In Quay, H. C. and Werry, J. I. (Eds.): *Psychopathological Disorders of Childhood.* New York, Wiley, 1972, pp. 173-233.

Wing, J.: Diagnosis, epidemiology, etiology. In Wing, J. (Ed.): *Early Childhood Autism.* Oxford, Pergamon Pr, 1966, pp. 3-50.

Wing, L.: The handicaps of autistic children: a comparative study. *J Child Psychol Psychiatry, 10:*1-40, 1969.

Wing, L. and Wing, J.: Multiple impairments in early childhood autism. *J Autism Child Schizophr, 1:*256-266, 1971.

Wolff, S. and Chess, S.: A behavioral study of schizophrenic children. *Acta Psychiatr Scandin, 40:*438-466, 1964.

Wright, H.: Observational child study. In Mussen, P. M. (Ed.): *Handbook of Research Methods in Child Development.* New York, Wiley, 1960.

Chapter 3

THE AUTISM SCREENING INSTRUMENT FOR EDUCATIONAL PLANNING
Background and Development

DAVID KRUG, JOEL ARICK AND PATRICIA ALMOND

Part I   Background

IN 1976, the HEW Region X Developmental Disabilities Office funded a grant through the Autistic Education Program and later through Good Samaritan Hospital for the purpose of developing and field testing an instrument that could be effectively used at the public school level to identify autistic children. A need had been demonstrated in this area, since the instruments then available tended to consist primarily of checklists that did not provide quantifiable or reliable educational placement information (David, 1975). Certain disciplines, such as medicine, appropriately contended that a complete medical and neurological evaluation by a medical staff familiar with autism was essential for establishing the diagnosis of autism (Ornitz and Ritvo, 1976). This stance is necessary for establishing diagnosis, but appears far too restrictive for public school screening procedures designed to facilitate educational placement.

Requirements for an educationally useful tool include ease of use, time involvement, and valid and reliable information that supports educational placement. The Autism Screening Instrument was developed with these requirements as constraints.

During the development of the instrument, it soon became apparent that several subcomponents, each capable of standing independently, would be required. The first component, a checklist of nonadaptive behaviors, provides a valuable general picture of how an individual "looks" in comparison to other

This research was supported by HEW Grant #13,631.

populations of handicapping conditions. This capability to "profile" the child's behavior was accomplished by quantifying the behavior characteristics on the checklist. The remaining four subcomponents of the instrument were developed as direct observation tools in which the individual is required to perform certain tasks or is observed in a standardized setting and his/her performance is coded. These four subcomponents are as follows: a vocal sample, a social interaction assessment, a functional education assessment, and a learning rate assessment.

The Autism Behavior Checklist: Subcomponent One

Checklists are a favorite tool of behavior scientists because they can be easily and quickly used and can provide a large amount of useful information simply. However, a common weakness with this type of instrument is that only one dimension of behavior is recorded: either occurrence or nonoccurrence. On these checklists, items are generally marked yes — the behavior occurs — or no — it does not. No differentiation of value between the items on these checklists is made. One method for eliminating this problem is to statistically attach weighted scores to every item so that the checklist will provide an additional dimension of information.

The Autism Behavior Checklist incorporates weighted scores to assist in quantifying the data obtained. Numbers from one to four follow each behavioral descriptor. A behavioral characteristic with a weighted score of four is the highest predictor of autism, and a weighted score of one is the lowest predictor of autism. The behavioral characteristics, for purposes of developing a behavioral profile, have been separated into five diagnostic categories: sensory, relating, body and object use, language, and social and self-help.

Based on the specific behaviors checked and the frequency of items checked, a behavioral profile is plotted. This profile may aid in differentiating individuals who have been diagnosed autistic from other handicapping conditions.

Sample of Vocal Behavior: Subcomponent Two

Language assessment, according to some studies, may be the best single predictor of autism (Lotter, 1974). The detection and evaluation of language delay, however, needs to be precise and discriminative as severely mentally retarded children may appear to exhibit the same general delayed language profiles as autistic children (Baker, Cantwell, Rutter, and Bartak, 1976).

The many studies that have reported on the speech of autistic children have substantiated that autistic speech is different from that of other speech delayed children (Bartak, 1975; Frith, 1970; Hermelin, 1971), but the IQs of the students involved in most of these studies were in the normal range and the children were verbal (Baker et al., 1976). Detailed and specific studies of low functioning autistic children have been conducted (Cunningham, 1968), but analysis was limited to those with "higher level" verbal behavior. Comparative analysis of the vocal similarities and differences of low IQ preverbal autistic and severely mentally retarded children were not discovered in a review of pertinent literature.

A high correlation between a unique vocal profile for preverbal autistic children and the characteristics commonly associated with autism will greatly aid in making a differential diagnosis between autism and mental retardation a reality. Preliminary findings suggest that obtaining a reliable sample of spontaneous utterances from preverbal autistic and severely handicapped individuals does provide valid information supportive of differential diagnosis.

Interaction Assessment: Subcomponent Three

Of the four "essential features" listed in the National Society for Autistic Children's (NSAC) Definition of the Syndrome of Autism, number four, "disturbances of the capacity to appropriately relate to people, events, and objects" may be the most difficult for the evaluator to objectively document. These disturbances are characterized by the following: lack of cooperative play, lack of expected responses to adults and peers, immature response or responses only in the presence of strong social cues, impaired ability to utilize objects or toys in an age-appropriate manner, and stereotypic or perseverative use of objects and toys.

Because a variety of observation methodologies are available, including frequency counts, anecdotal recording, and time sampling, the evaluator may be confused by which method to select, which behavior to observe, and once the data are recorded, how to interpret them in support of differential diagnosis and school placement.

Several considerations must be addressed in order to provide a direct observation tool that yields such data. Patterson and Maerov (1978) recommend tailoring a code system that will "test hypotheses about limited aspects of behavior" as well as examine the behavior "for interdependencies with environmental events." Since the objective is to differentiate students diagnostically on their ability to relate, the tool must provide evaluators with a functional procedure for describing a student's interaction or relation to "people, events, and objects." In addition, the tool must allow for comparisons across cases and the identification of relationships between demographic variables and patterns of the students' interactions (Mash, Terdal, and Anderson, 1973). Such a tool may also have the potential of evaluating treatment through the demonstration of behavior change.

It has been common in the past to use self-help and adaptive behavior checklists as instruments for measuring this area. The Interaction Assessment was designed to look at relating through direct observation of the students' responses to an adult in a play setting.

The procedures and rationale used to develop the Interaction Assessment have initially presented reliable data supportive of a differential diagnosis between autism and severe mental retardation. As with most direct observation procedures, it reflects the efforts of others in the field concerned with systematic observation and reliable coding of social behaviors. The methods of observation and recording adapted for use with this assessment were drawn to a great extent from the work of Mash, Terdal, and Anderson (1973).

Based on their rationale, three decisions were made about the construction of the observation procedures. It was decided that the tool would be used to record general classes of responses rather than recording discrete responses, that behavior sampling would be used rather than continuous recording, and that behaviors would be scored in context rather than in isolation.

The professionals who completed Interaction Profiles on students attended a 30 minute workshop in which training in use of the Interaction Assessment subtest was conducted. Video tape reliability training and scoring procedures were completed at the workshop. Before ending the workshop sessions, 95 percent agreement of scoring was required.

Educational Assessment of Functional Skills: Subcomponent Four

The Educational Assessment (EA) is a quick routine designed to probe a child's functioning level in five areas: in-seat, receptive language, expressive language, body concept, and speech imitation. In order to take the EA, the individual must have certain entry level behaviors, which include staying seated, keeping hands in lap, and looking at specified objects. In addition, disruptive behaviors that are incompatible to test taking must be absent in order for a successful administration of the EA.

The information from the EA will provide guidelines for beginning work with the individual.

The *In-Seat* activity is included as a separate subtest and given full weight with the other four subtest areas because of its important implications. The individual who is able to remain in his/her chair with no struggle to escape is exhibiting behavior that is essential to further test taking. An effort would be made to retain the individual who struggles to escape and to see if he/she will work through the attempt and become cooperative. In such a case, however, the individual would still be scored zero for in-seat.

The *Receptive Language* subtest items were selected for their ability to probe an individual's understanding and response to a variety of auditory and verbal stimuli (Kent, 1975; Hedrick, 1975). The items were selected from various developmental scales below the age of forty-two months.

The *Expressive Language* subtest items were also drawn from developmental scales below age forty-two months. These items are designed to elicit expressive (verbal/sign/gestural) responses to queries about the student's immediate environment.

The *Body Concept* subtest items evaluate motor imitation skills and body identification knowledge. The intent of this subtest is to probe the individual's general knowledge level of self, gained either by instruction or vicariously from his/her environment. Information from this subtest is particularly useful for program development.

The *Speech Imitation* subtest items are designed to evaluate an individual's ability to articulate a variety of vocalizations. Information gained from these subtest items is designed to aid in beginning language programming (Hedrick, Prather, and Tobin, 1975).

Prognosis of Learning Rate: Subcomponent Five

Of the many baffling characteristics of autism, perhaps the most critical detriment to effective education is the exceptionally slow learning acquisition rate found among many of these children. One learning characteristic that could adversely affect learning rate has been identified as "stimulus overselectivity." Lovaas, Schreibman, Koegel, and Rehm (1971) identified this learning pattern and found that among "normal," retarded, and autistic students only the autistic students demonstrated extreme stimulus overselectivity, i.e. autistic children are so selective in attention that they have trouble learning to respond to stimuli in context. In a follow-up study, Wilhelm and Lovaas (1976) found that stimulus overselectivity was not a characteristic restricted only to autistic populations. They found the phenomenon to be present in a population of severely retarded students, but to a lesser extent. Schreibman (1975) concludes that the learning problem of stimulus overselectivity was so pronounced in her six autistic students that nontraditional methods of instruction were required to teach them.

Arick and Krug (1978) report on a study to examine programming needs; the study found that the autistic students required four times more trials to learn the first step of a sequencing task than the remaining five steps, producing a significant learning-to-learn curve.

In light of this previous research, the learning task was developed to analyze the autistic students' learning rates and stimulus overselectivity compared to other diagnostic groups and to assess educational learning potential. The learning task is a simple two-step black/white sequencing task. The task can be administered to any student who is physically able to pick up a plastic chip or at least attempt to pick up the chip.

There are several phases for teaching, beginning with hand shaping and ending with a posttest for stimulus overselectivity. An individual child's learning rate will dictate the length of time needed for this subtest. The learning task can take a quick 15 minute session or it may be necessary to administer the learning task in four 15 minute sessions, depending on the student's learning rate. The learning task enables an educator to compare the learning acquisition rate of students performing at a similar functional level on a standardized learning task and to make judgements regarding placement.

Part II   Development

To assist in establishing content items for the *Autism Behavior Checklist,* behaviors commonly associated with autism were selected from the following instruments: Rimland's E-2 Form, the British Working Party's Checklist, Creak's Nine Points, the Behavior Rating Instrument for Autistic and other Atypical Children (BRIAAC), Rendle-Short and Clancy's Checklist, Polan and Spencer's Checklist, Lotter's Checklist, Lovaas' Checklist, and Kanner's Syndrome (DeMyer, 1971). From the above instruments, a total of fifty-seven behavior descriptors were selected, reviewed, and some in cases, rewritten. The checklist was then edited by fourteen internationally recognized experts in the field of autism. Based on their feedback, individual behavior descriptors were reworded, added, or deleted. The revised checklist was then presented to 3,000 professionals in the field of special education. From this activity 1,049 completed checklists were obtained.

In order to analyze content validity for the items used in the checklist, each behavior descriptor was cross-tabulated for its frequency of occurrence across each population (chi-square 2 × 2 tables). Each behavior descriptor was then ranked according to its gamma and phi score for predicting autism, and this new ranking was used to establish weighted scores by the production, reduction, and error (PRE) statistics.

Seventeen behavior descriptors had a gamma score above 0.54. These seventeen behavior descriptors were assigned a weighted score of 4. Seventeen behavior descriptors were equal to or below 0.53 and above 0.40, and were assigned a weighted score of 3. Sixteen behavior descriptors were equal to or below 0.40 and above 0.18, and were given a weighted score of 2; and seven behavior descriptors were equal to or below 0.18 and were assigned a weighted score of 1. By this method, the weighted score of 4 was determined to be the highest predictor of autism, and the weighted score of 1 the lowest predictor.

The format and procedures for obtaining the data for the Sample of Vocal Behavior subtest were based on several studies describing the language characteristics of verbal autistic children as well as descriptions of language development in preverbal normal intelligence children, and several salient characteristics were selected for study. These characteristics were selected because they could be found in samples of preverbal utterances and also because they were characteristics suggestive of autism.

The first category selected for investigation was divided into two parts: First Use utterances and Self-Repetitions (Wolff and Chess, 1965; Cunningham, 1968; Nakazima, 1970). The second category selected was divided into Communicative utterances and Noncommunicative utterances (Wolff and Chess, 1965; Cunningham, 1968; Savage, 1965; Hintgen and Bryson, 1972; Menyuk, 1974). Mean Length of Utterance (MLU) is commonly reported in language sampling studies and is frequently the major deciding factor for measuring development (Hedrick et al., 1975). Because the target population is basically preverbal, a MLU score was not an appropriate characteristic for this group, so the initial study investigated the proportion of babbling utterances to utterances containing words, phrases, and sentences (Menyuk, 1974).

The procedure for sampling preverbal utterances is adapted from several standard language sampling procedures (Johnson, Darley, and Spriesterbach, 1963; Lee, 1975; Brown, 1973; Cunningham, 1968). Based on these guidelines, a sample of fifty utterances was selected, and the free unstructured setting suggested by the procedures provided a starting point.

Sixty-one students were evaluated in several assessment areas: previous diagnosis, autism severity, functional performance levels, language age, and chronological age. All children had been independently evaluated and received a previous diagnosis of either autistic or severely handicapped non-autistic by inter-disciplinary school district or medical evaluation teams within one year of the study. Severity of autism was evaluated by the Autism Behavior Checklist subtest. Functional performance levels were determined on each individual through the Educational Assessment of Functional Skills subtest. The mean number of tasks passed ($\times$ = 28) by the sixty-one students was used as a performance criterion for further selection of the experimental matched populations. Language age was used to match the experimental groups: it was obtained by the student's teacher or a school psychologist's evaluation of the student's expressive and receptive language ability on one or more of the following: the Sequenced Inventory of Communication Development, the Peabody Picture Vocabulary Test, the Test of Auditory Comprehension, Alpern-Boll, Boehm, NPI Developmental Scale of Language, and the Slosson. Chronological age was obtained from the students' medical records and utilized to define the two age groups within each sample population.

Analysis found the autistic groups with significantly more babbling units than the non-autistic groups; preschool F (1, 7) = 5.64, p <0.05; school age, F (1, 12) = 18.9, p <0.001. A total score was derived by adding together the negative forms (repetitions, noncommunications, and babbling units) in each of the three categories: variety, function, and vocalization complexity for each student. Analysis found the autistic group with a significantly higher total score: preschool, F (1, 7) = 7.01, p <0.05; school age, F (1, 12) = 26.87, p <0.01. An analysis within the babbling units only found the school age autistic group with a significantly higher number of vowel-consonant utterances than the school age non-autistic group, F (1, 12) = 4.84, p <0.05. No significant differences in any of the other specific areas of babbling were found at p <0.05. An analysis within the intelligible utterances found the autistic preschool group with significantly fewer intelligible words, F (1. 7) = 6.1, p <0.05; and the autistic school age group with significantly fewer intelligible phrases, F (1, 12) = 5.83, p <0.05, and sentences, F (1, 12) = 4.84, p <0.05.

The procedures and rationale used to develop the *Interaction Assessment* have initially presented reliable data supportive of a differential diagnosis between autism and severe mental retardation in the area of social development.

Interaction Assessment data of forty students were collected for purposes of standardization. An analysis of this total sample's Interaction Profile found the following F-ratios and significance levels (Table 3.I).

A multiple regression analysis of the total sample population between the Interaction Assessment and the Autism Behavior Checklist found those students with higher Autism Behavior Checklist scores to also have high levels of No Response behaviors, r = .614, p <0.01.

Mean scores of the total samples' Interaction Profile by each matrix cell is shown in Table 3.II.

Initial standardization of the *Educational Assessment* has been done with a population of handicapped individuals composed of forty-one autistic and thirty-one severely handicapped persons. Preliminary evaluation of the results shows that the mean total score on the Eductional Assessment achieved by the autistic

TABLE 3.I

F-RATIOS AND SIGNIFICANCE LEVELS

	TOTAL SAMPLE EVALUATION	
Behavior Category	F-ratios	Significance Level
Interaction	4.95 (1,29)	$p < 0.05$
Independent Play	13.2 (1,29)	$p < 0.001$
No Response	13.15 (1,29)	$p < 0.001$
Aggressive Negative	2.81 (1,59)	Not Significant

TABLE 3.II

TOTAL SAMPLES
BREAKDOWN OF DIAGNOSTIC GROUPS
BY BEHAVIOR CATEGORIES AND PHASES

ADULT PRESENT PHASES	DIAGNOSTIC GROUP	MEAN SCORES			
		INTERACTION	CONSTRUCTIVE INDEPENDENT PLAY	NO RESPONSE	AGGRESSIVE NEGATIVE
Active Modeling	autistic	2.5	2.583	10.542	0.083
	severely handicapped non-autistic	4.375	7.375	4.25	0.00
Passive No Initiation	autistic	1.042	2.792	11.917	0.0
	severely handicapped non-autistic	2.313	9.625	4.75	0.0
Direct Cues	autistic	6.708	1.25	7.79	0.0
	severely handicapped non-autistic	10.875	2.56	1.438	0.062

sample was 21.4 and the mean score achieved by the severely handicapped group was 32.6. A tentative conclusion is that in addition to facilitating educational programming, the Eductional Assessment provides information that supports making differential placement decisions between autism and the condition of severely handicapped.

The Prognosis of Learning Rate subtest has evolved from three previous investigations undertaken by the authors. Arick and Krug (1978) investigated the learning acquisition rate of autistic children utilizing the Non-Speech Language Initiation Program (Non-SLIP), (Carrier and Peak, 1975) materials and teaching format. The investigation found strikingly significant learning-to-learn curves in the autistic population with an unusually high number of responses to learn the first step of any new task. Arick and Krug's (1978) comparison of the mentally retarded subjects used by Carrier and Peak found the autistic group required six times more responses than the retarded group to learn the first step of the task investigated. A second investigation of learning rate utilized a two-step symbol sequencing task with ten different shapes randomly presented, which allowed only the color of the symbol to discriminate the sequence. This study reliably separated the learning rates of mildly and moderately handicapped populations, but was found to be too difficult a task for the severely handicapped population; thus learning rates could not be compared.

The third investigation, begun in the autumn of 1977, simplified the task and allowed both the color and the shape to be the discriminative stimuli for identifying the correct sequence. In addition, only two symbols were used, and the student who failed at the randomized stimulus presentation method was given further trials utilizing a fixed position method. This third investigation is the basis for the current standardization procedures and normative data. In this study, forty-one professionals were asked to randomly select autistic or severely handicapped nonautistic students and administer the Learning Rate subtest. From this activity the learning rate data of seventy-two students were collected and analyzed for purposes of standardization. As the standardization process proceeds and the population increases, the normative data will be updated and more complex statistical analysis can be utilized.

A chi-square analysis found that significantly fewer autistic students met criteria on Hand Shaping, Random Position (A), and Fixed Position (B) than the nonautistic group, $\chi^2 = 4.37$, $p <0.05$; $\chi^2 = 9.05$, $p <0.01$; $\chi^2 = 7.2$, $p <0.01$. No significant difference was found at steps C and D (see Figure 3.1).

An analysis of variance found preverbal subjects had significantly greater total responses than the verbal subjects on Random Position (A) and Fixed Position (B), $F = 15.61$, $p <0.001$; $F = 8.02$, $p <0.01$.

A further analysis of preverbal subjects only found the autistic preverbal subjects with significantly more total responses on Fixed Position (B) than the nonautistic preverbal subjects. $F = 16.78$, $p <0.001$.

An analysis of the linear relationship between the subjects' language age and their total responses on Fixed Position (A) found a relationship of $r = 0.91$, $p <0.000001$, in that those subjects with the lowest language age required the most responses to learn Fixed Position (A). A strong relationship was also found between the Educational Assessment subtest and the

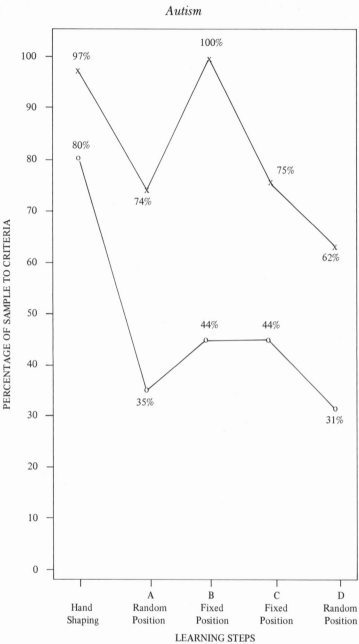

Figure 3.1. Diagnostic Profiles. 0 = autistic, X = non-autistic severely hand-icapped.

Fixed Position (A) of the Learning Rate subtest at $r = 0.78$, p <0.0001, in that the subjects with the lowest scores on the Educational Assessment required the most responses to learn the Fixed Position (A).

Summary

The ASIEP was developed to fill a void existing in tests available for severely handicapped autistic and severely handicapped nonautistic children. Analysis of first year standardization data indicates that this instrument reliably performs differential screening of autistic children, provides information valuable for making educational placement decisions, and is effective for use on a pre- and posttest basis for evaluating pupil progress.

During this third year of the development of this instrument, testing of additional students is continuing in order to further analyze correlations between subtest scores, total score profiles, diagnosis, and other demographic data. It is anticipated that the various subtests of this instrument will aid researchers in describing their subject populations clearly and will greatly enhance the placement of severely handicapped children into appropriate education programs.

REFERENCES

Arick, J. R. and Krug, D. A.: Autistic children: a study of learning characteristics and programming needs. *Am J Ment Defic, 83(2):*200-202, 1978.

Baker, L., Cantwell, D., Rutter, M., and Bartak, L.: Language and autism. In Ritvo, E. (Ed.): *Autism: Diagnosis, Current Research, and Management.* New York, Spectrum, 1976.

Bartak, L., Rutter, M., and Cox, A.: A comparative study of infantile autism and specific developmental receptive language disorders. *Br J Psychiatry, 126:*127-148, 1975.

Brown, R.: *A First Language: The Early Stages.* Cambridge, Mass., Harvard U Pr, 1973.

Carrier, J. and Peak, T.: *Non-SLIP.* H. & H. Enterprises, Lawrence, KS, 1975.

Cunningham, M.: A comparison of the language of psychotic and non-psychotic children who are mentally retarded. *J Child Psychol Psychiatry, 9:*229-244, 1968.

David, A.: Childhood psychosis: the problem of differential diagnosis. *J Autism Child Schizophr, 5(2):*129-138, 1975.

DeMeyer, M., Churchill, D., Pontius, W., and Gilkey, K.: A comparison of five diagnostic systems for childhood schizophrenia and infantile autism. *J Autism Child Schizophr, 1(2):*175-184, 1971.

Frith, V.: Studies in pattern detection: I. Immediate recall of auditory sequences. *J Abnorm Psychol, 76:*413-420, 1970.

Hedrick, D., Prather, E., and Tobin, A.: *Sequenced Inventory of Communication Development.* Seattle and London, U of Wash Pr, 1975.

Hermelin, B.: Rules and language. In Rutter, M. (Ed.): *Infantile Autism: Concepts, Characteristics, and Treatment.* Great Britain, Whitefriars Press, 1971.

Hintgen, J. and Bryson, C.: Recent developments in the study of early childhood psychoses: infantile autism, childhood schizophrenia, and related disorders. *Schizophr Bull, 5:*8-55, 1972.

Johnson, W., Darley, F., and Spriesterbach, D.: *Diagnostic Methods in Speech Pathology,* chapter 7. New York, Har-Row, 1963, 160-200.

Kent, L.: *Language Acquisition Program for the Retarded or Multiple Impaired.* Champaign, Illinois, Res Pr, 1974.

Lee, L.: *Developmental Sentence Analysis.* Evanston, Illinois, Northwestern U Pr, 1974.

Lotter, V.: Factors related to outcome in autistic children. *J Autism Child Schizophr, 4:*3, 1974.

Lovaas, O., Schreibman, L., Koegel, R., and Rehm, R.: Selective responding by autistic children to multiple sensory input. *J Abnorm Psychol, 77:*211-222, 1971.

Mash, E., Terdal, L., and Anderson, K.: The response-class matrix: a procedure for recording parent-child interactions. *J Consult Clin Psychol, 40:*163-164, 1973.

Menyuk, P.: Early development of receptive language: from babbling to words. In Schiefelbusch, R. L. and Lloyd, L. L. (Eds.): *Language Perspectives – Acquisition, Retardation, and Intervention.* Baltimore, Univ Park Pr, 1974.

National Society for Autistic Children: *Definition of the Syndrome of Autism.* Approved by the Board of Directors and the Professional Advising Board, July 1977. Submitted by Edward R. Ritvo and P. J. Freeman.

Ornitz, E., and Ritvo, E.: The syndrome of autism: a critical review. *Am J Psychiatry, 133:*211-224, 1976.

Patterson, G., and Maerov, S.: Observation as a mode of investigation. In Reid, J. B. (Ed.): *A Social Learning Approach to Family Intervention, Volume II. Observation in Home Settings.* Eugene, Oregon, Castalia Pub, 1978.

Savage, V.: Childhood autism: a review of the literature with particular reference to the speech and language structure of the autistic child. *Br J Disord Commun, 3:*75-87, 1968.

Schreibman, L.: Effects of within-stimulus and extra-stimulus prompting on discrimination learning in autistic children. *J Appl Behav Anal, 8:*91-112, 1975.

Wilhelm, H., and Lovaas, O.: Stimulus overselectivity: a common feature in autism and mental retardation. *Am J Ment Def, 81:*26-31, 1976.

Wolff, S., and Chess, S.: An analysis of the language of fourteen schizophrenic children. *J Child Psychol Psychiatry, 6:*29-41, 1965.

Chapter 4

A PROCESS FOR ASSESSING THE FUNCTIONAL HEARING OF THE AUTISTIC CHILD

HARRIETT SLIFE KABERLINE

IN THE COMPREHENSIVE assessment of autistic children, the possibility of additional handicapping conditions must be considered. The evaluation of hearing is one of the important aspects in the identification and differential diagnosis of autistic children. There are several primary reasons for considering the functional hearing of the autistic child. Two of these reasons are inherent in the diagnostic criteria of autism developed by Rendle-Short, namely, (1) acts as deaf, and (2) prefers to indicate needs by gestures (Lewis, 1978). The National Society for Autistic Children also includes in its definition of autism the "disturbance of speech, language and cognitive capacities" (Ritvo, 1977). In addition to these diagnostic criteria, parents of autistic children often report that their initial concern about their child arose because they thought the child did not hear. Since hearing is so important to the natural development of speech and language, a process used to determine functional hearing in autistic children is presented.

Within this process, both informal and formal evaluation procedures are considered in the following four areas: (1) Parent Interview; (2) Observation; (3) Subjective Audiological Assessment; (4) Objective Audiological Assessment.

Parent Interview

A high risk population can and should be evaluated by obtaining a careful prenatal history and postnatal physical assessment. Initially, a parent interview should be conducted to provide screening information regarding prenatal, paranatal, and post-

79

natal factors that can affect a child's hearing, thus identifying that child as a high risk child.

During pregnancy, maternal diseases or chemical inhibition may cause damage to the fetus with resultant sensorineural hearing loss. Some causative factors include maternal rubella, Rh incompatibility, toxemia, syphillis, Asian influenza, diabetes mellitus, heredity, prematurity, and certain drugs (Konigsmark, 1971). A recent study completed by the Office of Demographic Studies at Gallaudet College states that maternal rubella is the cause of 33.5% of the hearing losses of children in the United States (Trybus, 1977-78).

A difficult birth can sometimes damage the hearing mechanism of the infant. The use of forceps and other instruments during delivery has been known to damage the outer or middle ear producing hearing impairment. Anoxia, jaundice and low birth weight can have traumatic effects on the physical development of a newborn. Some of these effects include the possibility of damage to the hearing mechanism (Konigsmark, 1971).

More emphasis has traditionally been placed on postnatal causal factors of hearing loss in young children than on prenatal and paranatal causative factors. The most common diseases that surface in regard to childhood illnesses are measles and mumps. Three and four-tenths of all hearing losses in children are caused by these two childhood diseases. Of the more complex diseases, meningitis, encephalitis, and high fevers can cause severe damage to the inner ear. Eleven and two-tenths of the hearing losses are caused by meningitis and 5 percent by high fevers (Trybus, 1977-78).

Many medications have an ototoxic effect on both children and adults. The following drugs, which may be ingested by the mother especially in the first trimester of pregnancy or given to an infant to treat infection, may cause sensorineural hearing loss: mycin drugs including streptomycin, dihydrostreptomycin, neomycin, kanomycin, gentamycin; salicylates, quinine, thalidomide, and ethacrynic acid (Konigsmark, 1971).

The severity and impact of conductive hearing losses are more difficult to appreciate and realize than sensorineural hearing losses. A conductive hearing loss is defined as "any dysfunction of the outer or middle ear in the presence of a normal inner ear" (Newby, 1972). Factors related to conductive hearing losses include otitis media, an inflammation or infection of the middle ear, and a diversified group of structural anomalies of the ear canal and middle ear ossicles. Congenital otitis media is associated with three high risk categories: (1) newborns with cleft palate; (2) premature infants; and (3) delivery associated amnionitis (Jaffee, 1971). The conductive hearing loss in the newborn may persist into infancy and early childhood and yet still be unidentified by parents or physicians. The problems associated with these hearing losses may include the late onset of speech, impaired speech, impaired language development, learning disabilities, and perhaps even altered behavior.

It is important at this point to stress that none of the causative factors previously discussed will always create a loss of hearing. The possibility exists that with the occurrence of any one of these elements, physical problems could arise. Therefore, in the identification of a high risk population, it is essential to know what types of medical information to elicit when conducting a parent interview so that the determination of the functional hearing of the autistic child can be more easily diagnosed.

The developmental milestones are the next considerations to be documented in a parent interview. There are several scales or checklists of infant or child behavior that are valuable for assessment:

Bayley Scales of Infant Development
The Psychological Corporation
304 E. 45th Street
New York, New York 10017

Denver Developmental Screening Test
Ladoca Project and Publishing Foundation, Inc.
East 51 Avenue and Lincoln Street
Denver, Colorado 80216

Projects KIDS
3801 Herschel
Dallas, Texas 75219

Vision Up
6025 Chestnut Drive
Boise, Idaho 83704

Checklists:
  Speech & Hearing Checklist
  Can Your Baby Hear?
  Doctor, Is My Baby Deaf?
    from: Alexander Graham Bell Association
          3417 Volta Place, N.W.
          Washington, D.C. 20007

Included in the appendix is the Parent Questionnaire developed at the University of Colorado Medical Center by Marion Downs. This questionnaire is a useful screening instrument that is easily administered and provides valuable information. All of these checklists, scales, and questionnaires provide for the progression of behaviors exhibited by most children at respective stages of development. If the autistic child does not respond auditorily, as these developmental scales indicate, an audiological assessment should be obtained.

After the comprehensive parent interview regarding prenatal, paranatal, and postnatal causative factors of hearing loss, it should be determined whether the child has ever had speech. If the child talked at one time but stopped using speech for communicative purposes, the child is not deaf. Some degree of hearing is required in order to learn speech in a natural way. However, the autistic child's hearing ability must still be determined by formal methods.

Observation

The second area to be considered when attempting to determine the functional hearing of an autistic child is observation. When observing the autistic child's responses to various sounds, certain things should be noted. First, many autistic children ignore loud noises or voices. However, they may respond to sounds in another room by either trying to locate the sound, or ceasing or changing their activity. As an example, the child may ignore the parent's question, "Would you like to eat?" but when a bag of potato chips is opened in another room, the child runs in and gestures for some chips. If a child is continuously unresponsive to loud sounds, one must question his hearing ability. However, if the child indicates awareness to sound outside of his immediate environment, he cannot be severely hearing impaired.

Many autistic children demonstrate hypersensitivity to unique sounds such as blenders, pop tops, toilets, and nail scratching. They often have an affinity for motors in refrigerators or washing machines. One must be certain that the child is responding to sound and is not responding tactilely to the vibrations of the motors. If the child always imitates the actions involved in making these objects produce sound or if he always touches the objects as they produce sound, the child might not be hearing but responding tactilely to the vibrations made by each object. Another important observation to note is if the child indicates an awareness to these sounds when another person elicits the sound and the child does not see this occur. As an example, if the child's mother turns on the blender when the child cannot see her do this, but is within hearing distance, does the child react to this sound and try to locate it or does he ignore it?

During free play situations, many autistic children choose to entertain themselves with records or radios. Observation should determine whether the child is responding to the sound from the instrument, the spinning motion of the record, or the vibrations from the radio.

Some children can be conditioned to respond to music in a teaching situation. They may not answer verbally, but will press a bar or button for the reward of a musical passage. Others will dance or rock to music, but will ignore voice. With some autistic children, the presentation of a tone at 3,000 Hz will evoke self-stimulation activities.

If documentation of responses to various sounds is carefully obtained in the areas previously described, the possibility of a severe hearing loss or deafness can be eliminated quickly. This documentation can best be made by recording the types of sounds to which the child responds, the number of times the child responds to each stimulus, and the setting in which the child responds.

Determination of echolalia should be included as part of the observation. Many autistic children demonstrate an echolalic quality in their language. They fail to generate any of their own language and instead respond with various degrees of imitation to questions and answers. If a child is echolalic, he is able to hear well enough to develop language. If a child appears mute, a language sample can sometimes be obtained by putting a tape recorder in the child's room at night. Some autistic children verbalize when not in the presence of adults. Again, if any speech or echolalic responses are obtained, the possibility of a significant hearing loss is remote.

More formalized testing may be indicated after conducting a parent interview and observing the child. An accurate assessment of hearing is a very complicated task with noncooperative children. Many formal measures routinely used in audiological evaluations are extremely difficult to use because of the autistic child's behavior. The assistance of a creative and imaginative audiologist should be elicited to accurately assess the hearing of an autistic child. Therefore, subjective and objective assessment techniques available to the audiologist are described for reference purposes.

Subjective Audiological Assessments

Subjective methods of assessment require a great deal of cooperation on the part of the child. In light of the fact that some of the symptoms of autism include lack of eye contact, standoffish manner, resistance to change in routine, and strong resistance to any learning, this task becomes very difficult (Lewis, 1978). The results will therefore be questionable depending upon the cooperation and interactions of the child. A brief description of subjective methods follows.

Pure Tone Audiometry is used to determine how loud a sound must be before it is heard. With this information, an audiologist can identify and measure hearing loss. In order to determine this, the child is seated in a soundproof booth and tones of selected frequencies are presented from an audiometer to the subject via earphones. The mere act of putting an autistic child in the confining space of the booth and placing earphones on the child makes this formal assessment technique difficult. Once the earphones are in position and the tone presented, the child must indicate a response in some overt manner such as hand raising or dropping coins in a container. This requires cooperation and the establishment of rapport between the audiologist and the child. Responses obtained through administration of tones through earphones indicate the functioning of the hearing mechanism by air conduction. These responses will show how well sound is conducted from the outer ear to the inner ear.

If an air conduction test indicates a hearing loss, bone conduction testing must be administered to determine whether the loss is due to conductive or sensorineural factors, or perhaps a combination of the two. This test is performed by placing a bone conduction vibrator on the mastoid process of the temporal bone and presenting pure tones at selected frequencies. This procedure also requires the cooperation of the child (Newby, 1972).

Pure Tone Audiometry can also be administered by sound-field testing in a soundproof booth without earphones. The pure tones are presented from the audiometer through room speakers. This technique measures air conduction responses binaurally. The autistic child might offer less resistance to this type of audiological testing. Observations of the child to auditory stimuli are possible even if the child will not respond in a conditioned manner (Newby, 1972).

Speech Audiometry can determine at what level of loudness a child indicates an awareness of speech (Speech Reception Threshold) and how well the child discriminates or understands speech. These two factors are predictors of educational success in the development of language. The utility of this test battery will depend on the autistic child's capabilities for speech and language (Davis and Silverman, 1970).

Play Audiometry is a form of conditioned response used successfully with young children and difficult-to-test children. It involves the presentation of a visual clue with an auditory stimulus. An example of this type of testing is beating a drum with the simultaneous presentation of a pure tone at a selected frequency and decibel level. When the child begins to associate the drum with the tone, stimulus substitution may be used. The same pure tone signal is administered without the visual clue and the child is taught to respond with his hand. This technique involves the child more actively than traditional pure tone testing and would perhaps be used more successfully with autistic children (Davis and Silverman, 1970).

Tangible Reinforcement Operant Conditioning Audiometry (TROCA) establishes a working relationship without the examiner present. Positive reinforcement is given for appropriate responses to auditory stimuli. The child presses a button when he perceives a sound; candy or cereal is dispensed if a response occurs within the appropriate time delay of the stimulus presentation. TROCA is a valuable technique because interpersonal contact is avoided and the autistic child has the opportunity for interplay with mechanical equipment with which he is often intrigued.

Another subjective testing procedure that can be employed is *Behavioral Observation Audiometry* (BOA). The examiner observes gross responses to sounds presented in a free field setting. The use of earphones and voluntary conditioned responses are not necessary for this assessment. Often when pure tones are presented within the speech frequencies of 500 Hz, 1,000 Hz, and 2,000 Hz, the tones are meaningless to a young child. Therefore, more observable responses may be obtained by using warbled tones in a free field setting. Other sounds that will secure a greater chance for responses from an autistic child include the following: (1) the child's mother's voice; (2) music; (3) noisemakers (because he plays with these and is thus familiar with the sounds); and (4) environmental sounds such as machines, horns, vacuum cleaners, blenders, and lawnmowers. Since many autistic children have an affinity for these objects, there is a greater chance that they will respond in some way to these sounds. Although responses obtained in this type of situation will not provide an accurate assessment of the child's hearing, they will eliminate the possibility of deafness and will provide a level of awareness to sound (Pollack, 1970).

Figure 4.1 shows a chart that may be used in any testing situation as a checklist of observable behaviors. When the child is presented with auditory stimuli, note any of these changes in behavior that indicate an awareness to sound (Gerber, 1971; Newby, 1972; Pollack, 1970).

CHANGE IN BEHAVIOR

Name: _____
Address: _____
Parents: _____
Birthdate: _____
Date: _____
Examiner: _____
Reliability _____

	startle response	cessation of activity	alteration of activity	widening of eyes	shutting the eyes	covering the ears	body movement	facial grimaces	crying	cessation of crying	localizing sound	change in breathing rate	change in sucking pattern	walking toward speaker from which sound is emitted

COMMENTS: _____
_____
_____

Figure 4.1. Checklist for Observable Behaviors.

Objective Audiological Assessments

Easier and more reliable types of audiological assessments useful with an autistic child involve objective methods. These methods require less cooperation and interaction on the child's part and almost no relationship building prior to the administration of the tests. Three objective assessments are briefly described for your reference.

Impedance audiometry provides an evaluation of the middle ear pathology. Since some autistic children indicate a hypersensitivity to sound, impedance testing can also provide a measure of the child's recruitment and yield some information about hearing sensitivity. This method requires the child to remain still and can be administered with the child sedated. Since this test is a purely physical measurement, no active participation is required by the child (Davis and Silverman, 1970).

A cribogram is used in some hospitals to test the hearing of newborn babies. Transducers attached to cribs monitor the infant's response to sensory stimulation. This is a particularly important test to perform on all high risk infants.

Brain Stem Evoked Response Audiometry is becoming the most common and valid objective measure used with infants and difficult-to-test children. Stimuli are presented through electrodes attached to the skull. The average of the brain waves in response to the auditory stimuli is recorded on an electroencephalogram (EEG). This objective assessment does not require interaction or active participation on the part of the child. Therefore, uncooperative behavior will not interfere with the administration of the test (Davis and Silverman, 1970; Gerber, 1971).

Summary

When considering the differential diagnosis of the autistic child, it is necessary to determine why the child acts like he is deaf, does not use speech for communication purposes, prefers to gesture, and/or has a developmental lag in language. The assessment of the child's hearing is an important part of this diagnosis since hearing is necessary for the natural development of speech and language. A process has been described for reference purposes for all caregivers concerned with the determination of functional hearing in autistic children. This process focuses on the need to use a unique approach in the assessment of hearing in a difficult to test population.

Information must be elicited from parents in an attempt to identify a high risk population. After a careful history has been obtained, certain developmental milestones related to the use of hearing must be evaluated. Then, observations must be documented relating to types of responses to sound in specific situations. If there is still a concern about the child's ability to hear after these informal procedures have been considered, more formal assessment measures should be used. Both the subjective and objective methods of auditory assessment described in this chapter should be explored with regard to the ability of the child to interact and cooperate in a formal testing situation.

It is important to remember that many options exist in the process of assessing hearing in difficult-to-test children. Above all, the process should be child centered and considerate of the individual needs of this unique population of children.

APPENDIX

PARENT QUESTIONNAIRE

(Answer Yes if you have very definitely seen your child do these things even once or twice. If you have never seen him do them, answer NO.)

BIRTH TO FOUR MONTHS

	YES	NO

1. Does he startle to a sudden sound such as a cough, a shout, a dog bark, or a handclap? (Discount responses to a door slamming, the stamp of a foot, a loud airplane or truck noise, and other vibrations.)

2. When he is sleeping in a quiet room, does he stir or awaken, when someone speaks or a noise is made near him? (Some babies are constantly in noisy surroundings, and such infants tend to inhibit their responses unless they have been in quiet for some time.)

3. When he is crying or fretful, does he appear to calm down even momentarily when you speak out of eye-shot or when music starts up or when a sudden loud noise occurs?

4. At three to four months, does he occasionally seem to make feeble beginning head-turn toward a sound, or move his eyes in its direction?

4-8 MONTHS

1. Does he turn his head and eyes toward a sound on one side of him that is out of his peripheral vision? (At 4 months, he should begin to turn directly to the side.)

2. In a quiet situation, does he change expression or widen his eyes when he hears a fairly loud sound or voice?

3. Does he briefly enjoy ringing bells or squeezing noise-makers or shaking a rattle?

4. By six months, does he seem to talk or babble to persons in response to their speaking or making noises?

5. By six months, does his babbling include four different sounds? (Although a deaf baby's babbling sounds just like a normal hearing baby the first few months, by six months he usually uses only one or two gross vowel sounds.)

8-12 MONTHS

1. Does he turn directly and quickly toward an interesting soft noisemaker or to his name called or to a "sh-sh" out of his peripheral vision?

2. Does he use different pitches in his babbling?

3. Does he make several different consonant sounds in his babbling?

4. Does he seem to enjoy music and respond to it by listening or bouncing or vocalizing?

If you have answered No to any of these questions at the present age level of your child, his hearing should be checked at an Audiology Clinic.

REFERENCES

Davis, Hallowell and Silverman, S. Richard: *Hearing and Deafness.* New York, HR & W, 1970.

Downs, Marion: Parent questionnaire. *Conference on Newborn Hearing Screening 1971.* Washington, D.C., Alexander Graham Bell Assoc.

Gerber, Sanford: Neonatal auditory testing: a review. *Conference on Newborn Hearing Screening 1971.* Washington, D.C., Alexander Graham Bell Assoc.

Givens, G. D. and Seidermann, M. F.: Middle ear measurements in a difficult-to-test mentally retarded population. *Ment Retard, 15:*40-42.

Jaffee, M. D., Burton, F.: Hereditary and congenital factors affecting newborn conductive hearing. *Conference on Newborn Hearing Screening 1971.* Washington, D.C., Alexander Graham Bell Assoc.

Konigsmark, M. D., Bruce W.: Hereditary and congenital factors affecting newborn sensorineural hearing. *Conference on Newborn Hearing Screening 1971.* Washington, D.C., Alexander Graham Bell Assoc.

Lewis, Kay R.: *Rendle-Short Criteria for Autism – Screening/Referral Form.* Texas Research Institute of Mental Sciences, Developmental Services Section, 1978, Houston.

Lloyd, Lyle and Fulton, Robert: *Auditory Assessment of the Difficult-to-Test.* Baltimore, Williams & Wilkins, 1975.

Lloyd, L., Spradlin, J., and Reid, M.: An operant audiometric procedure for difficult to test patients, *J Speech Hear Dis, 33:*236-245.

Newby, Hayes A.: *Audiology.* New York, Appleton-Century-Crofts, P.H., 1972.

Pollack, Doreen: *Educational Audiology for the Limited Hearing Infant.* Springfield, Thomas, 1970.

Ritvo, Edward and Freeman, B. J.: National Society for Autistic Children — definition of the syndrome. July, 1977, *J Am Acad Child Psychiatry.*

Silva, D. A.: Multihandicapped children's preference for puretones and speech stimuli as a method of assessing auditory capabilities. *Am J Ment Def, 83:*29-36, 1978.

Stein, Laszlo K.: An electrophysiological test of infant hearing. *Am Ann Deaf, 121(3):*1976.

Trybus, Raymond J.: *Probable Cause of Hearing Loss.* Washington, D.C.: Office of Demographic Studies, Gallaudet College, 1977-78.

II.
INSTRUCTION

Chapter 5

A MULTIPURPOSE COMMUNICATION SYSTEM

Modified for the Autistic Total Communication (M.A.T.C.)

ANITA MARCOTT-RADKE

IN THE BRIEF HISTORY of related research examining the syndrome of autism, the lack of language and communication development within this population has been consistently identified as a salient feature. The various types of speech and language disorders exhibited by the autistic have been investigated and reported (Shapiro et al., 1970; Wolff and Chess, 1965; Churchill, 1978), but with little conclusive evidence that would provide a consistent description of the specific characteristics of their language pathology. The three most commonly used descriptors are mutism, echolalia, and severe language delay. The use of these three generalized terms suggest that language characteristics of the autistic have been found to be idiopathic among individuals.

Upon review of individual case studies, a wide range of individual differences within the three major descriptors can readily be observed. Some autistic students, though verbal, are severely delayed in receptive and expressive language. Others are verbal in that they are echolalic, but are receptively limited, while still others remain mute with questionable communicative abilities.

The purposes of this chapter are as follows:

(1) To give speech and language pathologists, educators, and other interested individuals an awareness of the importance of the development of communication skills to the total development of autistic students;

(2) To describe segments of total communication and provide

an overview of the selected signing system, SEE II (Signing Exact English); and

(3) To provide insights into the applications and modifications of the SEE II Program as it has been modified for the autistic (M.A.T.C.).

With autistic students, as with any population, communication is a basis for learning. In a higher conceptual framework, communication skills become that of an organized process called language. Many autistic students do not exhibit behaviors that demonstrate a concept of the use of functions of communication. Consequently, without intervention, the autistic student does not develop an organized language system.

Initially, it is essential to teach many autistic students the importance of a communication exchange. The term *exchange* implies that a specific action by the student can elicit a response by the teacher/clinician and vice versa. Many of these students do not spontaneously initiate the simplest exchanges, such as looking at, pointing to, or pulling the teacher/clinician to a desired object. Other students may imitate some of the teacher/clinician's gestures, such as crossing their arms or scratching their heads. These students do not have an understanding of the symbolic meaning of specific gestures such as pointing, yet have learned to imitate gestures nondiscriminately.

There are two types of exchanges; one that indicates reception and understanding and the other, which expresses symbolic information through the use of a sign. The usual gestural response for receptive activities is either pointing to or handing the object to the teacher/clinician. In a receptive exchange the teacher/clinician places several objects on the table. A foil or undesirable object may also be included. In order for the student to participate in the exchange (s)he must remain stationary long enough to look at the items, make eye contact with the teacher/clinician, and attend while receiving a directive, i.e. "Show me what you want." The student must then comply with the directive by either making a gesture response, such as pointing to an object, or by allowing the teacher/clinician to prompt the gesture response. Teacher prompts and cues are often necessary to attain these behaviors when beginning an exchange. Therefore, the teacher/clinician must begin to develop the prerequisite learning skills of in-seat behaviors, compliant behaviors, and eye contact behaviors when beginning an exchange and continue this procedure while exchanges are expanded.

Some autistic students will frequently appear oblivious to exchanges initiated by others. Without any behavioral interventions, these students become so involved in their autistic behaviors, such as self-stimulating noises or hand flapping, that communication initiations made by others pass unnoticed. The students do not seem to recognize and assimilate the meaning of these gestures in a symbolic manner. To reiterate, it is important to develop some prerequisite behaviors for learning with autistic students at this level, namely in-seat or stationary position behavior, compliance, and eye contact. This does not imply that a student must be able to maintain these behaviors, e.g. for a five minute period prior to communication training. It does, however, designate that with or without prompts, a student must be able to relate appropriately for a long enough period to complete the exchange. In an effort to establish the student's functioning level, (s)he should first be given the opportunity to respond spontaneously. If spontaneous gestures are not present, the teacher/clinician should begin programming at the appropriate level of student functioning, e.g. begin with imitation if the student can perform imitatively, and work up to spontaneous task completion.

Such intervening strategies include the following steps:

(1) If a response does not occur spontaneously, the teacher/clinician gives the student a visual cue such as the starting position of the gesture. One modification that has been successful with some students is holding the object near the area where the sign is formed. Likewise, photographs and line drawings of the starting position of the sign have been successful cueing instruments for some students.

(2) Should the student still not respond, the complete gesture is then presented for imitation.

(3) If the student still does not imitate the gesture, the teacher/clinician then manipulates the student's hands by shaping them into the desired gestural position.

The progress of a student's response on daily communication lessons can be measured on the basis of this hierarchy using the four categories of responses — spontaneous, cued, imitated, or manipulated. This process will be further described in the section entitled Applications and Modifications of the M.A.T.C. SEE II System.

TOTAL COMMUNICATION: HISTORY AND INVESTIGATION OF A SPECIFIC SYSTEM, "SIGNING EXACT ENGLISH"

The label *total communication,* which is a term indicating a special educational methodology utilized in the education of the deaf, has been borrowed and modified for our purposes. Total communication typically includes many of the following elements: the use of speech, a sign system, finger spelling, auditory training, speech reading, amplification, etc. There are two basic types of sign systems currently in existence: a sign-concept system (American Sign Language — AMESLAN) and a sign-word system (Signing Exact English — SEE II) with several options within the two basic types. The system currently being implemented in the Developmental Learning Program for the Autistic operated by the Wayne County Intermediate School District and Garden City Public Schools in Michigan is Signing Exact English or the SEE II system. This signing system was chosen because it translates exactly into English, including morphemic and syntactic functions. The transition from a sign-word system to spoken and written English is easier than with a sign-concept system for students who have some verbal skills, who are learning to read, or those who may become verbal through the use of signs.

Constant modifications in the presentation of the SEE II system are necessary in order to meet the individual need of autistic students. Thus, the name Modified for the Autistic Total Communication (M.A.T.C.) has been generated to label the communication system used in the Developmental Learning Program. Essentially, the technique consists of the simultaneous presentation of sign and verbalization, with one sign for each word plus markings for prefixes, suffixes, and other morphological structures. Unlike the Total Communication developed for the deaf, amplification is not used and no formal speech reading is included. The modifications will be discussed in the following section.

Applications and Modifications of the M.A.T.C. SEE II Program

When communicating with the autistic student, the goal of the teacher/clinician is to sign and to speak in short, complete, and grammatically correct sentences. The key words of verbalization are signed simultaneously when introducing a M.A.T.C. program to a student. As a student becomes more familiar with signing, the teacher/clinician usually signs and verbalizes the entire sentences. However, there are some students who are gesturally echolalic and will attempt to imitate all the teacher/clinician's gestures. In these cases, the teacher/clinician gives the student a directive for appropriate hand behavior, i.e. hands folded or hands on the table, and signs only the key words of the verbalization. With some students, it is necessary to continue this approach as a basis for their M.A.T.C. program. Other gestural echolalic students learn to tolerate a gradual increase in the number and complexity of signs presented while maintaining appropriate attention and hand behavior. They learn to receive and decode short complete sentences that are signed by the teacher/clinician and others.

The manner in which the signs are presented and emphasized may vary from student to student. For example, in the sentence, This is a ball, the teacher/clinician may stress the sign for ball using any of three methods: (1) by repeating the word and sign several times, (2) by pointing to the ball after each repetition, or (3) by encompassing the ball with his/her hands while making the sign. These methods of emphasizing the sign visually help the student make the symbolic associations between the spoken word, the sign, and the object. In this case, the iconicity of the sign for ball also provides a visual image that closely approximates the object itself. However, not all signs are visually similar to the actual object, in which case other associations can sometimes be utilized.

Criteria for Choosing a Core Vocabulary

There are several criteria that should be considered when choosing a core vocabulary for an individual M.A.T.C. program, the first of which is the relevancy of an object or activity to the student. An object or activity may be relevant if (1) it is motivating to the student, (2) it is an activity within the student's daily living routine which he has not resisted, or (3) it may be easily reinforced in the educational and home environment. A turn to jump on the trampoline may be highly motivating for one student who enjoys gross motor activities, is not afraid of the trampoline, and has access to the activity in his/her daily routine. Therefore, it may be a good source for vocabulary for that particular student. However, if the student seems fearful of the trampoline, is reluctant to participate in gross motor activities, or has little opportunity to experience the trampoline, the choice of that sign for the student's core vocabulary might lead to failure. Likewise, food items would not be an appropriate initial vocabulary choice for a student who demonstrates an aversion to eating. The choice of vocabulary items that relate to daily living activities facilitates the student's learning of those signs, increases his/her development of daily living skills, and therefore would be an appropriate choice.

The second consideration is the iconicity of the sign. Is there a visual association between the sign and the concept being expressed? There are several ways in which this visual association can occur. A sign can present a visual image of the object it represents. As discussed previously, the sign for ball is made by forming the shape of the ball with both hands. A sign can also depict an action relating to the concept being expressed. For example, the sign for hammer is made by hammering in the air with an upright closed fist, as if holding a hammer. Similarly, the sign for jump is made by having the index and middle fingers of the dominant hand "jump up and down" on the palm of the nondominant hand. These signs illustrate the image or action of the noun or verb, affording more concrete stimuli. Signs that include the manual alphabet as a component are sometimes selected when appropriate for a specific student. For example, the sign for *shoe* is made by tapping together two hands that are each depicting the letter *s* as it is made in the manual alphabet. This type of visual association is used when a student has some reading abilities, but is used less frequently than the other types of visual associations.

The third consideration in choosing a core vocabulary relates to motor movements necessary to form the sign. Is the sign easy to form or can it be modified to a less difficult or complex motor movement? The modification must retain the essence of the sign while not duplicating another sign. For example, the sign for *bike* is made by placing both hands in a fist position and rotating them as if peddling a bicycle. This sign is usually easy for students to make. While the sequence of motor movements required to form the sign for *pop* is complicated, it can be easily modified without losing its integrity. Therefore, by eliminating portions of the sign, the motor movements have been simplified but the integrity of the sign has been retained.

Although no hard and fast core vocabulary list can be established as appropriate to all students, the following are often included: favorite foods, toys, and activities, in addition to daily living tasks and essential communications necessary for expression of basic needs, such as bathroom, toilet, or drink. Occasionally there are students who do not seem to prefer any items or activities, in which case the teacher/clinician selects activities pertinent to the student's environment and daily living routine. Repetition of these activities during work sessions helps to reinforce the student's performance on the tasks.

Hierarchy of Basic Skill Development for a M.A.T.C. Program

Essentially, a concrete syntactic approach to basic language development serves as a guideline for the M.A.T.C. hierarchy. The first exchanges are comprised of specific nouns selected on the basis of their concreteness and relevance to the individual student. Once a student has achieved a small repertoire of nouns, concrete action verbs are then introduced. Reversed chaining, a process whereby the student completes the final portion of a sentence, is often utilized to acquire two or more word combinations. From this point other significant language structures, such as prepositions and adjectives, are taught to those students demonstrating such cognitive capacity. Caution is essential in choosing the core vocabulary within each category. As the prognosis for any autistic student's cognitive development is guarded, it is imperative that the vocabulary and concepts taught be consistently relevant to the student's daily needs.

A framework of generalized skill development is utilized in programming for students in M.A.T.C. This skill sequence is arranged from simple to difficult in communication tasks both receptively and expressively. Program modifications are made to meet the individual needs of the students in relationship to their cognitive status, age, and prognosis. Further individualization occurs through vocabulary selection within each category. Guidelines for modifications have not been developed since they are specific to the individual needs of the student, and therefore, clinical judgement must be exercised in each case. [This skill hierarchy has been disseminated at the two symposium sessions on M.A.T.C. programming and is available through the Developmental Learning Program.]

Students with low cognitive abilities do not progress through the entire hierarchy. A breakdown often occurs when transference from the concrete to the abstract is required. These students frequently require the use of real objects or a demonstration of actions in order to assign meaning to signed and verbalized communication. Many remain at the one word/sign utterance level with a core vocabulary of a few basic nouns and/or verbs. The presentation of pictures as stimuli for these students is often too abstract. Some students can be taught to match real objects to the pictures of these objects. A student's ability to acquire this transference from concrete objects to abstract pictorial representations is largely dependent upon that student's cognitive development and perceptual abilities. Innovative teaching techniques and materials offer a student more opportunities to make this transference when traditional methods have proven to be ineffective.

Evaluating Performance on M.A.T.C. Signing Sessions

It is essential to closely monitor student progress in the M.A.T.C. program. Data sheets are a critical part of this program as the teacher/clinician must be able to consistently evaluate student progress or lack of it in order to make program adjustments. The majority of M.A.T.C. data sheets have one factor in common, the inclusion of qualitative measures of student responses. The following are the four hierarchal categories presented: spontaneous, cued, imitated, and manipulated responses. Three types of cues are defined: signed, verbal, and physical within the category of cued responses. Figure 5.1 illustrates a typical M.A.T.C. data sheet that can be used for many activities, while other type data sheets have been specifically developed on an individualized basis.

The teacher/clinician records the performance objectives, e.g. John will sign for the following common objects ten out of ten times. The objects for which John is requested to sign are listed under the specific tasks. The teacher/clinician then presents the object and asks, "What is it?" If the student spontaneously signs the appropriate word, a slash is placed through the *S*. If a cue is required, a slash is placed through the corresponding *C* and the number 1, 2, or 3 is entered above the *C* to note the type of cue

M.A.T.C. DATA SHEET

Student:_____

Performance Objective:_____

SPECIFIC TASKS																					COMMENTS
1.	S	C	I	M	S	C	I	M	S	C	I	M	S	C	I	M	S	C	I	M	
2.	S	C	I	M	S	C	I	M	S	C	I	M	S	C	I	M	S	C	I	M	
3.	S	C	I	M	S	C	I	M	S	C	I	M	S	C	I	M	S	C	I	M	
4.	S	C	I	M	S	C	I	M	S	C	I	M	S	C	I	M	S	C	I	M	
5.	S	C	I	M	S	C	I	M	S	C	I	M	S	C	I	M	S	C	I	M	
6.	S	C	I	M	S	C	I	M	S	C	I	M	S	C	I	M	S	C	I	M	
7.	S	C	I	M	S	C	I	M	S	C	I	M	S	C	I	M	S	C	I	M	
8.	S	C	I	M	S	C	I	M	S	C	I	M	S	C	I	M	S	C	I	M	
9.	S	C	I	M	S	C	I	M	S	C	I	M	S	C	I	M	S	C	I	M	
10.	S	C	I	M	S	C	I	M	S	C	I	M	S	C	I	M	S	C	I	M	
TOTALS:																					
Dates:																					

Key: S = spontaneous   C = cued: (1) sign, (2) verbal, (3) physical
      I = imitated   M = manipulated

Figure 5.1. General M.A.T.C. Data Sheet.

Autism

M.A.T.C. DATA SHEET

Student: _____

Performance Objective: John will sign for the following common objects 10/10 times _____

SPECIFIC TASKS

Task	S	C	I	M	S	C	I	M	S	C	I	M	S	C	I	M	S	C	I	M	COMMENTS
1. Plate	S	C¹	I	M	S	C	I	M	S	C	I	M	S	C	I	M	S	C	I	M	
2. Cup	S	C	I	M	S	C²	I	M	S	C	I	M	S	C	I	M	S	C	I	M	
3. Spoon	S	C	I	M	S	C	I	M	S	C	I	M	S	C	I	M	S	C	I	M	
4. Soap	S	C	I	M	S	C	I	M	S	C	I	M	S	C	I	M	S	C	I	M	
5. Toothbrush	S	C	I	M	S	C	I	M	S	C	I	M	S	C	I	M	S	C	I	M	
6. Hat	S	C	I	M	S	C	I	M	S	C	I	M	S	C	I	M	S	C	I	M	
7. Sock	S	C	I	M	S	C	I	M	S	C	I	M	S	C	I	M	S	C	I	M	
8. Pencil	S	C	I	M	S	C	I	M	S	C	I	M	S	C	I	M	S	C	I	M	
9. Car	S	C	I	M	S	C	I	M	S	C	I	M	S	C	I	M	S	C	I	M	
10. Shoe	S	C	I	M	S	C	I	M	S	C	I	M	S	C	I	M	S	C	I	M	
TOTALS:	40	30	20	10	50	30	10	10													
Dates:		11/19				11/20															

Key: S = spontaneous   C = cued: (1) sign, (2) verbal, (3) physical

  I = imitated   M = manipulated

Figure 5.2. Sample Data Sheet.

used. The number one (1) represents a signed cue, two (2) represents a verbal cue, and three (3) represents a physical cue. The same slash procedure is used for imitative or manipulated responses. At the completion of ten responses, the number of each type of response is tallied and a percentage of spontaneous, cued, imitated, and manipulated responses is readily available. Figure 5.2 provides a sample data sheet that includes data for two daily sessions. Comparisons can therefore be made on day to day performances.

This basic data sheet is amenable to many activities and performance objectives. Similar data sheets are utilized for receptive activities, e.g. daily living skill sequences, which provide step-by-step directions for tasks such as setting the table and brushing the teeth.

Placement of Students in a M.A.T.C. Program: Criteria

When a student meets one or more of the following criteria, (s)he may be considered for placement in a M.A.T.C. Program:

(1) By the age of five years or older, the student has exhibited

little or no spontaneous verbal skills. The chronological age of five is supported by research as a determining criteria, but may vary with individual students based upon clinical judgements.

(2) A verbal student who exhibits difficulty with word retrieval.

(3) A student who exhibits little or no comprehension of the names of common objects or simple directives regardless of age.

(4) The student who exhibits prelinguistic behaviors as assessed in Part I, II, and III A of the Developmental Learning Program Prelanguage Inventory, but who as yet does not speak. As a minimum, these skills should include object permanence, responses to environmental stimuli such as auditory, tactile, and visual input and an emerging concept of the functions of a few common objects. Without this conceptual framework, it is unlikely that the student has the cognitive capacity essential to formulate and assimilate an organized communication system.

It is not necessary that a student be able to imitate signs to be considered for placement in a M.A.T.C. program since the student may be manipulated to form the signs until the motor pattern is learned. A student is usually allowed an extended trial period at the manipulation level before making a change in program assignment.

There are additional instances when M.A.T.C. may be implemented with a student. Verbal echolalic students sometimes benefit from such a program when traditional interventions for echolalia have not yielded any significant change. These students may also be gesturally echolalic in that they imitate the gestures of the teacher/clinician, but without apparent assignments of symbolic meaning. Some of these echolalic students have benefited from M.A.T.C. while others have not. As yet, we have not been able to determine prognostic indicators.

M.A.T.C. programs have also been utilized with verbal students who withdraw or become noncompliant when verbalization is requested. M.A.T.C. is then used to promote communication in a positive and nonthreatening manner. The increase of the students' verbal output is the desired outcome. No student participating in this program has regressed or shown a loss of skills, and the larger percentage have shown considerable progress.

There are some instances in which a student participating in a M.A.T.C. program will become increasingly verbal, and, consequently, the signs for learned vocabulary are faded. Signs are then used to teach only new vocabulary as necessary.

These guidelines and criteria have evolved from a trial and error process in programming for students in the Developmental Learning Program. It is necessary to apply clinical judgement in addition to the defined criteria for M.A.T.C. placement for some students. Clinical judgement includes a close examination of a student's developmental rates in skill areas other than language and an evaluation of the effect of interrupting behaviors on the student's ability to learn. This additional information helps the teacher of the speech and language impaired decide on program placement if there has been a question of the value of M.A.T.C. for a particular student. Although M.A.T.C. has not proved effective for every student to whom it has been prescribed, in no instance has it been found to be detrimental. Therefore, a M.A.T.C. Program may be prescribed for a trial period with the inclusion and integration of a backup system, such as a photo or picture card system.

REFERENCES

Churchill, D.: *Language of Autistic Children.* Washington, D.C., V. H. Winston and Sons, 1978.

Shapiro, T., Fish, B., and Ginsberg, G.: The speech of a schizophrenic child from 2 to 6. *Am J Psychiatry, 128:*1408-13, 1972.

Wolfe, S. and Chess, S.: An analysis of the language of fourteen schizophrenic children. *J Child Psychol Psychiatry, 6:*29-41, 1965.

Chapter 6

THE CONCEPT OF GENERALIZED IMITATION

Implications for Developing Curricula for the Autistic Child

SUSAN JOHNSEN DOLLAR

THE AUTISTIC POPULATION is one of the smallest defined subgroups in the field of special education. It has been estimated that autism occurs in about four or five out of every
10,000 children (Rutter, 1965). For this reason, little interest and
research was generated for many years. This paucity of information forced many of these children into the back wards of institutions where they received little or no educational programming.
The prevailing attitude seemed to be that there was little that
could be done for the autistic child. With the development of
behavioral technology, parent advocacy groups and legislation
focusing on the needs of children with the most severe handicaps, public and professional views have begun to change. Within the last fifteen years, it has been demonstrated repeatedly that
the autistic child can in fact learn (Ulrich, Stachnik and Mabry,
1966; Sloane and MacAulay, 1968; Ullmann and Krasner,
1965).

Problems seem to arise in the generalization of specific skills
from the training situation (Allyon and Azrin, 1968; Lovaas,
1966). Autistic children seem to over select or attend to only one
of several characteristics of a concept (Donnelen-Walsh, 1977;
Lovaas, 1971). Frequently, the characteristic may not even be
essential to the concept. For example, the autistic child who can
only dress himself/herself when in the presence of a particular
teacher or within a definite learning space has not learned the
concept of the dressing operation. She/he may have discrimin-

105

ated the teacher or the situation as an essential characteristic of the concept. If the teacher who signals the operation leaves, what happens to the skill that was "learned?"

The purpose of this chapter is to examine a way of developing curricula for the autistic child that reduces the probability of mislearning or attention to irrelevant cues. The approach requires the teacher to make an initial analysis of the concept to be taught to ensure that all irrelevant characteristics are varied within the teaching sequence. Before looking at what to teach the autistic child, it might be helpful to identify the characteristics of a *concept*.[1]

Concept Characteristics

First, concepts cannot be abstract: each example (instance) of a concept has certain observable characteristics. Therefore, any given concept, e.g. shoe, toothbrush, person, is defined by referring to the observable, common characteristics of the collected examples used to present the concept. Put another way, the examples presented comprise or present a concept because there will always be some characteristics which we group together to form a unique set of shared characteristics. This unique group of features defines the concept and is not shared by any other concept.

Second, concepts cannot be taught through a single example. The teacher's initial role in concept teaching is to structure the environment, e.g. verbal instruction and objects, so that various examples of a concept are shown to have a set of shared characteristics. For example, the teacher may present a picture of a star and say, "This is an example of a 'hunk.'" Next, she/he may present a picture of a tree and say, "This is also a 'hunk.'" At this point, does the learner know what a "hunk" is? The star and the tree could be examples of a number of different concepts. "Hunk" could be Christmas objects, solid objects, or pointed objects. Even though the teacher may have presented positive examples of the concept, the two examples cannot teach the

---

[1] The idea of a *concept* is generated from the works of Becker, Engelmann and Thomas (1975); Bruner, Goodnow and Austin (1967); and Dollar and Dollar (1976).

concept. Each example has many characteristics in addition to the ones defining the concept. For this reason we always talk about groups or classes of instances used to present a concept.

Third, the teacher must never vary or change the determined essential or defining characteristics and must *always* vary the unimportant characteristics of examples. This point follows directly from earlier comments about the fact that it is the common or unvaried characteristics of examples that signal behavior. As an example, suppose that the teacher intended to teach the concept of *shoe*. In teaching *shoe*, the teacher presents a variety of instances; however, the teacher never varies the characteristic of color. In fact, each group of instances presented share the common characteristic of being brown. In this example, characteristics such as color, position, size, etc., do not change the meaning of *shoe* and must be varied.

Fourth, the essential characteristics of concepts are relative. As an example, how would you determine how big is *big?* An eagle is big in comparison to a set of category containing all birds. An eagle is small in comparison to the set of things that fly. It is important to know what concept set or category we are teaching. To further illustrate the key point of determining essential characteristics by comparing concepts, suppose that the only shapes you planned to teach were *triangles* and *circles*. The only needed essential characteristic to differentiate the two concepts would be *straight lines* for triangle and *curved lines* for circle. To increase the complexity of the concept, assume that the concept set includes not only circles and triangles but also includes squares as well. Given the addition of *squareness* to teach, we can no longer direct the learner's attention to the *straight side* characteristic previously used to teach triangle. Straight side may no longer be the only essential characteristic of triangle because another concept in the concept set now shares the straight side characteristic. We could choose to define triangle as three straight sides and square as four straight sides. Given the addition of *rectangles* to teach, rectangles and squares have four sides, and both share the straight side characteristic with triangles. Thus, we would have to change the essential characteristics of squareness to include four, straight and equal sides in order to teach the difference between square, rectangle and triangle. Therefore, the essential characteristics of a concept may be defined only after you determine the higher order concepts. Essential characteristics are relative because they may change depending upon what other concepts are members of the same higher order set.

Tasks should include both positive and negative examples of the concept. It is impossible to present every example of any single concept. In teaching, you present a group of examples that are a sample of all possible examples. For instance, you select a sample of triangles to present rather than present all of the triangles in existence. To learn the concept correctly, the child must be presented with the range or boundaries of the concept. To demonstrate the boundary of a concept, the learner must be shown *nonexamples* or *not instances*. The limitation of triangle can be shown by presenting circle and square as not instances. The not instances chosen are from the other concepts in the concept set. Presenting a shoe as a not instance of triangle would be inappropriate because shoe and triangle are not in the same concept set. Put another way, shoe and triangle instances do not share any common relevant characteristics. Concepts that are members of the same higher order concept set are likely to confuse the learner if the critical differences between each concept are not taught.

If a teacher understands the idea of a concept, she/he can determine what is important for the student to discriminate from the presented instances and what instances are needed to ensure generalization. With an analysis, a listing of essential and irrelevant characteristics are generated. These irrelevant characteristics can later be systematically varied in developing a sequence of presentation.

Difference Between Task and Concept Analysis

This approach to the development of skill training sequences varies from the present and most prevalent task analysis procedures. In task analysis, terminal and prerequisite behaviors are specified and placed in a logical sequence. For example, take the self-help skill of tying shoes. Some analyses of this task have specified thirty-six behavioral pinpoints. As the child reaches criterion on one pinpoint, she/he moves to the next pinpoint until "mastery" is obtained. Using this approach, the student learns to tie a shoe. The "shoe," in one case, was a model provided by the developers of the program.

It is questionable whether or not the student could tie other shoes, shoes on his/her own feet, or even shoes with different laces. With concept analysis the concepts of *shoe, lace, bow,* plus the operation of *tying* would be analyzed and systematically varied within the sequence to further generalization. For the most part, curricula based upon task analysis begins with no concept presentation at all and proceeds directly to having the learner perform tasks that relate to the unpresented concepts. It is not surprising that a student may only learn to tie the model shoe and may have to be retaught to tie other shoes in different situations. The major purpose for looking at the analysis of concepts as a means for developing training curricula for the autistic child is to provide an efficient way of transferring skills across tasks, settings, and people.

The Concept of Generalized Imitation

To illustrate the approach it may be helpful to examine the concept of *generalized imitation*. Imitating the behavior of another person is one of the most important operations an autistic child can learn since many skills are acquired in this manner.

In analyzing a concept, the first step is to collect a series of teaching instances that identify the current characteristics of the concept. To review, those characteristics held constant are called essential; those that are varied are called irrelevant. Let's examine one case study to demonstrate the analysis procedure:

> To train imitation, the teacher would give the signal "Do this" and follow it with an action to be imitated. The first task was to raise her left arm. Susie did not respond. The teacher reached out and raised Susie's left hand, then gave her food. The teacher put Susie through the steps of the response. After doing this several times, the teacher began to fade out his help until Susie was responding on her own.
>
> The second response to be imitated was tapping the table with the left hand. The teacher said, "Do this," and tapped the table. Susie raised her hand. "Do this" had become a signal for raising her hand, not tapping the table. Physical prompting was used once again until she could tap the table when the teacher did. The teacher then went back to saying, "Do this," while raising his left hand. Susie tapped the table. For a series of

trials, the teacher went back and forth between the two responses to teach Susie that "Do this" was the signal to look at what I do and do it. Imitation involves the operations of looking and doing what you see someone else doing. At first, "Do this" was a signal for Susie to raise her hand. Then, "Do this" was a signal to tap the table. By going back and forth between the two tasks, she could only be right if she looked at what the teacher was doing.

The next task was to tap her chest with her left hand. She learned a little faster, but was still confused when the teacher went back to hand raising and tapping. When all of the tasks were performed on signal, a new task was introduced. Each new task was learned more quickly. By the time 50 tasks had been taught, Susie was imitating more than half of all new tasks on first presentation. She was learning the operation, the generalized procedure of matching her behavior to that of the teacher. By the time 130 tasks had been taught, she was imitating almost every new task on first trial. The only tasks she had trouble with were ones that were physically difficult for her, like walking while balancing a book on her head.

Part of the way through the training, she was taught to imitate whole chains of responses. The teacher would say "Do this" and then tap the table, walk across the room, and clap his hands. Then Susie would do each action in sequence.

Late in the training, when she would imitate almost anything, the teacher said "Do this" and made the sound "Ah." Susie would not do it. Imitation had been an operation controlled by "Do this" and a visual signal, not an auditory signal. The examples of the imitative operation had not been taught. She had not been taught to imitate sounds. To get imitation of sounds going, the teacher put the sound in with a chain of actions. He said, "Susie, do this." He got up from his chair, walked to the center of the room, turned toward Susie, said "Ah," and returned to his seat. Susie got up, went to the center of the room, faced the teacher, and began a series of facial and vocal responses out of which eventually came something close enough to "Ah" to merit reinforcement. The basis for teaching Susie to talk (through verbal imitation) has been started (from *Teaching 2: Cognitive Learning and Instruction* by Wesley C. Becker, Siegfried Engleman, and Don R. Thomas. © 1975, Science Research Associates Inc. Reprinted by permission of the publisher).

Using this example, the concept of generalized imitation would include the following essential characteristics:[2] one teacher is present; there is a signal for the imitative response, "Do this"; the response is followed by a similar or same response; one observer (Susie) is present; the setting where the response is

---

[2] For the purpose of this chapter only a single example is used. To make a more thorough analysis of the concept, multiple examples should be examined.

made appears to be constant; reinforcement (food) followed successful performance. The characteristics that were varied or irrelevant to the concept were the responses(s) that was imitated, the number of responses imitated following the "do this" signal, and the modality of the signal.

After identifying the essential and irrelevant characteristics from the example, the second step is to determine which essential characteristics need to be varied to avoid mislearning. In this case, if the setting and model are held constant, Susie may learn to imitate responses only within a single situation. It is important that Susie imitate not only at school but at home; not only the teacher, but the parent or other students. Susie may also need to learn to imitate when others are present, e.g. in the family, in the classroom. Consequently, the number of models and observers will also need to be varied. It does seem that some kind of stimulus control of the imitative response is essential. By observing autistic children, one learns that they do imitate a variety of responses. However, most of these responses are deemed maladaptive or inappropriate to the situation. It is important that desired responses be elicited by appropriate cues although the cues may vary. Simply stated, when Susie is asked to imitate, she imitates. Eventually these cues may become less explicit in indicating when imitation is appropriate.

The third step is to make a list of the characteristics of the concept. Characteristics of generalized imitation would appear to be the following:

Essential	*Irrelevant*
1. Signal present for imitative response	1. Signal may be verbal, non-verbal or less explicit
2. Response is followed by another similar (same) response	2. Content of and modality of response
3. Association of reinforcement with a model or signal for the imitative process	3. Person who is model
4. Attention to model(s)	4. Situation where imitative response occurs
	5. Physical presence of reinforcer
	6. Number of models or observers

The fourth step is to compare the concept with other concepts in the same set. A refinement of the concept of generalized imitation could be determined as other concepts within the same set are identified. For a further analysis, the reader is referred to Gerwitz and Stingle (1968) who do contrast the concepts of identification and introjection with the concept of imitation.

Finally, once the concept is specified, the teacher plans the program sequence. In determining a sequence, the teacher needs to follow two important rules:

1. Separate, as far as possible, those tasks in the sequence that are difficult to discriminate from one another. For example, the operations of *jumping* and *hopping* have more characteristics in common than jumping and *walking*. Consequently, if these were responses that you wanted the learner to imitate you would teach the concept of jumping, then several other concepts, before hopping. At that point you would contrast the two operations to direct the learner's attention to specific differences.

2. Tasks should systematically vary one irrelevant characteristic at a time. In the case of Susie, only the content of the response was varied initially. Next, the number of responses that followed the signal was varied and, finally, the mode was varied. If the teacher systematically varies all of the irrelevant characteristics, the child will learn the essential characteristics of the concept.

Summary

The following are some important points that have been made in this chapter:

1. Autistic children do learn but have difficulty in generalizing what they learn.

2. This lack of generalization may be due to the autistic child's attention to irrelevant as opposed to essential characteristics of the concept.

3. To determine what are essential characteristics, the curriculum developer or teacher needs to do an analysis of the concept.

4. Once the concept is analyzed, the teacher can then follow the sequencing rules to systematically vary irrelevant characteristics.

Many questions remain unanswered. Is it more efficient to teach basic skills through concept analysis, task analysis or both processes? What measure should be used in determining when to begin varying irrelevant characteristics? How many irrelevant characteristics can be varied at one time with the autistic child? Will the essential characteristics of the concept vary depending upon the population?

One of the major responsibilities of the educator toward the autistic population is to find the best means for teaching critical skills. Hopefully, the ideas presented in this paper will lead to new areas of research in the developing of effective teaching programs.

REFERENCES

Allyon, T. and Azrin, N.: *The Token Economy.* New York, Appleton-Century-Crofts, 1968.

Becker, W., Engelmann, S., and Thomas, D.: *Teaching 2: Cognitive Learning and Instruction.* Chicago, SRA, 1975.

Bruner, J., Goodnow, J., and Austin, G.: *A Study of Thinking.* New York, Wiley, 1967.

Dollar B. and Dollar, S.: *Learning Opportunities for Teachers.* Austin, Texas, Accommodative Instructional Systems, 1976.

Donnellan-Walsh, A.: The autistic child in the public school classroom. In Gilliam, J. (Ed.): *Teaching the Autistic Child.* Austin, Texas, Texas Society for Autistic Citizens, 1977, pp. 5-37.

Gerwitz, J. L. and Stingle, K. G.: Learning of generalized imitation as the basis for identification. *Psychol Rev, 75:*374-397, 1968.

Lovaas, O. I.: Acquisition of imitative speech by psychotic children. *Science, 151:*705-707, 1966.

Lovaas, O. I., Schreibman, L., Koegel, R. and Rehm, R.: Selective responding by autistic children to multiple sensory input. *J Abnorm Psychol, 77:*211-222, 1971.

Rutter, M.: Medical aspects of the education of psychotic (autistic) children. In Western, P. T. B. (Ed.): *Some Approaches to Teaching Autistic Children.* Oxford, Pergamon Pr, 1965, pp. 61-74.

Sloane, H. N., Jr. and MacAulay, B. C.: *Operant Procedures in Remedial Speech and Language Training.* Boston, 1968.

Ullmann, L. P. and Krasner, L.: *Case Studies in Behavior Modification.* New York, HR & W, 1965.

Ulrich, R., Stachnik, T. and Mabry, J.: *Control of Human Behavior.* Glenview, Illinois, Scott, 1966.

Chapter 7

TEACHING SIMPLE DISCRIMINATIONS WITHOUT ERRORS

Wesler H. Perlman

What is a Discrimination?

W E SAY THAT A CHILD is discriminating between things in the environment when the child demonstrates that he/she can reliably tell the difference between two things. To "tell the difference" is not restricted to a verbal response. Matching a red block to a red block in a setting where red and green are present is to tell the difference between two things. To name the colors is also another way to tell the difference between two colors.

A Way to Teach Discriminations

Applied Behavior Analysis introduced a systematic way to teach discriminations. Typically, if one was interested in teaching the difference between red and green, we rewarded the child for matching red to red in the presence of red and green. The placement of red and green in the stimulus array was randomized to guard against position preference developing. Repeated presentations of red continued until the child reached criterion (twenty correct consecutive responses or 95% correct for a session of fifty trials). Once criterion was reached, green was then taught in the same fashion. When green reached criterion, then red and green were presented in a mixed fashion. Typically, at this point a significant decrease in correct responses takes place. Often, the child responds at a chance level. Over a period of perhaps hundreds of trials the child would learn to match red to red and green to green. Sometimes discriminations taught in this way may never be learned by the child. Nevertheless, when the discrimination was learned, many errors were made. In a very practical sense, the more errors a child makes,

114

the fewer things he can learn for a specified time frame. It has been said that we learn from our errors and that it is a natural part of the learning process. It is true that we learn from our errors, but some of us learn to make another error from a previous error. Such seems to be the case with autistic and retarded youngsters. To make no errors is also natural if the environment happens to be arranged in that manner.

Errorless Learning

Terrace made a breakthrough in laboratory research by teaching discriminations errorlessly. This was done by fading along some dimension (intensity, hue, etc.) of the stimulus. This concept stimulated much research and became the foundation for many teaching regimes. True fading procedures rely on some costly device to fade the stimulus or teacher preparation of many sequenced materials to fade the stimulus. These procedures have been very effective, but very costly to deliver in terms of money and time invested.

Terrace's focus of control had to do with the stimulus, with little attention given to the response. Errorless learning techniques are certainly not limited to fading some aspects of a stimulus.

A new way to teach discriminations without errors has evolved. It involves more precise control of the relationship of the stimulus and response components. The environment is arranged in such a way that it is almost impossible to make an error. Therefore, the consequence becomes a much less salient feature of teaching a task; that is to say we supply consequences, but do not rely so heavily on them when teaching a task. The arrangement of the environment, in and of itself, makes the occurrence of an incorrect response highly unlikely.

How We Got to Where We Are

Let us return to the example we talked about earlier — teaching a child to match red to red or green to green in the presence of red and green. When red and green meet criterion, their presentations are mixed and a significant decrease in correct responses takes place. We were shaped to start at this point, because we saw that we had not taught anything up to that point as evidenced by the child's behavior. Therefore, our point of departure from standard teaching was to start off by teaching both response presentations mixed from the beginning. We thank the many autistic, retarded, and other handicapped children for shaping our behavior and telling us how to teach them.

Purpose

The purpose of this chapter is to present a procedure for teaching discriminations without errors. It certainly is not and does not claim to be exhaustive. This paper is not experimental in the sense that particular hypotheses were not tested. It is scientific and is based upon data. Much of the data is anecdotal. There is no experimental design, because it is not an experiment. This is simply a presentation of a procedure that is a practical tool for teaching basic form discriminations, color discriminations, same-different concepts, labeling objects, etc., without errors.

Procedure for Errorless Learning

The procedure is best understood by the accompanying data sheet. In this example, we will use a very simple discrimination—matching three-dimensional colors. After the basic procedure is presented, a brief discussion of teaching more difficult tasks will be presented.

The following are key descriptors: stimulus array, stimulus presented, order of presentation, response made by student.

> *Stimulus Array* — objects, color, etc., that are in the child's view on the desk; the desk top is divided into two equal parts by marking with masking tape.
>
> *Stimulus Presented* — object, color, written word, spoken word, etc., that is presented to the child that begins the trial.
>
> *Order of Stimulus Presentation* — the systematic order or pattern in which stimuli are presented. For example, a 1:1 presentation is an alternating of stimulus A and B (A, B, A, B, etc.). A 2:2 presentation patterns stimulus A and B in this fashion: A, A, B, B, A, A, B, B. A 1:1:2:1:1

presentation patterns stimulus A and B in this fashion:
A, B, A, A, B, A, B, B, A, B.

Response Made by Student — placement of color to appropriate color in stimulus array or putting word card on appropriate object.

What Do We Want the Child to Do Terminally?

When the child is presented with a red block, we want the child to put the red block that is presented next to the red block in the stimulus array and when the child is presented with a green block, we want the child to put the green block that is presented next to the green block in the stimulus array. The position of the stimuli in the stimulus array are randomized on each trial. The order of presentation is also randomized.

Position I — constant position of stimulus or stimuli in stimulus array. Stimulus A on left, stimulus B on right (red on left, green on right). (See data sheet in Appendix.)

Position II — constant position of stimulus or stimuli in stimulus array. Stimulus B on left, stimulus A on right (green on left, red on right). Level A — (see data sheet) Position I, one color in stimulus array.

A_1 — order of presentation 1:1 (A, B, A, B or red, green, red, green)

Criterion (in order to move to A_2) — ten consecutive correct responses (five red, five green).

Sequence of trial 1 (top view of desk);

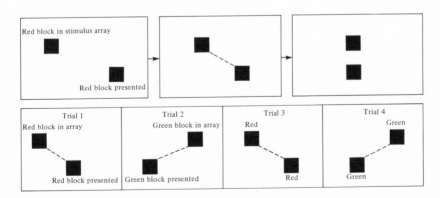

A₂ — Position I, one color in stimulus array 2:2 order of presentation A, A, B, B, A, A, B, B (red, red, green, green, red, red, green, green).

Criterion — eight consecutive correct responses.

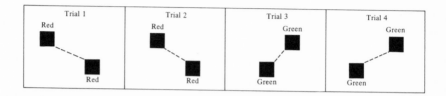

A₃ — Position I, one color in stimulus array 1:1:2:1:1:2:1:1 order of presentation A, B, A, A, B, A, B, B, A, B (red, green, red, red, green, red, green, green, red, green).

Criterion — ten consecutive correct responses.

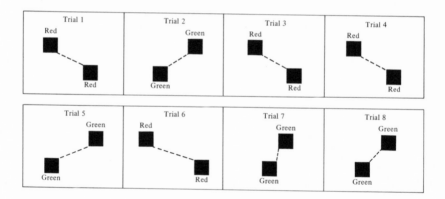

Note: the *order of presentation* is the only difference among A₁, A₂, . A₃. Level B — Position I, two colors in stimulus array.

B₁ — Position I, two colors in stimulus array, 1:1 order of presentation, A, B, A, B (red, green, red, green).

Criterion — ten consecutive correct responses (five red, five green).

If student makes an error, give student one more chance. If student makes a second error, go back to the former simpler level (in this case A₃).

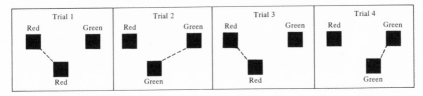

B$_2$ — Position I, two colors in stimulus array, 2:2, order of presentation, A, A, B, B, A, A, B, B (red, red, green, green, red, red, green, green).
Criterion — eight consecutive correct responses.

B$_3$ — Position I, two colors in stimulus array, 1:1:2:1:1:2:1:1, order of presentation A, B, A, A, B, A, B, B, A, B (red, green, red, red, green, red).
Criterion — ten consecutive correct responses.

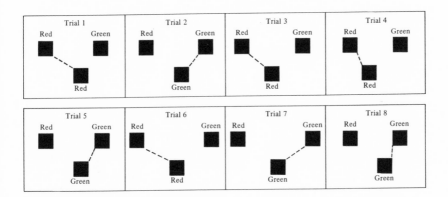

Level D — Position II, two colors in stimulus array. (Note: Level C was skipped because only one color in stimulus array.) If student makes an error at this point, give the student one more chance. If student makes second error, go to Level C_3.

D_1 — Position II, two colors in stimulus array, 1:1, order of presentation A, B, A, B (red, green, red, green).

Criterion — ten consecutive correct responses.

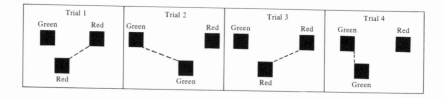

D_2 — Position II, two colors in stimulus array, 2:2, order of presentation, A, A, B, B, A, A, B, B (red, red, green, green).

Criterion — eight consecutive correct responses.

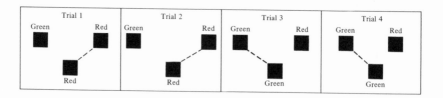

D_3 — Position II, two colors in stimulus array, 1:1:2:1:1:2:1:1, A,B,A,A,B,A,B,B,A,B (red, green, red, red, green, red, green green, red, green).

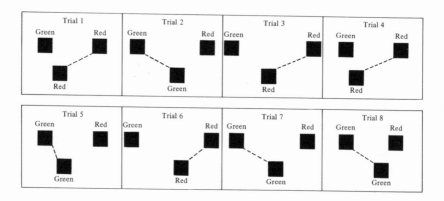

At this point, the order of presentation and the placement of colors in the array are both randomized. If an error is made, give the child one more chance. If a second error is made, go back to former level of training. Typically, once a student completes the entire sequence, no further training is needed.

Extensions

We have had the pleasant experience of teaching many autistic youngsters different types of discriminations using the procedure. Usually, it requires eighty to ninety trials to teach a discrimination pair. We have taught youngsters to label objects with word cards in a matter of twenty minutes. Prior to this training, these were youngsters in which literally thousands of trials and hundreds of hours were invested to teach such a simple discrimination. Despite this, many times these youngsters never learned the task.

We have taught three-dimensional shapes in relation to two-dimensional shapes, two-dimensional colors in relation to two-dimensional colors, discriminating between B and D, receptive labeling of objects (word cards, signs, verbal), expressive labeling of objects, same and different concepts, spatial relations and simple commands (pick up, push).

Prerequisites — In our example (matching colors).

1. Sitting at desk.
2. Attending — looking at the stimulus presented and the stimulus array. The child should not be given the opportunity to manipulate the stimulus presented unless he/she is attending to the stimulus presented. This becomes much more of a problem when the stimulus presented is auditory. The next section will discuss such related problems.

Things Inherent in the Task that Affect Difficulty of the Task

If things in the stimulus array are very similar (pen and pencil), then the discrimination between them is more difficult. Therefore, at the beginning of training, use objects that are very dissimilar and then proceed to more closely related shapes. In other words, make the task easy by making the difference between things very obvious.

Autism

The nature of the stimulus presented can have a big effect on the difficulty of the task. For example, if we wanted a child to label an object (cup) with a word card (cup), the stimulus presented would be the word card. Since the stimulus presented is visual, we have a better idea of whether or not the child is attending to the stimulus presented. Also, it is easier for a child to attend to a visual stimulus as opposed to an auditory stimulus because of its permanence. The auditory stimulus is evanescent — it is there and gone. Perhaps a way to increase the probability of attending to an auditory stimulus is to arrange an additional cue announcing the beginning of a trial. If we say *cup, the child is to pick up the cup. The stimulus presented is the word cup.* The stimulus array consists of a cup and a ball. The response made by the child is to pick up the cup. This would be called receptive labeling. In the example of the word card, in relation to the cup, the response made by the child is placing the word card on the cup. If we were asking a child to label objects expressively, we lose much control over the production of the response. The stimulus presented is always the same (What is this?). We circumvented this when teaching the same-different concept. First, we taught it receptively by putting two same objects on the left and two different objects on the right. The stimulus presented was "Pick up same" or "Pick up different." This receptive training served to bridge the gap for expressive labeling. Signs in their pure form are evanescent, but, because they are visual signs, they can be made more permanent during training.

A Word of Thanks

A special thanks goes to all the children, parents, students, and staff at the Center For Behavioral Studies in Denton, Texas at North Texas State University for their support.

APPENDIX

Child's Name: _____ Date: _____

Trainer's Name: _____ Length of Session: _____

Reinforcer Used: _____ Reinforcement Schedule: _____

POSITION I

A. Objects Used	Order of Presentation	1 Color of Stimulus Array
Red-left — — — Green-right	A_1 1:1	
— — —	A_2 2:2	
— — —	A_3 1:1:2:1:1	

POSITION II

C. Objects Used	Order of Presentation	1 Color in Stimulus Array
Red-right — — — Green-left	C_1 1:1	
— — —	C_2 2:2	
— — —	C_3 1:1:2:1:1	

B. Objects Used	Order of Presentation	2 Colors in Stimulus Array
— — —	B_1 1:1	
— — —	B_2 2:2	
— — —	B_3 1:1:2:1:1	

C. Objects Used	Order of Presentation	2 Colors in Stimulus Array
— — —	D_1 1:1	
— — —	D_2 2:2	
— — —	D_3 1:1:2:1:1	

Randomization of Presentation   and   Randomization of the Array

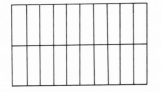

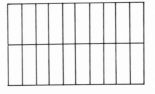

Chapter 8

CURRICULAR MATERIALS FOR AUTISTIC CHILDREN

KITTY DORSEY

T HE OBJECTIVE of this chapter is to present an overview of selected commercially available curricula that are applicable for use with autistic students. The presentation does not reflect all materials available, nor does it reflect materials from all companies and projects that produce this type of material. It is intended only to apprise educators of the range and extent of materials available.

The following criteria were used in the selection of materials included:

1. Curricula that was developed for, or has been used with, the specific populations functioning as severely/profoundly handicapped and/or multiply handicapped.
2. Curricula that meets the needs of this population at some developmental age between birth and adulthood.
3. Curricula that addresses the spectrum of skill areas, or one or more of the specific skill areas necessary for independent functioning.
4. Curricula that contain specific objectives correlated with suggested teaching activities or strategies.
5. Curricula that may be used by professional staff, supportive staff, paraprofessionals, ward attendants, or parents.
6. Curricula that are available commercially or available upon request.

The following annotations are descriptions of the materials presented.

BCP Method Cards

Developer: The Special Education Management System (SEIMS) by the Santa Cruz County Office of Education, Santa Cruz, California.

Publisher: VORT Corporation
P.O. Box 11132
Palo Alto, California 94306

Format: Five books.

Developmental Level: Age and label free.

Content Areas: Self-help, motor, communication, social, and learning skills.

Goal: To provide instructional programs and methods to match each of the strands and objectives included in the BCP (Behavioral Characteristics Progression) assessment.

Description:

The five BCP method books contain more than 2,200 teacher-developed instructional methods. Each method is correlated to a BCP objective and includes the following:

BCP strand number
BCP objective number
Title of activity
Pupil abilities required
Interest level
Pupil grouping
Activity length
Number of adults required

Suggested materials and/or equipment (in most cases, the methods do not require commercially available materials or equipment)
Step-by-step instructions

BCP Method Book 1 – Self-help Skills contains 371 methods for the following BCP strands: Feeding/Eating, Drinking, Toileting, Grooming, Dressing, Undressing, Nasal Hygiene, Oral Hygiene, and Self-identification.

BCP Method Book 2 – Motor Skills contains 534 methods for the following BCP strands: Sensory Perception, Visual Motor,

Gross Motor, Orientation, Mobility, Wheelchair Use, Ambulation, and Swimming.

BCP Method Book 3 – Communication Skills contains 500 methods for the following BCP strands: Auditory Perception, Prearticulation, Language Comprehension, Language Development, Listening, Sign Language, Finger Spelling, and Speech Reading.

BCP Method Book 4 – Social Skills contains 467 methods for the following BCP strands: Attendance/Promptness, Adaptive Behaviors, Impulse Control, Interpersonal Relations, Responsible Behaviors, Personal Welfare, Self-Confidence, Honesty, Social Eating, Attention Span, and Task Completion.

BCP Method Book 5 – Learning Skills contains 420 methods for the following BCP strands: Reading, Math (computation), Practical Math, Writing, Spelling, and Reasoning.

EBSCO, IEP-1, Personal Competencies

Authors: Numerous classroom teachers.

Publisher: EBSCO
1230 First Avenue North
Birmingham, Alabama 35203

Cole Supply
P.O. Box 1717
Pasadena, Texas 77501

Format: Kit; Approximately 160 instructional method cards, two cards of teacher instructions, and a pad of fifty profile tracking charts.

Developmental Level: Students who function as severely and profoundly handicapped and low-functioning trainable mentally retarded.

Content Areas: Personal competencies, self-help skills.

Goal: To provide instructional exceptional prescriptions and instructional method cards for the teacher of the severely and profoundly impaired.

Description:

The *IEP-1, Personal Competencies Program* provides cards with hundreds of proven, sequenced instructional methods in the following areas:

Toothbrushing	Eating
Nose Blowing	Social Eating
Personal Safety	Drinking
Self-awareness	Toileting
Social Speaking	Grooming
Gross Motor A	Dressing
Gross Motor B	Undressing

Each instructional card contains the following:
    The long-term goal area
    A short-term instructional objective
    A list of instructional methods
    Prerequisite skills necessary
    Resources needed (resources and materials that would nor-
        mally be found in a classroom)

All instructional objectives are listed on a form to allow for easy
data collection. These Profile Tracking Charts are provided in
pads of fifty in the kit. All teacher instructions are provided on
two cards at the front of the kit. Also included is a card of general
instructional suggestions for the teacher.

The *EBSCO, IEP-1,* is easily accessed through any assessment
utilized.

EBSCO, IEP-2, Program on Behavioral, Attitudinal and Pre-Academic Competencies

Authors: Numerous classroom teachers.

Publisher: EBSCO
1230 First Avenue North
Birmingham, Alabama 35203

Cole Supply
P.O. Box 1717
Pasadena, Texas 77501

Format: Kit; Approximately 180 instructional method cards, two cards of teacher instructions, and a pad of fifty profile tracking charts.

Developmental Level: Special education students of junior high school age, students who function at the higher range of trainable mental retardation, and young mildly impaired students with behavioral disorders.

Content Areas: Behavioral, attitudinal, and preacademic competencies.

Goal: To provide instructional exceptional prescriptions and instructional method cards for the teacher of the severely and profoundly impaired.

Description:

The *IEP-2, Program on Behavioral, Attitudinal and Pre-academic Competencies* provides cards with hundreds of proven, sequenced instructional methods in the following areas:

Handwriting
Eye Motor Coordination
Functional Arithmetic
Reasoning
Auditory Perception
Sensory Perception
Listening
Adaptive Behavior

Self-control
Person-to-person Relations
Attention Span
Task Completion
Attendance/Punctuality
Honesty
Self-confidence

Each instructional card contains:
 The long-term goal area
 A short-term instructional objective
 A list of instructional methods
 Prerequisite skills necessary
 Resources needed (resources and materials that would nor-
  mally be found in a classroom)

All instructional objectives are listed on a form to allow for easy data collection. These Profile Tracking Charts are provided in pads of fifty in the kit. All teacher instructions are provided on two cards at the front of the kit. Also included is a card of general instructional suggestions for the teacher.

The *EBSCO, IEP-2*, is easily accessed through any assessment utilized.

Functional Speech and Language Training for the Severely Handicapped

Part I: Steps 1-9, Persons and Things
Part II: Steps 10-29, Actions With Persons and Things
Part III: Steps 30-42, Possessions and Color
Part IV: Steps 43-60, Size, Relation and Location

Authors: Doug Guess, Wayne Sailor, and Donald M. Baer.

Publisher: H & H Enterprises, Inc.
P.O. Box 1070-C
Lawrence, Kansas 66044

Format: Four books with scoring forms.

Developmental Level: Persons who lack language skills whether they are referred to as autistic, brain-damaged, or profoundly retarded.

Content Areas: Language.

Goal: To provide a comprehensive language training program for the severely handicapped.

Description:

The manuals eliminate the need for specialized facilities or specially trained teachers. The program can be used in settings ranging from institutions to the home. The only prior knowledge the trainer needs is some understanding of behavior management techniques. The program has been made as specific as possible while still retaining the flexibility necessary to meet the needs of individual students.

The manuals include examples of scoring forms and example trials to help the language trainer understand the process. Specific instructions are given in the techniques for conducting training sessions and in how to recognize when the child is ready to progress to each new step. Also included are tables for converting scores to percentages to make progress reporting easier. Detailed instructions explain the process of summarizing the sessions and graphing progress so that the teacher, parents, or others concerned with the child's education may chart the progress of the child through the program. Different students progress at different rates, but the training must be done in sequence without skipping steps, because the later manuals build on the skills acquired in the earlier manuals.

The price of each training manual includes one set of scoring forms. Each child in training will need a set of scoring forms. Forms for each part are different.

Initial Expressive Language Program

Authors:	John J. McDonnell, H. D. Fredericks, and David Grove.
Publisher:	Teaching Research Publications Monmouth, Oregon 97361
Format:	Kit; Teacher's Manual, Student Placement Tests and Data Sheets, more than 300 picture cards.
Developmental Level:	The handicapped student of any chronological age who has no language or speaks in phrases of less than five words.
Content Areas:	Expressive language.
Goal:	To provide teachers and parents with language material that can be used to train handicapped children in expressive language.
Description:	

The objective of the program is to teach the student to speak in phrases consisting of more than five words. There are eight sections in this language program:

Establishment and Maintenance of Eye Contact
Motor Imitation
Motor and Vocal Imitation
Verbal Imitation of Consonants and Vowels
Verbal Imitation of Consonants and Vowel Chains
Verbal Imitation of Words
Identification of Objects and Action Words
Word Chaining through Imitation

The Teacher's Manual includes a general overview of the principles of learning involved in the application of this program. Also, there are sections that give the functions and directions for use of both the Student Placement Tests and the Data Sheets.

For each of the eight phases of the program, the trainer is provided the following information:

Terminal behaviors
Prerequisite behaviors
Materials required
Procedure (introduction, recording the data, cues, placement
in phase, progression through steps, alternative treatment
approach, steps, transfer of learning, consequating)
The kit also contains over 300 picture cards that are required in
various phases of the program.

Instructional Programming for the Handicapped Student

Authors: Daniel R. Anderson, Gary D. Hodson, and Willard G. Jones.

Publisher: Charles C Thomas, Publisher
301-327 East Lawrence Avenue
Springfield, Illinois 62717

Format: Book.

Developmental Level: Severely handicapped students.

Content Areas: Appearance, arithmetic, attending, cleanliness, concept, domestic and vocational, dressing, eating, miscellaneous, motor, sight vocabulary, socialization, speech and language, toileting, and writing skills.

Goal: To provide professional persons who provide direct educational services to the handicapped and those who train others to work with the handicapped student an extensively validated training program in behavior management skills suitable for use in a variety of educational settings.

Description:

More than 100 validated instructional programs appropriate for use with the handicapped student are presented. Emphasis throughout these programs is on the development of fundamental behavioral skills often lacking in the more severely handicapped student. Physically, the text is divided into three parts:

Part I deals with developing sound instructional programs for the purpose of either eliminating undesirable student behaviors or developing new and desirable ones.

Part II consists of an anthology of instructional programs appropriate for use with the handicapped student.

Part III contains an annotated bibliography of references to commercially available instructional programs, journal articles, and textbooks, which discusses techniques useful for modifying a wide variety of student behaviors.

The Karnes Early Language Activities

          Author: Merle B. Karnes.

       Publisher: GEM
                    Generators of Educational Materials,
                    Enterprises
                    P.O. Box 2339
                    Station A
                    Champaign, Illinois 61820

          Format: Kit: Teacher's Manual, 200 activity cards.

Developmental Level: Children functioning at the eighteen to
                    thirty-six month level in language.

   Content Areas: Four areas of language skills — motor,
                    visual, auditory, and verbal.

            Goal: To assist professionals, paraprofessionals,
                    or parents in center or home-based day
                    care and preschool programs, and
                    teachers of handicapped children in the
                    initial stages of language development.

     Description:

The Karnes kit is a set of 200 activity cards divided into four
areas of language skills: motor, visual, auditory, and verbal. The
cards contain 1,000 activities that are arranged in order of difficulty within a category and across categories.

Each activity card has a lesson plan format which includes the
following:
   Behavioral objectives
   Materials, whether teacher-made or commercially available
   Procedures which explain setting, appropriate interaction,
      reinforcement, and other hints
   Criteria of performance to be met
   Activities to strengthen and help maintain the objective

The manual includes a format for recording progress of the
student based on the master sequencing of the activities across
objectives. Also included are sections on adaptations, techniques

to stimulate language development, suggestions for successful lessons, and management techniques.

Language Acquisition Program for the Retarded or Multiple Impaired

Author: Louise R. Kent.

Publisher: Research Press
2612 North Mathis Avenue
Champaign, Illinois 61820

Edmark Associates
13241 Northup Way
Bellevue, Washington 98005

Format: Manual.

Developmental Level: Severely retarded children.

Content Areas: Language.

Goal: To provide an operational manual for the teaching of language to severely retarded children.

Description:

The program consists of a variety of tasks that are sequenced according to presumed difficulty. Within three major sections, "Pre-Verbal," "Verbal-Receptive," and "Verbal-Expressive," are several phases that are further analyzed into parts. The "Pre-Verbal" section deals with the acquisition of prerequisite attending behaviors and motor imitation. The "Verbal-Receptive" and "Verbal-Expressive" sections include selected receptive and expressive skills, such as pointing to body parts, finding objects named, naming colors, and counting disappearing objects. The language may either be oral or manual, depending on the handicapping conditions and the age level of the student.

The manual includes complete instructions for each part of the program. These instructions include an initial inventory, test-teach procedures, final inventory and retention checks (this includes criteria level where applicable), presession preparation, and data recording.

The entire system is based on training procedures that involve the principles of reinforcement theory. Through the use of a token economy, the system increases the likelihood that certain behaviors will recur and be maintained.

Learning Staircase

Authors: Lila Coughran and Marilyn Goff

Publisher: Teaching Resources Corporation
100 Boylston Street
Boston, Massachusetts 02116

Format: Kit: Administrator's manual, 568 task cards for twenty modules, assessment inventory systems (AIS), report forms for parents, and grid pad for record keeping

Developmental Level: Three to six years

Content Areas: Language, cognitive, motor, and self-help skills

Goal: To provide accurate and specific diagnosis of individual children.

To provide a planned and systematic individualized curriculum based on prescriptions derived from these diagnoses.

To provide for evaluation of the results of the program to aid in further placement and/or programming for each child and to aid in accountability procedures if needed.

Description:

The following twenty curriculum modules are included in the Learning Staircase program:

Toilet Training	Vocabulary
Pre-Verbal	Same and Different
Gross Motor	Classification
Fine Motor	Time
Body Image	Sequence
Spatial Relationships	Number Concepts
Colors	Reading Readiness
Adjectives	Auditory Memory
Verbal Comprehension	Auditory Perception
Verbal Expression	Visual Memory

Each module is composed of a number of tasks or objectives (ranging in number from nine to eighty-two per module). Each task is presented on a separate task card which contains —

The objective, or *task*, which states what the child will be able to do upon completion of the task.

The approximate *developmental age*, which indicates the typical age at which most children accomplish the task.

The *method* for teaching the task.

The *criterion*, or standard, by which success for that task may be judged.

Specific *materials* to be used to implement the method.

The teacher's guide provides the teacher with a management system for implementing the total program. It also provides relevant references for each of the curriculum modules. The two appendices contain a scope and sequence of the total program which lists each module, the levels within each module, and the units and tasks within each level; and a listing of commercially available materials which could be used with each curriculum module.

Murdoch Center C & Y Program Library

A Collection of Step-By-Step Programs for the Developmentally Disabled

Authors: Andrew J. Wheeler, et al.

Publisher: Psychology Services
Program Library
Murdoch Center
Butner, North Carolina 27509

Format: Set; Manual (includes instructions, staff training and monitoring package, list of programs), complete set of 350 programs, and fifty each of baseline and training data sheets.

Developmental Level: Severely and profoundly retarded children and young adults.

Content Areas: Self-help, residential, and social skills; fine motor coordination; preacademics; and academics.

Goal: To develop a training system that:
1. Is usable by all training staff (regardless of academic background) at the Murdoch Center.
2. Contains a simple and efficient method of data collection that does not require a great deal of time or paper.
3. Contains a large number of programs at a very basic level and more complex skills broken down into very small steps.
4. Contains programs written in enough detail that varied trainers could implement them in consistent fashion.

Description:

Virtually the only prerequisite for training staff in learning to use the system is fundamental literacy. The system is easily mastered because it contains only two general teaching methods:

backward chaining and general shaping. The methods are unique in another aspect in that no verbal cueing is used in either method.

Another feature that leads to greater independence is the constant placement of stimuli. Because the initial command is only given once and is immediately followed by the student's performance, either cued or not, that verbal stimulus becomes discriminative for initiation of that performance. Also, reinforcers always follow the last step in the chain, not the actual step being trained.

The single data sheet can show up to 110 sessions' data on one side of a paper. It is self-graphing. Trainers complete their data sheet for each session by circling a letter that indicates degree of cueing or independence. No additional observer is required, and minimal time is needed for record keeping.

The collection has more than 350 programs, ranging from skills as simple as "pick-up — Palmer" to "Use of Calculator." Programs are written so tightly that little ambiguity exists regarding which movement is required at each point of the program.

The programs are grouped into the seven categories listed above. Self-help, preacademics, and academics are divided into subcategories. The categories and subcategories for all programs are coded by letter abbreviations. The final part of most programs' code is a numeral, which provides a unique code for each program within an area.

Each program format contains the following:
   Task (the exact name of the program)
   C & Y Program Library Number
   Page —— of —— (indicates how many pages the program has)
   Rev. (indicates revision date, if any)
   Specific Target Behavior (the behavior goal)
   General Instructions (the teaching method to be used)
   Prereq. (the prerequisites for the program)
   Materials (equipment and materials needed to carry out the
      program)
   Goal or Step — Student Behavior (task analysis of what the
      student will do)

Method — Trainer Behavior (the necessary actions of the trainer to produce the desired student behavior at each step)

Non-Slip

Non-Speech Language Imitation Program

Authors: Joseph K. Carrier, Jr., and Timothy Peak.

Publisher: H & H Enterprises, Inc.
Box 3342
Lawrence, Kansas 66044

Format: Kit; Program Manual, Word Symbols, Symbolic Sentence Tray, Program Instruction Cards, Picture (Stimulus) Cards, Word Cards, and Data Sheets.

Developmental Level: Students who have essentially no speech other than basic gestures or utterances.

Content Areas: Communication.

Goal: To help a trainer identify specific strengths and weaknesses in the learner's behaviors and to train the most critical requisite skills for language and communication.

Description:

Non-Slip is a mechanism to prepare nonspeech students for entrance into traditional communication programs. The Non-Slip Program Manual provides a description of prerequisite skills necessary for the program, including instruction on acquisition of those skills, i.e. manipulation of symbols. The authors give illustrations of adaptations that can be made to accommodate certain handicapping conditions.

The *Non-Slip* Program consists of twelve subprograms and includes a pre- and posttest for each. Also included in the manual is a set of recommendations for the transfer of the student into a regular communication or speech program.

Portage Guide to Early Education, Revised

Authors: Susan M. Bluma, Martha S. Shearer, Alma H. Frohman, and Jean M. Hilliard.

Publisher: The Portage Project
Cooperative Educational Service
Agency 12
412 East Slifer Street
Portage, Wisconsin 53901

Format: Kit; checklist of behaviors on which to record an individual child's developmental progress, a card file listing possible methods of teaching these behaviors, and a manual of directions for use of the checklist and card file as well as methods for implementing activities.

Developmental Level: Birth to 6 years.

Content Areas: Infant stimulation, socialization, language, self-help, cognitive, and motor skills.

Goal: To enhance a developmental approach to teaching.
To include several areas of development, using color coded cards.
To provide a method of recording existing skills and those learned during intervention.
To provide suggestions on how skills can be taught.

Description:

The *Portage Guide to Early Education* was developed to serve as a guide to teachers, aides, nurses, parents, or others who need to assess a child's behavior and plan realistic curriculum goals that lead to additional skills. The behaviors listed on the checklist are based on normal growth and development patterns. The materials were designed for normal children ages birth to six and handicapped children of any age with behaviors common to preschool children.

Behaviors in each area are initially assessed and indicated on the checklist. When a child misses ten to fifteen items in a row, the evaluation stops, and the instructor chooses the skills to begin teaching with the use of the card file. Each card is labeled according to —

  Category (content area)
  Age level (for normal development)
  Title (or skill to be taught)
  "What to Do" (a list of various activities to teach the skill). The instructor reads over the suggestions given and chooses the one which would be the most effective in teaching the child.

Information is given in the manual for developing behavioral objectives, task analysis (which is only used to an extent on the cards), cueing, teaching procedures, correction procedures, reinforcement, and prerequisites for learning.

The Potomac Program

A Curriculum for the Severely Handicapped, Deaf, Hearing Impaired, Non-Verbal

Authors: Sarah Hyde and Deborah Engle.

Publisher: Dormac, Inc.
P.O. Box 752
Beaverton, Oregon 97005

Format: Notebook.

Developmental Level: Severely handicapped, deaf, hearing impaired, or nonverbal.

Content Areas: Matching, categorization, sequencing, gross motor skills, fine motor skills, sign language, introduction to hearing aids and auditory training, and introduction to speech.

Goal: To train for specific skills and learning to learn (students are encouraged to solve problems and create order).

Description:

Each of the eight curriculum areas includes the following elements:

Cover page
Flow charts
Behavioral objectives
Subobjectives (teaching steps)
Activities
Explanatory illustrations
Evaluation sheets

After the student has completed Matching, Categorization, and Sequencing, s/he will be ready to begin basic math programs and/or programs presenting nonmath conceptual skills. Upon completion of Gross Motor Skills, Fine Motor Skills, and Sign Language, the student may enter structured language programs. Introduction to Hearing Aids and Auditory Training and Introduction to Speech will prepare the student for speech training.

Explanations of flow charts, curriculum structure (behavioral objectives, subobjectives, and activities), and illustrations apply to all sections of the curriculum. Evaluation sheets, because they are designed to reflect progress toward short-term goals within certain subject areas, are explained in the individual section notes. Sample forms are included.

**Performance Objectives for Preschool Children and
Preschool Curriculum Cards**

Developer: Part of the Project "An Upper Penninsula
Comprehensive Program for Preschool
Handicapped Children."

Publisher: Adapt Press, Inc.
808 West Avenue N
Sioux Falls, South Dakota 57104

Format: Kit; Manual of sequenced objectives,
more than 1,000 activity cards.

Developmental Level: Birth through six years.

Content Areas: Prereading skills (auditory discrimination, auditory memory, visual discrimination, visual memory, and beginning sounds), math skills, language and speech skill, self-care skills, social skills, gross and fine motor skills.

Goal: To provide the teacher with one teaching and measurement technique for a developmental sequence of learning objectives.

Description:

The performance objectives are based on age/level skills found in a variety of materials. All age level skills are based on the normal child's growth and development. The authors suggest the following use of the performance objectives:

1. Evaluate the child with standardized instruments to determine approximate age level functioning and potential areas of deficit.
2. Screen the child with performance objectives at his/her age/skill level until a teaching level is ascertained.
3. Screen the child in other skill areas to determine if teaching should occur in other areas as well.
4. Select the specific performance objectives to be used with the child.

5. Refer to the cross-referenced curriculum card to determine if there is a suitable teaching technique or develop a teaching technique.

Performance objectives are found either by age or by skill area. Each card contains —

A restatement of the Performance Objective

A teaching technique for that skill

Materials needed

A means of measuring whether the child has attained the performance objective

Project More

Daily Living Skills Curriculum

Developer: Under the direction of James R. Lent, George Peabody College, Nashville, Tennessee.

Publisher: Hubbard
P.O. Box 104
Northbrook, Illinois 60062

Format: Fifteen booklets.

Developmental Level: Severely retarded and trainable mentally handicapped ages three to eighteen years.

Content Areas: Personal, home, and community skills.

Goal: To teach, in a systematic, integrated sequence, an ever expanding number of vital skills, beginning with personal care and progressing to home care, then to activities outside the home. The continuity of program development is intended to provide an increasing individual independence.

Description:

Each of the daily living skills programs consists of a teacher's handbook with step-by-step procedures dealing with a single skill as part of the integrated total curriculum. Each of the programs is complete within itself, including instructions for teachers, teaching strategies, correction procedures, motivational systems, and record-keeping components.

The teaching strategies follow a consistent format:
1. Each skill is broken down into small ordered steps or increments.
2. Instructions are provided for offering four kinds of help: no help, verbal help, demonstration, and physical help.

All instruction is based upon the premise that the least amount of help possible should be offered. The object is to get the student to perform independently and with less and less help. Extensive testing and simple recording devices determine when the student has met the criterion of maximum self-sufficiency and independence.

Reinforcers are recommended throughout the training procedure. They must immediately follow correct response and must be selected for their effectiveness with individual students. In general, positive social reinforcement is suggested, although tangible rewards may be used. Punishment is never recommended.

Thirty *Project More* programs are in progress or projected. Programs currently available are:

Care of Eyeglasses
Complexion Care
Care of Simple
  Injuries
Eating
Face Shaving
Feminine Hygiene
Hair Rolling
"How to Do More"
  Curriculum
  Guide

Hair Washing
Hand Washing
Leg and Underarm
  Shaving
Nose Blowing
Showering
Toothbrushing
Use of Deodorant

The Radea Program

Specific Skills Development Program

Developer: Dallas County MH/MR Center.

Publisher: Melton Book Company
111 Leslie Street
Dallas, Texas 75207

Format: Kit; teaching manual for testing and remediation, 564 task cards, four cassette
tapes, twenty-nine picture cards, ten
Radeagraphic sets, fifty task trial sheets,
1,000 daily progress charts, fifty individual progress profiles, 280 Radea
manuscript pages.

Developmental Level: Birth through seven years.
Each of the five areas is divided into four
levels:

Level I   — zero to two years
Level II   — two to three and one-half
years
Level III   — three and one-half years
to five years
Level IV   — five to seven years

Content Areas: Visual perception, auditory perception,
perceptual motor, oral language, and
functional living. The sixth area, special
problems, includes toilet training, behavior, and sequences of activities designed to eliminate common problems,
e.g. inappropriate repetition of words,
self-stimulatory behaviors.

Goal: To increase the adaptive behavior of the
child by structuring the rate and direction
of change.

Description:

The Radea Program is composed of structured, developmentally
sequenced tasks. Based on Jean Piaget's theory of cognition, a

student learns skills by progressing from experiences with real objects to experiences with representations of real objects, e.g. pictures, models, and photographs, and then to experiences with symbolic representations of objects, e.g. oral and written language.

Each of the 503 basic task cards contains a separate task. Each task uses task analysis to define each activity's component parts. Each component is learned separately using the success of the first as an aid in learning the second.

Each task card contains five kinds of information:
1. The *task objective* states the skill to be taught.
2. The *sequence of steps* lists activities that assist the teacher in training the objective and indicates when reinforcers must be given.
3. Suggested *materials* facilitate teacher preparation before instruction begins.
4. The *mastery criteria* are given to help the teacher determine whether the objective has been met and the skill learned.
5. The *grouping* suggests optimum size of a group working on the particular task.

The Radea Program – Supplementary Materials

Radea Implementation Module (RIM)

Format: Kit; Set of seven wooden blocks (for color and size discrimination), set of twenty-five Radeashapes, set of four piece shape puzzles, set of more than 550 Radea Picture Cards with index, set of boy and girl paper dolls with clothing for dressing.

Goal: To provide materials essential to the use of the Radea Program.

Radea Support Materials (RSM)

Format: Set of round wooden beads, set of numbered wooden blocks, two sets of plastic alphabet letters (upper and lower case), Dressy Bessy doll, Dapper Dan doll, set of plastic noisemakers, set of toy cars, pull-apart toy, cookie sheet (reflective), two cloth bandanas, set of measuring cups, set of poker chips, wooden pegboard with pegs, set of plastic fruit, two wooden puzzles.

Goal: To provide the teacher or trainer with the ideal support materials necessary to facilitate the use of the Radea curriculum on a daily basis.

Radea Teacher Training Program

Format: A vinyl-bound trainer's manual with step-by-step instructions for presenting six training sessions, manuals for ten participants, and a one-week loan of the filmstrip/cassette "Overview" and three videotapes.

Goal: To train professional and paraprofessional staff members in the effective use of the Radea Program.

The six training sessions are as follows:
1. The *Overview* (a filmstrip/cassette introduction to the entire program).
2. *Behavior and the Behavioral Objective* (a videotaped presentation defining a behavior and a behavioral objective).
3. *Behavior Management* (a videotaped presentation of behavior management).
4. *Piaget and Child Development* (a written narrative of the philosophical constructs on which the Radea Program is based).
5. *Observing and Recording* (a videotaped presentation showing the correct use of recording materials).
6. *Testing and Remediation* (a written narrative describing the correct use of the Testing and Remediation instrument).

Santa Clara Plus

Developer: The Santa Clara School District, Santa Clara, California.

Publisher: Richard L. Zweig Associates
20800 Beach Boulevard
Huntington Beach, California 92648

Curriculum of Texas, Inc.
900 Old Koenig Lane, Suite 129
Austin, Texas 78756

Format: Kit; 242 readiness recipe cards containing 664 activities, forty blank cards for adding favorite activities, forty-seven spirit masters, teacher's manual, IDT (Inventory of Developmental Tasks), and Observation Guide.

Developmental Level: Three to seven years.

Content Areas: Social/emotional development, motor coordination, visual motor performance, visual perception, visual memory, auditory perception, auditory memory, language development, conceptual development, and games.

Goal: To provide instructional activities (prescriptions) correlated to the sixty tasks identified by the Santa Clara Inventory of Developmental Tasks to improve ease of administration and to increase effectiveness.

Description:

The Santa Clara Plus is arranged in the order of skills measured by the Santa Clara Inventory of Developmental Tasks. The activities are grouped in approximate ascending level of difficulty within each strand of tasks. The activity tasks were created by *EARLY YEARS MAGAZINE* in their "Green Pages" feature.

The sequence for use of the Santa Clara IDT and the Santa Clara Plus are as follows:

1. Use the more than 100 new affective activities in the "social/emotional development" section of the Santa Clara Plus to help each student develop self-image (this is the new section that is not a part of the IDT).
2. Use the test section of the original Santa Clara IDT to determine cognitive skills each child in the class does not know.
3. Correlate the student deficits with the Santa Clara Readiness Recipe cards and spirit masters for instructional activities for each childs' level. Learning activities can be directed by the teacher, a teacher's aide, a parent, a volunteer, or an upper-grade student tutor.

The following is the format for the recipe cards:

1. Title of skill needed
2. Numerical order of card in kit
3. Behavioral objective for activities on this card
4. Materials needed for the specific activity. (Materials common to a classroom such as pencils, paper, and scissors are often assumed.)
5. Suggested size of group
6. Developmental strand
7. First activity
8. Second activity
9. Third activity

Step by Step Dressing
A Handbook for Teaching the Retarded to Dress

Authors: Shirley Henderson and Mary McDonald.

Publisher: Suburban Publications
Box 3444
Champaign, Illinois 61820

Edmark Associates
13241 Northup Way
Bellevue, Washington 98005

Format: Book.

Developmental Level: One to five years.

Content Areas: Dressing skills.

Goal: To provide a handbook for teachers and trainers that uses the principles of behavior modification to teach dressing to retarded children.

Description:

Approximately half of the book describes dressing techniques with sections on dressing, undressing, and clothing types. All major items of clothing are covered. Testing and progress charts are detailed and task analyzed, but are easily understood and graded.

The following areas are covered in this book: developmental levels in dressing, techniques for teaching, gathering information about the child's skills and lags in this area, setting goals and writing lesson plans, and teaching and record keeping; a bibliography is included.

A Step-By-Step Learning Guide for Older Retarded Children

Authors: Vicki M. Johnson and Roberta A. Werner.

Publisher: Syracuse University Press
1011 East Water Street
Syracuse, New York 13210

Format: Book.

Developmental Level: Four to fourteen years, depending upon the degree of retardation.

Content Areas: Fine motor ability, self-care, language development, gross motor skills, perceptual ability.

Goal: To design learning tasks that enable the child to learn essential skills for development.

Description:

This book is designed to be used by parents, teachers, and paraprofessionals in teaching school-aged retarded children. Each of the nearly 300 learning tasks has a specific objective, and an explicit description of the procedures for performing each task is given. In addition, teaching techniques and behavior management are considered. While most of the activities can be done either at home or at school, one chapter is designed specifically for parents' use at home.

A Step-By-Step Learning Guide for Retarded Infants and Children

Authors: Vicki M. Johnson and Roberta A. Werner.

Publisher: Syracuse University Press
1011 East Water Street
Syracuse, New York 13210

Format: Book.

Developmental Level: Birth to six years.

Content Areas: Self-care, social behavior, gross and fine motor skills, language development, perception.

Goal: To provide learning tasks that enable the child to learn essential skills for development.

Description:

The book is designed for parents, teachers, teachers' aides, child care workers, and others who work with retarded children in the home, school, or institution. It consists of 240 learning tasks arranged in sequence, one or two to a page, with photographic illustration and precise description of the teaching procedure. Also included is a "Checklist of Present Abilities," which is correlated to specific task numbers to help ameliorate these specific deficiencies. Cueing, behavior shaping techniques, and sample daily schedules are also presented.

The Step System

Sequential Tasks for Educational Planning, Volume I

Developer:	Cajon Valley Union School District, Department of Special Education, W. D. Stainback, Director.
Publisher:	Cajon Valley Union School District Department of Special Education P.O. Box 1007 El Cajon, California 92022
Format:	Large manual.
Developmental Level:	Birth through thirteen plus.
Content Areas:	Independent living skills, physical development, recreational development, task skills, personal and social development, prevocational, academic, general, and speech and language skills.
Goal:	To provide a total instructional management system that follows the student from entry into a program, throughout his class activities, to succeeding classes in future years and as a permanent record. It is designed to fulfill all of the requirements of P.L. 94-142 and also to be precise, yet flexible and economical of time.
Description:	

The Step System is an attempt to offer efficiency to the process of the development of Individual Educational Programs. It is an attempt to forestall duplication of effort, need for repeated clerical chores and re-creation of fundamental instructional strategies. It is an effort to give the teacher a product that offers, on a single page, a functional diagnosis, a task-analyzed sequence of measurable objectives, a means of recording an instructional history, a report to the parent, an instructional management system, a means of evaluating student progress, and, when combined in aggregate with other STEPs, a means of evaluating an overall program.

The Step System is correlated to the BCP (Behavioral Characteristics Progression) assessment but is also an extension of it. The more than 10,500 objectives are divided into the nine skill areas listed above. A "Sample Blank Individual Education Program" is provided along with simple descriptions of the process necessary for the completion of it:

1. Determine general goal area,
2. Select a step,
3. Determine present level of educational performance,
4. Determine periodic objectives,
5. Determine the least restrictive environment, and
6. List evaluation results.

The classification of a step depends on the target behavior, the manner in which the objectives are sequenced, and the purpose for which the step is intended. There are four types of steps:

1. Task Analysis
2. Instructional Sequence
3. Curriculum Milestones
4. Mastery of a Single Behavior

Each of the over 10,500 objectives are listed with an indication as to the suggested step type as well as the age range for different types of students (regular class, learning handicapped, communication handicapped, physically handicapped, and severely handicapped). Flexibility is built into the system for teachers who need to add additional steps for specific students.

Steps to Independence

A Skills Training Series for Children With Special Needs

Authors:	Bruce L. Baker, Alan J. Brightman, Louise J. Heifetz, and Diane M. Murphy of the "Behavioral Education Projects" at Read House, Harvard University.

Publisher:	Research Press
	2612 North Mattis Avenue
	Champaign, Illinois 61820
	Edmark Associates
	13241 Northup Way
	Bellevue, Washington 98005

Format:	Five booklets: *Early Self-Help Skills, Intermediate Self-Help Skills, Advanced Self-Help Skills, Behavior Problems, Training Guide.*

Developmental Level:	Children with special needs.
Content Areas:	Self-help skills.

Goal:	To provide a parent training model for parents of special needs students that is based on behavior modification principles and is incorporated into easy-to-use manuals.

Description:

Each of the three *Self-Help* manuals follows an identical two-section structure, with the respective contents geared to meet the needs of varying levels of child ability. In the first section, "Principles and Methods," a general understanding of behavior modification is provided, as well as rationale for parent responsibility in teaching. In effect, someone completing only this section should have a good working knowledge of the language and practice of behavior modification and should also have decided upon —

1. A skill to teach.
2. A list of steps in that skill.

3. A time and place for teaching.
4. Appropriate teaching materials.
5. Appropriate rewards.
6. A strategy for recording progress.

They should be ready to begin teaching. While the outline for this first section is generally the same across the three manuals, the descriptions of the principles and methods in each are tailored to one of the three ability levels.

The second section, "Programs," is likewise tailored to these three skill levels and is designed to provide parents with concrete steps and suggestions to follow in teaching.

Behavior Problems covers behavior problem management in teaching sessions and elsewhere. The approach stresses specifying the problem behavior, measuring its occurrence, identifying the antecedents and consequences, and then developing a program to reduce the problem behavior and encourage desired behaviors. It focuses on problem behaviors characteristic of children with special needs, such as self-stimulation, self-abuse, and fearful behaviors.

The three *Self-Help* manuals and the *Behavior Problems* manual are designed for use by parents, staff members, or anyone else working with special children. The *Training Guide* is for use by counselors working with parents and teachers. It features a behavioral assessment guide that permits parents and teachers to determine the appropriate training manual for each child.

All of the manuals are written in clear, jargon-free style with step-by-step directions and many useful illustrations. Easy-to-use record keeping forms are also included.

Success Learning Programs

Self-Help Skills 1
Self-Help Skills 2
Education Skills
Physical Education Skills
Arts & Crafts and Recreational Skills

Author:	Laurence E. Payne.
Publisher:	Communication Skill Builders, Inc. 817 East Broadway P.O. Box 6081-E Tucson, Arizona 85733
Format:	Five notebooks.
Developmental Level:	Twelve weeks to thirteen years.
Content Areas:	Self-help, education, physical education, arts and crafts, and recreational skills.
Goal:	To provide a ready-made training program that will help the teacher of the exceptional child with the basic skills needed.

Description:

Each program is presented in a complete sequence that is easy to follow. It is recommended for use by aides, paraprofessionals, and parents, as well as by teachers, because the total teaching situation is arranged. Using easily obtained materials, the programs list prerequisite skills, automatically check the progress of the pupil, and provide clear, measurable objectives for completion. An easily maintained evaluation and recording system is included in each program.

The series covers the developmental ages of twelve weeks to thirteen years and is successful with small groups in the classroom or on an individual basis. Each skill that is presented to the student is developed using the simplest possible steps, in order for the child to learn without making mistakes. The format for each skill includes the following:

Instructional objectives; describes the skills the student will acquire upon completion of instruction, in observable terms.

Entering behaviors; describes prerequisite behaviors and skills.

Disruptive behaviors; lists those behaviors that will upset teaching and gives a step-by-step method of handling them.

Teaching techniques; listed in ordered sequence.

Pretests.

Pass criterion; standard of performance.

Steps.

Procedure.

Posttests.

These five programs were designed in actual teaching situations and are adaptable for individual children. They are recommended for use with Individual Education Program Plans. They are also recommended for use by parents in home programs.

Teaching the Moderately and Severely Handicapped

Curriculum Objectives, Strategies, and Activities
Volume I: Behavior, Self-Care, and Motor Skills
Volume II: Communication, Socialization, Safety, and Leisure Time Skills
Volume III: Functional Academics for the Mildly and Moderately Handicapped

Authors: Michael Bender, Peter J. Valletutti, and Rosemary Bender.

Publisher: University Park Press
Chamber of Commerce Building
Baltimore, Maryland 21202

Distributed by:
Edmark Associates
13241 Northup Way
Bellevue, Washington 98005

Format: Three volumes.

Developmental Level: Moderately and severely handicapped of all ages.

Content: Behavior, self-care, motor, communication, socialization, safety, leisure time, and functional academics.

Goal: To fill an existing need for a curriculum that adequately and comprehensively meets the myriad of needs of the moderately and severely handicapped child or adult.

Description:

Each of the content areas included in this curriculum are broken down into the following:
General objectives of the area.
Specific objectives with required performance level (criteria) and recommended observations.
Lists of suggested activities.
Also provided are teaching strategies and topical bibliographies

of suggested readings. Within each area, objectives and activities are listed for staff working with physically handicapped students.

The lists of suggested activities are developmentally sequenced. Indications are given for cues, reinforcements, cautions, suggested materials, and record keeping.

Training for Independence

Fundamental Self-Care and Functional Training for Daily Living

Developer: The Outreach and Development Division, Exceptional Child Center, Utah State University.

Publisher: Developmental Learning Materials
7440 Natchez Avenue
Chicago, Illinois 60648

Format: Kit; 8 programs containing instructions, charts for record keeping and reward badges.

Developmental Level: Retarded, physically handicapped, developmentally immature, and early childhood.

Content Areas: Self-help skills and behavior.

Goal: To respond to requests from parents and teachers for programs with precise, step-by-step instructions in the essential skill areas included.

Description:

The following are the *Training for Independence* programs:
Programs for Teaching —
The Independent Use of Zippers, Buttons, Shoes, and Socks.
Independent Dressing Skills.
The Counting of Objects.
The Identification of Coins.
The Recognition of Functional Words.
The Understanding of Functional Words and Phrases.
The Retention of Important Oral Phrases and Numbers.
When a Child Misbehaves.

In the seven skill programs, specific suggestions for correcting and praising, sample instructor and learner charts for recording progress, and a sheet of twenty-four colorful reward badges are included with each program. Each of the seven skill programs contains a pre-check to determine learner readiness, sequential lessons, and follow-up activities that expand and incorporate tasks into meaningful daily routines. The program for teaching word recognition includes two decks of cards on which functional words are printed in four colors and upper and lowercase letters. Support is systematically reduced throughout the lessons to promote learner independence.

Practical techniques for modifying and establishing appropriate behavior are given in the reference book WHEN A CHILD MISBEHAVES.

III.
MANAGEMENT

Chapter 9

SYSTEMS OF STRUCTURED EXCHANGE
Changing Families of Severely Deviant Children

MARTIN A. KOZLOFF

Introduction

The Role of Parents in the Service Delivery System

U NTIL VERY RECENTLY, children with severely deviant behavioral repertoires (for example, autistic, emotionally
disturbed, and mentally retarded children) were viewed and
treated within one or another variant of the illness model. They
were seen as either biologically impaired, in which case organic
therapies (such as ECT and chemotherapy) were used, or they
were seen as suffering from some form of psychological or
emotional impairment, in which case psychotherapeutic
methods were employed. Moreover, the role of parents in their
children's treatment was minimal, and for a number of reasons:

1. Despite the fact that the parents had been living with their
children for years and had had the most contact with them,
parents were not considered knowledgeable enough to greatly
influence the programs being conducted by professionals.
Treatment decisions, in other words, flowed from professionals
to parents. Consequently, the knowledge the parents had in fact
gained about the "operating characteristics" of their children
and about methods for helping them or for dealing with their
problems was rarely incorporated into the body of professional
wisdom. This may have contributed to the decades of intellectual
and therapeutic stagnation in the psychological and educational

From Martin A. Kozloff, Systems of Structured Exchange: Changing Families of
Severely Deviant Children, Sociological Practice, *1(2)*:1976, fall.

approaches to the treatment of children with severely deviant behaviors. Indeed, the prognosis for children as severely deviant as autistic children has been poor, with only a minority ever reaching a high level of social adjustment, even fewer entering paid employment, and the rest facing a life of confinement at home or in custodial institutions.

2. To the extent that children's problems, especially severely deviant behaviors, were regarded as organic in nature, the parents were considered rather irrelevant to their children's treatment. After all, the conventional wisdom stated, what did parents know about the nervous system. And besides, one cannot so easily repair a damaged nervous system.

3. On the other hand, when their children's problems were viewed from the psychogenic perspective, the parents were often blamed. The parents were thought to have been cold, punitive, or indifferent to their children, providing an environment with little stimulation, pushing their children too fast, or not encouraging independence in them. It should be pointed out that there was, and is, no solid evidence supporting the theories that see parents as central to the etiology of severe socialization disorders. Nevertheless, rather than allowing, or seeing the need for, parents to participate as co-therapists, many professionals felt that the parents needed psychotherapy along with their children, which, perhaps, they did, after having been blamed for their children's problems.

Contradictions and Change

By the early 1960s, a number of contradictions and dilemmas in the approaches for dealing with severely deviant children had become painfully obvious. First, it was clear that there were simply not enough professionals to help the large number of children who needed help (Arnstein, 1965; Mosher et al., 1970; Lindsley, 1966). Second, a number of studies indicated that the predominant theories and therapies (organic and psychogenic) were inadequate, if not, in fact, iatrogenic (Rimland, 1964, 1969; Frank, 1965; Wener et al., 1967; Levitt, 1957; 1963). Third, research began to show that unless parents were trained, the gains their children made in special educational or treatment environments did not readily generalize to other settings, and were not maintained for very long after the formal intervention had ended.

A fourth problem, of a theoretical nature, but having important implications for practice, was this: it no longer seemed reasonable to make neat distinctions between what was organic and what was environmental in nature. For a long time, homeopathy had been a predominant link between theory and diagnosis, on the one hand, and practice or treatment, on the other. That is, the alleged nature (or etiology) of the problem dictated the mode of treatment. Organic problems would receive organic therapies: psychological problems would receive psychotherapy. The problem was that while homeopathy had been in use for centuries, and had been quite successful, as the history of medical achievements indicates, the problems of severely deviant children could not be definitely traced solely to either organic or psychological factors. In effect, for decades, professionals had been treating hypothetical problems — minimal brain damage, emotional trauma, stimulus deprivation.

Heteropathy, an alternative to homeopathy, became possible with the emergence of applied behavior analysis and social-structural approaches to deviant behavior, e.g., structured exchange theory. The major assumption of heteropathy is that the alleged nature or etiology of a problem need not dictate the mode of treatment. For example, when a person is left without speech following a stroke, one does not usually repair the brain: one helps the person relearn speech. In other words, the physiological theory that explains the origin of the problem can be quite different from any learning theory that explains how rehabilitation works.

The early work of behavior analysts and behavior modifiers, such as Ayllon (1963), Ayllon and Michael (1959), Fuller (1949), Lindsley (1965), Isaacs et al. (1960), Bachrach et al. (1966), and Ferster and DeMyer (1962), made it clear that despite the differences in etiology, the disordered and deviant behaviors of the people these therapists worked with (autistic children, people with anorexia nervosa, chronic schizophrenics) could be remedied, in part, by changes in the social environment, specifically, those features of the social environment called contingencies of reinforcement or structured exchanges.

These therapists found that no matter how people had developed certain "symptoms" (such as not eating, mutism, bizarre gestures), the symptoms (behaviors) would begin to decrease and be replaced by pronormal behaviors when the environment was structured such that symptomatic behaviors were no longer reinforced and pronormal behaviors were systematically reinforced. What they demonstrated, of course, was something that their sociologist colleagues had assumed all along, namely, that social structure has powerful effects on behavior.

The work of these therapists, coming at a time when a great deal of money was being spent on new methods for helping severely deviant children, spawned a large number of programs in behavior modification for autistic, mentally retarded, delinquent, hyperactive, aggressive, and oppositional children. In addition, it stimulated a great deal of work with parents, teaching them to help educate and socialize their children.

However, the early work done within the behavioral approach, which rested on the principles and methods of operant conditioning, was not without its weaknesses. The following were the major ones:

1. Again, the direction of influence between the persons planning and implementing the new and hope-to-be beneficial reinforcement systems and the children was seen as one-way. While most operant conditioners would certainly admit that the therapist, teacher, or parent is, in turn, influenced by changes in the behavior of the children, the dimension of reciprocal influence (of exchange) remained merely implicit, except in the writings of a few.

2. An operant analysis of an environment (such as a family) produced a set of contingencies, each one being a statement of the relationship between certain features of the environment (e.g., the frequency of reinforcement for various behaviors, as delivered by parents) and certain features of the behavior of children (e.g., the frequency of cooperation versus the frequency of oppositional behavior). Such analyses, however, left out two important systemic features of the interaction between parents

and children, namely, that, as noted above, the behaviors of parents are reciprocally affected by changes in the behaviors of their children and that the various contingencies of reinforcement (e.g., cooperation-reinforcement, oppositional behavior-reinforcement, playing reinforcement) are themselves interconnected, such that a change in one contingency is likely to produce changes in others.

3. A major practical consequence of early operant conditioning analyses was that control was seen as resting with the persons who understood how contingencies operate. Such persons would be the only ones capable (or regarded as capable) of predicting, and hence rationally planning, behavioral change. At the same time, though, by failing to deal explicitly with the reciprocity of influence (structured exchanges rather than one-way contingencies) and with the interconnectedness of the exchanges in a system (which together constitute feedback loops that generate accelerating increases and decreases — positive feedback — or decelerating increases and decreases — negative feedback — in the system), an operant analysis would not be able to adequately predict long-term states of individual behaviors or of the system.

Structured Exchange Theory

By the mid-1960s, a number of sociologists, basing their work on the operant conditioning of Skinner and on the structured exchange theories of Homans (1961), Blau (1967), Emerson (1969), and others, began working to solve some of the problems of children with severely deviant behaviors. For example, Hamblin and his co-workers (1971) conducted programs for hyperactive hyperaggressive children, for normal children, for autistic children, and for children in inner-city schools. Ferritor et al. (1972) and Burgess et al. (1968) conducted programs in schools. Kozloff (1973, 1974) developed programs for parents of deviant children.

SOME PRINCIPLES OF STRUCTURED EXCHANGE THEORY. A few words about some of the basic principles of structured exchange theory and its connection with other theories in sociology are in order. In general, structured exchange theorists agree with the operant conditioners that reinforcers are a basic component of social systems, since reinforcers exert so much "control" over behavior. "Reinforcers" are all of the tangible and intangible "things" and events that persons will engage in behaviors to acquire (positive reinforcers) or to escape and avoid (negative reinforcers). Some reinforcers, such as food, water, warmth, and cold, seem to be reinforcers without prior experience. Hence, they are called "primary reinforcers." A taste for or aversion to other things, such as praise, money, and hairy spiders, on the other hand, must be acquired through interaction with other reinforcers. These, then, are called "conditioned reinforcers."

Equal in importance to the reinforcer is the link or arrangement between a behavior and the reinforcers that follow it. The arrangement is called a "contingency of reinforcement," which includes a description of the reinforcing event, the speed of its presentation or removal, the probability of its presentation or removal, and a description of events that signal that the link between behavior and reinforcer is either "on" (discriminative stimuli) or "off" (stimulus delta). The importance of the contingency has been demonstrated many times in studies that show that the strength of a behavior varies as a function of the arrangement between behavior and reinforcer, and not merely as a function of whether or not the behavior is reinforced. Thus, when reinforcers are presented at random, the specific behavior(s) under study may decrease in strength.

Within the perspective of structured exchange theory, the contingency of reinforcement is still a basic unit of the social system. Indeed, it is the basic unit of social structure. However, the contingency is viewed as a structured exchange, in that both parties (the person upon whose behavior the reinforcer is dependent and the person who is presenting or removing the reinforcer) are affected by it, both in the short and long run. *Structured* means that the exchange is a relatively durable, frequent, or predictable feature of the system.

Thus, if person A engages in some behavior and is positively reinforced (e.g., with praise) by person B, A's behavior will increase, or is likely to. Most important, if the change in A's behavior as a result of reinforcement is itself reinforcing for B, then B's behavior of reinforcing A will increase. In sum, the structure of the exchange (reciprocal positive reinforcement) will generate an accelerating increase in the behavior of both persons; that is, a positive feedback loop. (Of course, A's behavior might increase for other reasons besides "reinforcement" from B. But if B assumes that A's behavior change was caused by B's reinforcing A, B will superstitiously reinforce A.)

For structured exchange theorists, the different exchanges in a system are not isolated from one another. The introduction of a positively reinforcing exchange may also generate or alter other structured exchanges in the system. For example, when parents begin to reinforce behaviors of their children that they used to ignore, not only will the newly reinforced behaviors increase, but other behaviors of the children are likely to increase as well. And, reciprocally, the parents are likely to begin reinforcing other behaviors. Thus, one has a better chance of predicting long-term system change.

Finally, by describing the reciprocal influence in systems, control is no longer seen as a one-way process. Those who are teaching children are forced to see how their teaching behaviors (as well as their feelings) are affected by changes in the children's behaviors. And those who are training parents must see that parents are, at the same time, training them in how to train.

Note the crucial linkages here between various levels of a social system. The biologically based operating characteristics of the human species (indeed, of most, if not all, animal life) make possible the phenomenon of behaviors increasing as a function of contingent reinforcement (a psychological process). On an intermediate level (a social-structural level), the relationships between the behaviors of members of a system can be described in terms of structured exchanges. Finally, under certain conditions of structured exchange, the behaviors of members covary in such a stable way that the covariance (e.g., mutual acceleration) is itself a feature of the social system, a feature that we have called a positive feedback loop.

As for the connection between structured exchange theory and other approaches in sociology, notice that reinforcers can also be seen as resources in a social system. Hence, to the extent that some persons control access to, delivery of, and desire for (or aversion to) reinforcers, they can control the behaviors of persons who are desirous of or averse to the resources. Such control of resources, especially when it involves their unequal distribution, has often formed the basis of political-economic analyses, and seems to be the basis for the conflict theory tradition in sociology. Thus, it is possible to analyze the structure and function of social systems on many levels, from families, to schools, to communities, to nation states, in terms of the major ways (structured exchanges) in which resources are controlled and delivered, and of the effects of the structured exchanges in behavior.

A SYSTEM-ORIENTED TRAINING PROGRAM

For the past seven years, my co-workers and I have been developing and evaluating systems for socializing or educating severely deviant children and for training parents to conduct comprehensive educational programs in the home, to accelerate, generalize, and maintain the gains their children were making in school, to prepare the children for school, or to substitute for the lack of schools for their children. As with other research, ours indicated that there was no reason to believe that the parents caused their children's socialization or development to go awry or to stop. Indeed, the work of numerous biologically oriented researchers points to some initial or continuing neurological or metabolic malfunction.

What, then, is the role of sociology? Viewing the families in terms of structured exchanges, it is clear that certain structured exchanges common to every family we have worked with may worsen the children's behavior or may fail to promote or strengthen pronormal behaviors.

Types of Structured Exchanges in Families

We have found five types of structured exchanges. It should be noted that the exchanges described below also exist in families of "normal" children. The problem is that when coupled with the existing deficits of deviant children, the exchanges tend to produce either a worsening or a stabilizing of deviant behavior (as well as a worsening or stabilizing of the parents' counterproductive efforts to cope with the children's behavior).

ESCAPE. A predominant structured exchange is the one in which the parents reinforce disruptive behaviors (such as tantrums or head-banging) by cuddling the child, providing him with food, toys, TV, talking to him, chasing after or yelling at him when he behaves in these ways. In other words, the parents, finding the child's behavior highly aversive, are engaging in escape behaviors that will terminate the child's behavior. Usually, the child does stop the disruptive behavior for a short time, and this negatively reinforces (and strengthens) the parents' efforts to stop the child's behavior.

The tragedy of this exchange is that both parties are reinforced. The child is positively reinforced by the parents' attention (as well as by the food, toys, music), and the parents are negatively reinforced when the child temporarily stops the disruption. Over time, the reciprocal reinforcement built into the exchange results in the parents' and child's engaging in the exchange more and more often. Thus, the child spends more and more time being disruptive (as well as getting better and better at it), and the parents spend more and more time and energy trying to stop the child's disruptive behaviors.

Note that the above exchange is connected to other exchanges in the system. For the more family members engage in the escape exchange, the less time and energy (and behavior) are available for the parents to positively reinforce "good" behaviors.

PLACATION. A second type of structured exchange is one in which the parents learn to avoid the aversive behaviors of their child by providing the child with reinforcers before disruptive behaviors begin. In other words, the parents reinforce such behaviors as watching TV, aimless wandering, mild pushing and pulling, and gestures indicating that a tantrum is imminent. In this way, they minimize the short-run costs of having to bear so many episodes of tantrums, screaming, and self-injury. In the long run, however, they are wasting reinforcers that could have been used to strengthen pronormal behaviors, and are strengthening aimless and disruption-threatening behaviors.

MULTIPLE SIGNALS. In this exchange, the parents present the

child with a signal to change a behavior in some way (e.g., by asking the child to come to them or to answer a question). If the child does not comply with the signal, the parents are likely to repeat it, over and over, until the child finally complies or the parents give up. The latter is usually the case. The problem with this exchange is that each time the parents repeat the signal, they have reinforced the last episode of noncompliance (with their attention), thus making it even less likely that the child will comply in the future.

FAILURE TO REINFORCE PRONORMAL BEHAVIORS. Not only are parents very likely to reinforce problem behaviors, but they are also very unlikely to reinforce pronormal behaviors (except those that represent marked changes from their children's usual behavior patterns). Occasionally, the reason seems to be the parents' belief (drawn from the larger culture) that children should be good, and hence should not be reinforced for what they "ought" to be doing anyway. Usually, however, the reason seems to be that the parents are so overwhelmed by (and hypersensitive to) disruptive behaviors that they did not notice the few approximations to pronormal behaviors emitted by their children.

RELIEF. A major structured exchange between parents is one of relief-giving. Although parents sometimes argue with one another concerning the events that triggered a problem behavior that has just occurred, or each other's methods of handling it, a more common pattern is one in which each parent uses the other for some form of support or relief, for example, to watch the other children while one parent is busy with the deviant child, to give sympathy, or to come home from work to help with the deviant child in a time of crisis.

Although relief-giving is probably very important in maintaining the marital relationship, it does not necessarily mean that the parents are engaged in a cooperative effort to change the deviant behaviors from which they seek relief.

It must be said that this description of the major exchanges in families of severely deviant children does not imply that the exchanges are a function of parents' intellectual or "personality" deficits. In the absence of knowledge of how to change their children's behaviors, and of support and coaching in doing so, and given the extreme disruptiveness of the behavior, the best short-run solutions to their children's aversive behaviors may well be these structured exchanges. Sadly, the exchanges, since they involve the reinforcement of both parents and children, become more frequent and durable, decreasing the likelihood of beneficial change in the system, unless outside help is obtained. In effect, what one sees in families are people doing their best to keep their heads above water.

Design and Operation of the Training Program

The goals of our programs were to help parents of severely deviant children replace the counterproductive exchanges in their families with those that would promote, strengthen, and maintain pronormal behaviors, and to teach parents a wide range of skills for evaluating their children's educational needs, planning a comprehensive educational program, conducting teaching programs in seven skill areas (ranging from Learning Readiness through Motor Skills and Imitation, to Functional Speech, Chores, and Self-help Skills), and evaluating their progress and revising their programs accordingly.

Program Contract and Credit-Check System

An interesting counterintuitive feature of family systems (and possibly of all social systems) — and one predicted by structured exchange theory — is that beneficial changes in children's behaviors will not necessarily maintain their parents' teaching behaviors. The reason for this seems to be that at certain times the parents must invest a great deal of time and energy in return for very little reinforcement in the form of behavior change in their children. That is, the rate at which their children progress (and reinforce the parents) slows down as harder and harder behaviors (such as speech) are worked on. The same phenomenon applies to the training staff. It is a great deal of work to teach a second party how to teach a third party to speak. Consequently, in our project all participants (parents and staff) signed a contract that specified certain terms of the program. These included attending all meetings, being on time, completing all assignments, making home visits, and having materials prepared.

The successful meeting of the terms of the main program contract, and of any contracts written during the program, earned the participant a certain number of credits for that week. Each family and staff member also wrote three certified checks, in increasing amounts, to organizations they did not like. One parent held staff checks and kept track of staff credits. One staff member did the same for all families. Each week, credits earned during the past week were tallied, and if a minimum number had not been earned, one of the checks was mailed, and had to be replaced with another.

The purpose of the contract-credit-check system was to impart a businesslike air to the initial meetings, to show parents that the staff took behavior change very seriously, and to help all parties to maintain their behaviors during "lean" weeks. Interestingly enough, no parents objected to the system; some not only expected it of "behaviorists" but welcomed it.

Training Curriculum

Parents met as a group (four families per program) during three-hour, weekly meetings. The instructional phase of each program lasted approximately fifteen weeks. During each program, parents were taught two kinds of skills. First, throughout the program, they were taught how to replace counterproductive exchanges with structured exchanges that would help to replace their children's deviant behaviors with pronormal behaviors, and would help parents to motivate, reinforce, and maintain their own teaching and exchange-management behaviors. Second, at specific points in the program, parents were taught skills for evaluating the children, planning and conducting educational programs, taking data, and revising their programs.

In early meetings, parents were taught to evaluate their children's behavioral strengths and weaknesses using a "Behavior Evaluation Scale" (Kozloff, 1974). The evaluation enabled parents to determine which behaviors they needed to teach their children in each skill area. And parents were taught to use their evaluation in order to plan their children's educational program.

At this early stage, the parents also learned how to locate reinforcers, how to shape and prompt behaviors, and how to take
data.

Once the parents had acquired the basic evaluating, planning,
and teaching skills, and had begun to restructure the exchanges
in the family, they were taught to use their new skills to teach
behaviors in the different skill areas — behaviors such as eye
contact, cooperation, sitting, small and large motor activities,
motor and verbal imitation, functional speech, chores, and self-
help routines. Since the educational program had a curriculum
consisting of a rather large number of behaviors (ninety-nine), it
was possible for parents to tailor their educational programs to
their children's unique needs, and to participate in the same
program with parents of quite different children.

Meetings were similar in that they all involved (1) a review of
the past week's reading assignment (Kozloff, 1974); (2) the parents' presenting their data and discussing their progress or any
problems they might have had during the week; (3) a presentation by staff on the next week's topic (for example, how to teach a
certain behavior) by means of a short lecture, a demonstration,
role-playing, a film, or a videotape, and (4) a review of
videotapes made in the homes during the week, showing parents
working with their children according to a written contract
which specified their home program for that week.

At the end of each meeting, each family worked with its "behavioral consultant" (a staff member assigned to the family) to
plan and write a contract for the coming week's work and to
specify the time for a home visit. During the week, the behavioral
consultants made home visits to each family to (1) coach the
parents as they interacted with their children and each other; (2)
work with the children to demonstrate a teaching method; (3)
reinforce the parents for their work; and (4) make a videotape of
parents working with their children, for purposes of review at
the next meeting.

The instructional phase was preceded by a pretraining phase,
during which time baseline home observations were made (recorded on videotape) of parent-child interaction in various settings; parents were interviewed; and parents filled out question-

naires regarding the family history and parents' feelings and ratings of their competence as teachers. Pretraining data were used for both program evaluation and program planning (e.g., for specifying behaviors of children and parents that would have to be addressed during the program.)

When the series of instructional meetings was completed, a series of "maintenance" meetings and follow-up home visits was conducted. Such contacts were gradually faded out, to be replaced by phone calls.

Results

Numerical data on the programs consist of parents' scores on tests of conceptual and planning skills; parents' data on their children's weekly progress through the program; and videotape analyses of interaction during baseline, program, and follow-up. In addition, a large amount of information was gathered from telephone calls, interviews, home observation notes, and parents' logs and notes, which helped in the drawing of inferences about parents' feelings of confidence and competence, their hopes and fears, and their relationships with staff and with other families.

Progress of Parents and Children

Comparisons of the children's behaviors across baseline, program, and follow-up (based on scorings of the "Behavior Evaluation Scale," parents' data, and videotape analyses) indicate that very significant improvement was made in the different skill areas by all but two of the twelve children. Table 9.I compares behavior during baseline and at the end of the series of instructional meetings.

To summarize, all of the children began their educational programs in the Learning Readiness area (the first area in the sequence), with eight of the twelve children having virtually no functional speech, rarely or never imitating sounds or words, having very little or no skill at motor imitation, being extremely noncompliant, performing very few chores or self-help routines, and frequently engaging in disruptive and bizarre behaviors (tantrums, screaming, rocking, strange postures, self-injurious behaviors).

TABLE 9.I

PROGRESS OF THE CHILDREN IN DIFFERENT SKILL AREAS BETWEEN
BASELINE AND END OF PROGRAM

	Learning Readiness Baseline	End	Motor Skills Baseline	End	Motor Imitation Baseline	End	Verbal Imitation Baseline	End	Functional Speech Baseline	End	Chores and Self-help Baseline	End
Jimmy	1	4	1	3	1	4	1	4	0	3	1	3
Mark	0	3	0	2	0	3	0	3	0	3	0	2
Patti	0	3	1	2	1	3	1	3	1	2	1	2
Carl	0	3	0	3	0	1	0	1	0	1	0	3
Freddy	0	3	0	1	0	2	0	1	0	1	0	3
Chuck	2	4	4	4	4	4	4	4	4	4	1	3
Karen	0	2	0	2	0	2	0	1	0	1	0	2
Kim	0	1	0	0	0	0	0	0	0	0	0	1
Ted	0	3	1	4	0	4	1	3	0	3	1	3
Marty	0	3	1	3	1	3	1	3	1	3	1	3
Rob	0	3	1	3	0	3	0	3	1	3	1	2
Lynn	0	1	0	1	0	1	0	1	0	1	0	1

0 = virtually no skill; very low frequency or extreme noncompliance
1 = early stages of acquisition
2 = past early stages of acquisition, but progress is slow
3 = past early stages of acquisition; progress is fast
4 = learning at normal rate or has acquired the skill and normal frequency

Of the four children who had some functional speech, two children's verbal repertoires were predominantly echolalic (that is, they merely imitated what they heard); one child used several phrases and simple sentences (with poor articulation), and one child's verbal repertoire was nearly normal for his age. Ten, possibly eleven children, then, could be described as autistic or autistic-like. The one child with a nearly normal verbal repertoire was an "oppositional" child who did not pay attention to tasks for a sustained length of time (that is, until they were completed), did not reliably cooperate with simple requests, and frequently engaged in aggressive and tantrum behavior.

Although the children differed in their rates of improvement during the programs, by the end of the instructional series, ten of the twelve children had mastered or were making progress in the learning readiness skills; eight had progressed rapidly through the simpler small and large motor skills; seven of the eleven children who needed work on motor imitation were making progress in that area; all children were learning and per-

forming chores and self-help routines that they had not performed before, such as self-feeding, dressing, clearing the table,
and toileting; and all but two of the children were replacing their
long-standing patterns of noncompliant, disruptive, and aimless
behaviors with constructive small motor play and chores.

Perhaps most important in terms of their participating in and
learning from schools and other community settings, of the
eleven children who had severe verbal deficits (eight being virtually mute), six were making rapid or normal progress on
verbal imitation, and five were making progress on functional
speech. The other children were still working on behaviors considered prerequisites for learning speech.

With regard to parents' teaching skills, all of the parents had
learned to work together and individually to (1) plan teaching
programs; (2) spot and correct problems in their programs; (3)
prompt, shape, and reinforce behaviors; (4) replace problem
behaviors; and (5) take data on their children's progress. All
parents learned how to teach the learning readiness skills. Most
learned, in addition, how to teach motor skills, motor imitation,
and chores and self-help skills. About half of the families (those
whose children were behaviorally ready) also learned how to
teach verbal imitation and functional speech.

As for *changes in the structured exchanges* in the families, information from the parents (logs, charts, conversations) and
from direct home observations and videotapes made each week
showed that significant changes had taken place both during
teaching sessions and at other times and places. The most important and durable changes common to the families were in (1)
encouraging, requiring, and reinforcing pronormal behaviors,
using primary, social, and, most important, natural, activity reinforcers (instead of placating the children); (2) ignoring or timing
out the children when they engaged in disruptive behaviors
(rather than reinforcing such behaviors); (3) pinpointing and
reinforcing weak, but pronormal, behaviors (instead of "holding
out" for perfection or not recognizing such behaviors); and (4)
working as a team, to plan, evaluate, and implement teaching
programs, and to strengthen one another's behavior through
coaching and reinforcing.

Indeed, parents were often observed to use statements of

learning and exchange principles to initiate or correct their interactions with each other and with their children. For example: "Yeah, I'll have to reward him faster"; "He'll have to ask for it before he gets it"; "Reward him now!" (husband to wife); "Just ignore that" (wife to husband). It appeared, then, that some of the principles had become *norms* governing some of the new exchanges.

Finally, as to the *maintenance of behavioral change*, it is possible that once a program has ended and the inputs from staff have decreased, the parents will gradually teach less and less and may revert to unproductive methods of living with their children. To the extent that that happens, a training program has failed. Follow-up data, however, indicate that, in most cases, behavioral changes in parents and children are being maintained, and that further gains are being made.

Specifically, follow-up phone calls, home visits, and maintenance meetings showed that all parents required at least occasional advice on how to handle problems that had arisen or on pinpointing the next behaviors to work on; and that while about one-fourth of the families continued to work with their children at a high, steady rate that was similar to the rate during the program, three-fourths of the families' home programs went in cycles, with parents decreasing the number and duration of their daily sessions for several days to several weeks, and then returning to a more rigorous schedule.

Learning as an Input-Output System

For many years, applied behavior analysts, including myself, have utilized an experimental design with periods often arranged as follows: baseline — treatment — return to baseline — return to treatment — follow-up. In each period, they observed the covariation between very few (usually one) independent variables (such as frequency of reinforcement) and an equally small number of dependent variables (such as frequency of cooperation versus frequency of noncompliance). Thus, they compared the effects of different reinforcement contingencies on behavior through *time*, while trying to hold constant other variables.

Without question, this design was of great importance — scientifically (testing of theory), pragmatically (application of findings), and ideologically (for example, when a graph showed marked changes in behavior with each change of the contingencies, the behavior analysts and their audience became even more assured of the truth of their theory and its assumptions).

It is clear, however, that the design has serious flaws, and that it may have outlived its usefulness. First, a behavior is affected by more than one class of events, both historically and at any given moment. Reinforcement frequency is of demonstrated importance, but it is only one of many classes of observable events which affect the probability of a behavior in a system. Second, it is doubtful that all of the other independent variables in a system have ever been adequately controlled by constancy, except, perhaps, in a laboratory setting, thus raising the question of whether the graphs have been depicting causation or correlation. And third, although plotting change as a function of time (e.g., days) may convince a reader (and writer) that change has occurred, it is also very wasteful of information. Although behaviors do change through (or as a function of) time, they, it is hoped, do not change merely because of the passage of time, but, rather, because of changes in other events (inputs, such as reinforcement) that impinge on behavior through time.

Consequently, a final task in the parent training project was to develop a method for depicting and analyzing the behavior change process in a way that would (1) reflect its complexities and its systemic features; (2) have mathematical precision, yielding law-like generalizations; (3) retain applied capabilities (that is, be useful in setting or changing educational policy and practice); and (4) assess the relationships between dependent (output) and independent (input) variables more directly (that is, examine the relationship between an input and an output variable by plotting one against the other, and not both against time).

With the help of the project consultant, Dr. Robert L. Hamblin, who has pioneered in the mathematical analysis of social systems (Hamblin et al., 1973), the first steps were taken toward the development of a broader and more realistic perspective on the learning process as a system. Essentially, it was found that the videotapes made each week on the interaction of parents and children in teaching situations made it possible to record a large number of events of two classes: inputs (behaviors of parents, such as number of new tasks worked on, occasions to respond to a task, prompts, and reinforcements); and outputs (behaviors of the children, such as number of new tasks learned, disruptive behaviors, correct, incorrect, and approximately correct responses across and within the different skill areas of the educational program).

Although it is still possible to plot change in children's behaviors (outputs) over time, a decision was made to plot each output (learning) variable as a function of the input (teaching) variables, with all data being cumulative. In this way, it was no longer necessary to attempt to control by constancy, since day-to-day changes in a large number of inputs were being measured. For example, the cumulative number of new tasks learned could be plotted as a function of the cumulative number of new tasks worked on, occasions to respond (trials), prompts, and reinforcements. In this way, one learns how much (quantity) and at what rate change is occurring as a function of (cost of) the various inputs. The systems analyst hopes to find accelerations in pronormal behaviors as a function of the inputs, for example, that new tasks are being learned at a cost of fewer and fewer occasions to respond, prompts, and reinforcements. Such accelerations would indicate that the exchange system was an efficient one.

Graphs of each input-output link could also be used for spotting deterioration in the system. For example, if a graph showed that greater and greater amounts of reinforcement were needed to generate the learning of new tasks, the parent or teacher could institute a change in the exchange system so as to stop the deterioration before the child's progress was at a standstill and the parent or teacher, reciprocally, was "fed up" with teaching. Thus, one might try easier tasks, switch to more novel tasks and to new reinforcers, or prompt the child more often.

Figure 9.1 shows the progress of a four-year-old boy during the course of the training program. One of his behaviors (outputs) "cumulative tasks learned (TL)," is plotted as a function of his parents behaviors (inputs), "cumulative tasks presented

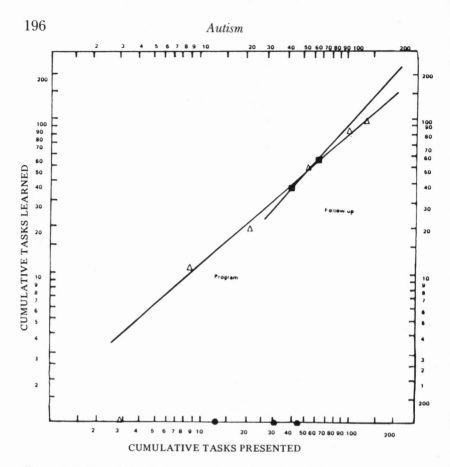

Figure 9.1. Cumulative tasks learned as a function of cumulative tasks presented to Ted, a four year old austistic-like boy. Each data point represents one session. Baseline (●–●), Program (△–△), Follow up (■–■). The X-axis represents the input from parents (cumulative tasks presented). The Y-axis represents the output from child (cumulative tasks learned).

(TP)." All plots are log × log coordinates. Plots having slopes greater than 1.0 depict positive acceleration showing efficiency in the exchange system and a process of positive feedback in which parents and children are learning from each other.

As can be seen from the figure, during the baseline period (before Ted's parents were trained) Ted was presented with a total of 48 new tasks over three sessions, and he failed to learn (or perform) any. During the program, however, he was presented with 130 new tasks, and learned almost 100 of them. Moreover, the slope of the line is almost 0.85, which shows that he was learning new tasks almost as fast as they were being presented to him. Since the line is seen as a member of the family of curves called power functions (which would be slightly curved were it plotted on rectangular coordinates), the partial equation for Ted's learning of new tasks as a function of new tasks presented during the program phase would be $TL = TP^{.85}$.

The line for Ted's learning during the follow-up period is most interesting, and heartening, for it shows that he was learning at a rate higher than that during the program. The slope (exponent) of that line is 1.05, with the partial equation being $TL = TP^{1.05}$. In other words, Ted's behavior during the follow-up was accelerating.

One last point should be made. An inspection of the graph shows that the variance explained by tasks presented is extremely high (something almost unique in sociological research). In fact, the same high explained variance is found in every relationship we have examined. Consequently, it is possible to predict with a great deal of accuracy, how much input will be required to produce a given amount of output.

Conclusions

The parent training project, to date, has yielded a number of important findings and opportunities. First, it has been shown that it is possible, with relatively little time and staff, to markedly alter patterns of exchange in families of severely deviant children, thereby providing parents with a great deal of skill as observers, planners, and teachers (at the same time, replacing feelings of frustration and hopelessness with feelings of competence and optimism) and helping their children to learn and perform many of the important behaviors required for participation in the community. Second, it has been shown that structured exchange theory provides a set of principles that can be used to design social environments that generate behavioral change. And finally, the method for conducting a mathematical analysis of the learning process that takes place within a system of structured exchanges not only describes the system in more detail, but yields law-like generalizations about the effects of structured exchanges on behavior, and can be used in the social sciences for predicting behavior change under given exchange conditions and for monitoring and altering the system in beneficial ways.

REFERENCES

Arnstein, H. S.: An approach to the severely disturbed child, pp. 1-7. In Weston, P. T. B. (Ed.): *Some Approaches to Teaching Autistic Children.* Oxford, England; Pergamon Pr, 1965.

Ayllon, T.: Intensive treatment of psychotic behavior by stimulus satiation and food reinforcement. *Behav Res Ther 1:*53-61, 1963.

Ayllon, T., and Michael, J.: The psychiatric nurse as a behavioral engineer. *J Exp Anal Behav, 2:*323-334, 1959.

Bachrach, A. J., Erwin, W. J. and Mohr, J. P.: The control of eating behavior in an anorexic patient by operant conditioning techniques, pp. 153-163. In Ullmann, L. and Krasner, L. P. (Eds.): *Case Studies in Behavior Modification.* New York, HR&W, 1966.

Blau, P. M.: *Exchange and Power in Social Life.* New York, Wiley, 1967.

Burgess, B. L., Clark, R. N., and Hendree, J. C.: An experimental analysis of litter procedures. *J Appl Behav Anal, 2:*71-77, 1971.

Bushell, D., Jr., Wrobel, P. A., and Michealis, M. L.: Applying "group" contingencies to the classroom study behavior of preschool children. *J Appl Behav Anal, 1:*55-63, 1968.

Emerson, R. M.: Operant psychology and exchange theory, pp. 379-405. In Burgess, R. L. and Bushell, D., Jr. (Eds.): *Behavioral Sociology.* New York, Columbia Pr, 1969.

Ferritor, D. E., Buckholdt, D., Hamblin, R. L., and Smith, L.: The non-effects of contingent reinforcement for attending behavior on work accomplishment. *J Appl Behav Anal, 1:*7-19, 1972.

Ferster, C. B., and DeMyer, M. K.: A method for the experimental analysis of the behavior of autistic children. *Am J Orthopsychiatry, 32:*89-98, 1962.

Frank, G.: The role of the family in the development of psychopathology. *Psychol Bull 64:*191-205, 1965.

Fuller, P. R.: Operant conditioning of a vegetative human organism. *Am J Psychol, 62:*587-590, 1949.

Hamblin, R. L., Buckholdt, D., Ferritor, D., Blackwell, L., and Kozloff, M.: *The Humanization Processes.* New York, Wiley, 1971.

Hamblin, R. L., Jacobsen, R. B., and Miller, J. L.: *A Mathematical Theory of Social Change,* New York, Wiley, 1973.

Homans, G. C.: *Social Behavior: Its Elementary Forms.* New York, Harcourt, Brace and World, 1961.

Isaacs, W., Thomas, J., and Goldiamond, I.: Application of operant conditioning to reinstate verbal behavior in psychotics. *J Speech Hear Dis, 25:*8-12, 1960.

Kozloff, M. A.: *Reaching the Autistic Child.* Champaign, Ill, Res Pr, 1973.

Kozloff, M. A.: *Educating Children with Learning and Behavior Problems.* New York, Wiley, 1974.

Levitt, E. E.: The results of psychotherapy with children: an evaluation. *J Consult Psychol, 21:*189-196, 1957.

Levitt, E. E.: Psychotherapy with children: a further evaluation. *Behav Res Ther, 1:*45-51, 1963.

Lindsley, O. R.: Operant conditioning methods applied to research in chronic schizophrenia. *Psychiatr Res Rep, 5:*118-139, 1956.

Lindsley, O. R.: An experiment with parents handling behavior at home. *Johnstone Bull, 9:*27-36, 1966.

Miller, L. K., and Miller, O. L.: Reinforcing self-help group activities of welfare recipients. *J Appl Behav Anal, 1:*59-65, 1970.

Mosher, L. R., Feinsilver, D., Katz, M. M., and Wierckowski, L. A.: *Special Report on Schizophrenia.* Washington, D. C.: U. S. Department of Health, Education and Welfare, April.

Rimland, B.: *Infantile Autism.* New York, Appleton-Century-Crofts, 1964.

Rimland, B.: Psychogenesis versus biogenesis: The issues and the evidence, pp. 702-735. In Plog, S. C. and Edgerton, R. E. (Eds.): *Changing Perspectives in Mental Illness.* New York, HR&W, 1969.

Wener, C., Ruttenburg, B., Dratman, M. L., and Wolf, E. G.: Changing autistic behavior: the effectiveness of three milieus. *Arch Gen Psychiatry, 17:*26-35, 1967.

Chapter 10

CASE MANAGEMENT/ADVOCACY FOR THE AUTISTIC INDIVIDUAL

F. STEVEN FEARING

THE TEXAS SOCIETY FOR AUTISTIC CITIZENS is a nonprofit, consumer advocacy organization that has served as a resource and catalyst for progressive changes in services for autistic Texans since its inception in 1976. While progress had been achieved in many areas involving statewide impact and interagency planning, the State Society recognized, in 1977, that their advocacy efforts were impeded by the lack of case-by-case counseling, follow-along, and referral services. In recognition of the systematic exclusion of autistic people from timely and appropriate services, the Interagency Task Force on Autism (1977) recommended the development of "case management/ advocacy services" to autistic children and their families. The Case Manager/Advocate (hereafter referred to as CM/A) was described as a "child care specialist, assigned to the family, to coordinate the many multi-disciplinary needs the child will face in years to come; a long-term counselor; a resource person; community advocate; referral source; friend in time of crisis. The case manager/advocate can develop the overall goals for the family including both long-range and short-term treatment programs individually formulated for the child. The case manager/advocate can ideally help provide continuity of care."

Funded in part by the Hogg Foundation in 1977, the Texas Society for Autistic Citizens piloted the Case Manager/Advocacy Project based on the recommendations of the Interagency Task Force report. The overall goal of the project was to test the efficacy of professional case management and advocacy on a state-wide basis as conducted by an agent outside the human delivery system.

This model of professional case-by-case advocacy, tied to the system concerns of a state-wide, nonprofit consumer group, had, to our knowledge, never been tried. With a very limited budget and a staff of only one, the project hoped to make at least a small difference for approximately twenty-five families and their autistic children. A major focus was preventing premature institutionalization.

Many Faces of Advocacy

Today there are many different agents of advocacy that operate within separate spheres of influence and provide particular kinds of expertise. Within the dimension of case or individual advocacy, one can find the citizen advocate, public and private ombudsman, the legal advocate, and case manager/advocate (Moore, 1976). Inevitably, all of these advocates will also involve themselves in class advocacy actions while working on behalf of the client or through their affiliation to an advocacy organization. In so doing, they may assume other duties, such as program broker or community organizer. However, officials from the Developmental Disabilities Office (DDO), the Bureau of Education for the Handicapped (BEH), and the National Institute of Mental Health (NIMH) have reviewed the disparate advocacy models and cited "an inevitable tendency toward case advocacy" (Roach, 1976).

For both class and case advocacy, there are basically three types of advocacy expertise or function: lay, legal, and professional (Boggs, 1976). The most significant prototype of lay advocacy may be the "Citizen Advocate" as developed by Wolf Wolfensberger during the late 1960s, now promulgated widely by the National Association for Retarded Citizens (NARC). Citizen advocacy is basically a one-to-one relationship between a trained volunteer and a mentally retarded or otherwise developmentally disabled person, who is known as a protege. Wolfensberger (1972) saw the citizen advocate as having "instrumental and expressive functions." Instrumental functions pertain to the management of the protege's daily life and the meeting of his basic maintenance needs. The facilitation of feelings of self-worth and the giving of affection and companionship are germane to the citizen advocate's expressive function. A national survey of 117 citizen advocacy programs recently conducted by NARC found, however, that citizen advocates were providing much emotional (expressive) support, but little of the much needed practical (instrumental) assistance (Addison, 1976). The survey also found that citizen advocates were serving clients in community settings, but not in large multi-purpose agencies. The DDO, BEH, and NIMH also concluded that "non-professional lay persons recruited to serve as advocates have experienced difficulty implementing an approach geared to systemic change" (Roach, 1976).

The legal advocate embodies the oldest use of the term — the act of representing one in the litigation or legal negotiation process concerning rights, grievances, or appeals. The CM/A provides consultation relative to the clients' due process rights and rights of access to social services. The legal model of "advocacy" is applied by the CM/A up to the point of courtroom representation. It behooves parents at that time to acquire a lawyer and form an advocacy triad with the CM/A providing the perspective of an agent for program monitoring. This advocacy triad has proven effective in bringing advocacy goals to their fruition.

The CM/A as described here aspires to the status of "professional," as opposed to a "lay" advocate, and has competence within the human delivery system. The case "manager" aspect makes use of the social work application of the medical model of patient management. The CM/A guides or directs the parent and/or client so that they do, or have done for them when necessary, what a professional considers appropriate to deal with their problems. There is an implied administrative meaning to this kind of management for the autistic individual. Diverse clinical input must be managed by clarification and service possibilities must be codified to bring a focus for action.

The basic thrust of case management and advocacy has in recent years received legislative mandate and congressional endorsement. The Developmental Disabled Assistance and Bill of Rights Act of 1975 (DD Act, Public Law 94-103), Section 113, calls for each state to "have in effect a system to protect and advocate the rights of persons with DD and . . . such system will (A) have the authority to pursue remedies to insure the protection of the rights of such persons . . . and (B) be independent of any state agency. . . ." Section 112 of the Act calls for a program coordinator who will be responsible for the implementation of the habilitation plan. The CM/A affiliated with the Texas Society for Autistic Citizens has served as a bridge between the mandated protection and advocacy system and the agency program coordinator. The CM/A has served as a primary link to the Protection and Advocacy System in Texas (P & A), and has established direct communication with the P & A on all relevant matters. The CM/A has disseminated P & A information and has served as a screening element for access to the P & A System. This has been done informally within the project design.

The CM/A model formally relates to the advocacy system mandated by Public Law 94-103, the Protection and Advocacy System of Texas, and the individual client as depicted in Figure 10.1. The family and the autistic client receive individual legal advocacy from the P & A System, individual lay advocacy from TSAC, and individual professional advocacy from the CM/A. The family may influence all of these various advocacy efforts through their own actions, as illustrated by the two-way flow of the arrows. The Developmental Disabilities Council in Texas provided finite "seed" money to TSAC while the funding to the P & A System by Public Law 94-103 is continuous. TSAC is connected to the P & A System by a delegate to its board.

Further endorsement for the case manager/advocate concept is contained in the President's Committee on Mental Retardation's (1976) new publication, *Century of Decision,* which calls for a personal representative for every mentally retarded person (and presumably every DD):

> Such a representative will serve as the person's agent in understanding and articulating his needs and in negotiating services which are at any time essential to meet the person's unique requirements. . . . Case workers or "case managers" are commonly assigned by service agencies to implement the delivery of services to persons in need.

The most recent and direct endorsement for case management came in the newly passed Rehabilitative Service Act of 1978

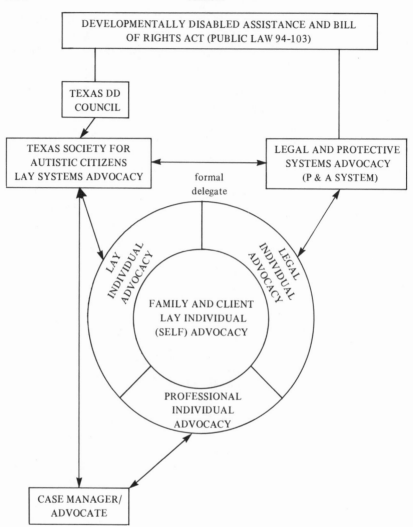

Figure 10.1. Case management/advocacy function within larger Advocacy System.

which contained the new Developmental Disability legislation. "Case management" was noted as one of the four priority service areas, "providing such services to persons with DD as will assist them in gaining access to needed social, medical, educational, and other services." The other three service areas acknowledged in this legislation were child development services (prevention, identification, and alleviation), alternative community living arrangement services, and nonvocational social-developmental services. It is significant that the work of a case manager/advocate would also engender the development of these service areas.

Format for Case Management/Advocacy

The specific objectives of the Case Management/Advocacy Project piloted by the Texas Society for Autistic Citizens is outlined as follows:

I. *Development Procedures for Individual Program Planning*
   A. Establish a "data base" on each client and maintain a problem oriented progress record of management and advocacy interventions. This data base includes family data, pregnancy, birth, and neonatal history, diagnostic and evaluation summaries, program history, "advocacy effort" history, developmental history adapted from Rimland's Form E-2, an adaptive behavior checklist, and the *Muskegon Index of Autistic Behavior.* This data base allows the parents to organize their thinking and medical records, perhaps for the first time.
   B. Encourage the creation of an interagency and interdisciplinary (as opposed to multidisciplinary) mechanism of service from an individual programmatic perspective, reducing the chronic role segregation experienced by parents and service providers. Facilitate the coordination of agency responsibilities and interagency communication with the parents as a full partner.
II. *Identify Gaps in Service Delivery System*
   A. Evaluate and problem solve in areas of eligibility, appropriateness, and effectiveness.
   B. Clarify the problems of identification, diagnosis, and referral as it relates to the need for early intervention and a smooth, predictable linkage to appropriate services.
III. *Advocate for Needed Services*
   A. Disseminate materials, general information, and suggested programmatic models and diagnostic tools to parents and service providers.

B. Assist in the development and design of appropriate public education programs for the autistic. Arrange for outside consultancy if mutually desired.

C. Form advocacy partnership with parents in all their negotiations with local school districts and other service providers and provide linkage to direct legal support if needed.

D. Assist in the adaptation and modification of existing community programs.

IV. *Provide Long-term Advocacy Relationship*

A. Provide continued information, referral, and follow-along to family and client with training for eventual self-advocacy.

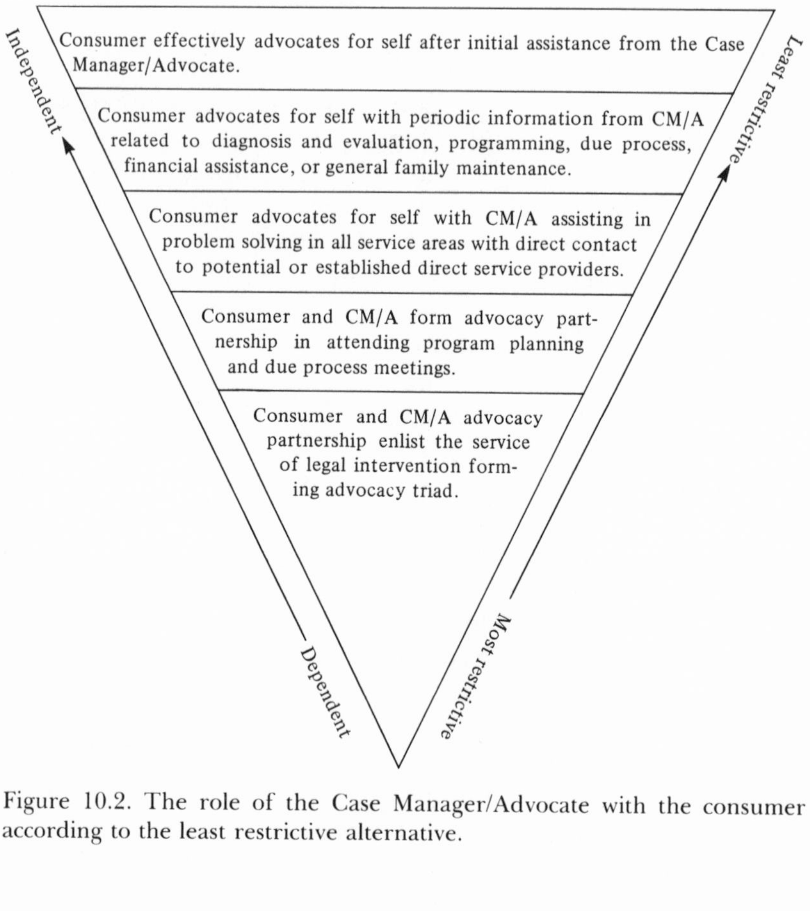

Figure 10.2. The role of the Case Manager/Advocate with the consumer according to the least restrictive alternative.

B. Assist in the utilization of community services and in a smooth transition from one service to the next as the client ages and his/her needs change.

Figure 10.2 illustrates how the Project objectives are implemented in a progression of increased advocacy activity. Some cases proceed from "independent" self-advocacy beginnings to the most "dependent" status. Nearly every client of the CM/A Project requires assistance in problem solving and direct interaction with service providers.

Values and Ideological Base

It is crucial for the advocate and obligatory for the service delivery system to operate from a value system or ideological perspective that recognizes the arbitrariness of deviance as defined by the larger culture. Deviance is a purely statistical phenomenon based on the occurrence of individual behavior in a particular context and is always relative to the "competencies" valued by the majority. Developmentally disabled individuals have a public "non-elected" deviance that must be viewed relative also to the often malevolent, consciously elected, "private" deviance of so-called normals (Gold, 1975).

The following beliefs must underlie the advocate's relationship to the developmentally disabled, autistic client (Jessing and Dean, 1977):

1. *Each person has value.* Regardless of their historical devaluation or obscurity, autistic people are as valuable as other people and should be afforded the same dignity and respect as all other human beings.
2. *The developmental theory.* Every autistic person is capable of growth and learning throughout his entire life. This is the crucial underpinning of special education.
3. *The normalization theory.* Through appropriate learning opportunities, the differences of people who have been devalued by society can be diminished and their images in society enhanced. The normalization principle requires the use of the most normal, "least restrictive" alternative to meet the needs of the autistic individual. The CM/A should be able to evaluate human delivery systems with regard to

normalization. Normalization can be "rated" by use of the "Program Analysis of Service Systems" (PASS) available from the National Institute on Mental Retardation, Toronto.

4. *Consumer participation.* The parents of the autistic person know his needs best, and establishing accountability of service delivery systems to parents and their representatives will lead to high quality services.

5. *Human and legal rights.* Autistic people are citizens with the same rights and responsibilities as other citizens of the same country and the same age. The CM/A needs to be familiar with the nature and definition of a broad range of personal rights and their basis in the Constitution, statutes, or other applicable standards. Areas of human rights include, but are not limited to, the following: the right to life, education, due process, medical care, the least restrictive living or treatment alternative, a guardian if necessary, rehabilitation, training or employment, marriage, sexuality, and procreation.

These ideologies should be the operating perspective of any human delivery system. The advocate must keep them foremost by influence and example. In addition to these values, the Case Manager/Advocate Pilot Project is based on three interlocking premises of case management that create a unique advocacy vehicle for autistic individuals and their families:

1. *Independence.* The CM/A is external to any service delivery system and therefore is not likely to be "co-opted" or "cooled out" by the system.

2. *Wholistic and client centered.* From this independent stance, the advocate can clarify and maintain the focus on the autistic individual as a "whole" person with diverse and changing needs throughout life and on the family unit as also an evolving, actualizing organism. The advocate takes this perspective across agency lines because each separate agency has only limited jurisdiction with regard to particular pieces of the autistic individual's personal development.

3. *Long-term relationship and follow-along.* Also implicated in

crossing agency lines is the need for an advocate to stay with the family over the long haul. As many service systems and agency personnel drop out of the picture, the case manager/advocate provides a continuous focal point for family support and life planning.

Needs and Numbers of the Autistic

The elucidation of the needs of autistic individuals and their families is still the primary role of any advocate for this particular developmentally disabled population. The advocate's first challenge is to educate himself, professionals, those in decision-making roles, and the general public. Although the case manager/advocate is concerned with the needs of individuals and their options in local areas, it may serve him to understand the numbers of the larger national problem. Prior to the passage of the Education for All Handicapped Children Act of 1975 (P.L. 94-142) congressional committees were told during testimony that more than half of the estimated 8 million handicapped children in the United States today do not receive appropriate educational services (*Educating All the Handicapped,* National School Public Relations Assoc., 1977). How many of these are autistic and what percentage of the autistic population is being denied service?

That is hard to know for sure. But of the nearly 100,000 autistic individuals in the United States[1] 80 to 90 percent are eventually institutionalized. That is a sobering beginning point in recognizing the lack of available resources. In 1974, the National Society for Autistic Children's Information and Referral Service, under contract with the NIMH, conducted a survey of the United States so that they could put together a directory of services (*U.S. Facilities and Programs for Children with Severe Mental Illnesses,* NIMH, 1974). It was found that under 5 percent of the 500 facilities and programs surveyed had a program specifically designed to serve persons with a diagnosis of autism! Only 58

---

1. This figure is based on the 4.5 in 10,000 incidence rate for a United States population of approximately 220 million. Bernard Rimland estimates 10 percent of these cases have Kanner's syndrome. Others consider the "autistic-like" to include considerably more than this figure.

percent would accept the autistic as a matter of policy, and many ruled out those who did not have good self-help skills or speech. Several states had no facilities that admitted the autistic as a matter of policy.

In Texas

Based on the 4.5 incidence rate, the Texas *State Plan for Developmental Disabilities* (1978) projected a state population total for autistic children ages zero to twenty at 1,836 for the fiscal year 1978 and an adult population (over twenty) at 2,622 for a total of 4,458. The plan broke it down another way by estimating that 1,656 children and 1,052 adults were in need of case management services. Over 1,600 autistic individuals were considered eligible for special education. Based on figures gathered through contact with the Texas Education Agency, fewer than 100 autistic children have been identified as receiving specialized educational services. Fewer than ten autistic programs are known to exist. So, it is estimated that 1,500 school-aged autistic children in Texas can be found in the following settings:

1. Private settings for the mentally retarded and emotionally disturbed.
2. Public school classes for the mentally retarded, emotionally disturbed, or multihandicapped.
3. State schools for the mentally retarded.
4. State hospitals for the mentally disturbed.
5. Still at home.

Oddly enough, the Texas DD Plan lists no autistic children being served in our state school and state hospital system. The lack of numerical data in this section of the state plan is indicative of the morass of diagnostic and funding mechanisms.

The report of the joint interim committee on special education to the 66th Texas Legislature (*Education for the Handicapped Children in Texas*, 1979) recognized the need "to bring legal definitions of handicapping conditions and diagnostic definitions together and apply them as a single definition" (p. 44). The new definition of autism contained within the upcoming *DSM III* should bring added clarity in this regard. "Autism, residual type" will be a welcome addition. It is noteworthy that the interim committee's recommended definition of autism establishes it as a separate category. They go on to say "The Committee has received compelling evidence that the nature of an autistic child's handicap is such that, if inappropriate programs are imposed upon an autistic child because of his classification in another handicap category, tremendous harm can be done to the child" (p. 75).

Each autistic individual requires a unique mix of services or treatments appropriate to his/her developmental constitution and behavior, personality and learning style, age, family or living circumstances, and locale of residence. The CM/A engages direct service personnel in program planning and life planning based on these individual variables. He solicits for new services and communicates with system managers within the context of general service needs. Awareness of the basic, naturally progressing service protocol encourages a "wide-lens" appreciation of what the autistic individual is all about. Information is power. When service personnel learn, for instance, that there is such a person as an autistic adult, their perceptions about all autistic individuals may change in fundamental ways.

It is not the author's purpose to chronicle here the many categories of social, medical, and educational services needed by autistic individuals throughout life. It should be generally understood that autistic individuals can be viewed chronologically in three broad categories of service needs:

1. Prevention, early identification, and early intervention (secondary prevention, zero to four years).
2. Education and treatment services, three to twenty-one years.
3. Adult developmental training, vocational training, and community residential alternatives.

The work of the CM/A in Texas has brought cause to focus on the following particular needs:

1. *Alternative residential facilities* with a naturalized home environment providing cost-effective, intensive, and quality

treatment. The "teaching home" model piloted by the Autistic Treatment Center in Dallas is one such environment.

2. The development of quality *educational programs* in low incidence areas of *rural Texas*.
3. *Provision of respite care and support services,* e.g. crisis and emergency, for families. The extended family, community based program of the Texas Treatment Center for Autism in Houston represents such a model.
4. *Financial support* for families.
5. The significant need for *information and referral,* as well as *advocacy assistance,* to clarify responsibilities, rights, and opportunities for the families of autistic individuals.

Advocacy and the Ubiquitous System

With tongue in cheek, Ruth Sullivan of NSAC's Information and Referral Service described the qualities needed by parent advocates. "It would have been considerably more helpful," she writes, "if when we were assigned to be parents of autistic children, we had been automatically endowed with motivation, wisdom, stamina, patience and persistence . . . " (Sullivan, 1978). She adds that it would also be helpful to have doctorates in law, medicine, public administration, psychology, and special education — with good health, good looks, and a first name friendship with members of Congress and state legislatures thrown in for good measure! Of all the qualities, she cites persistence as being the most important. However, when parents "take on" the system alone, this persistence may feel more like the curse of Sisyphus.

It has been suggested that in recent years the human delivery system has experienced a great influx of services to the developmentally disabled (Crosson and Chavan, 1977). This appears to be true at one level, in that there are more choices than there were ten years ago. The number of service alternatives for the autistic child has indeed increased, especially within the public school sector. Now there are a few isolated appropriate programs, whereas none existed before. In general, DD consumers are now faced with a wide variety of very fractionated services. This phenomenon of the human delivery system is accentuated for autistic individuals because their needs require the diagnostic or treatment intervention from so many different agencies that do not know or care to know one another. Some parents may feel better with the more familiar necessity of teaching their child at home, rather than challenging the system.

These parents may experience raised expectations for help with seemingly no clear course of how to proceed. They sense that the services are out there — but where? The service system is so complex that successful maneuvering within it is usually impossible for even the most dedicated and persistent consumers and parents. "Maximizing the use of available services presupposes knowledge of what services are needed, when they are needed, and what they are supposed to accomplish. Without some assistance, it is unreasonable to expect parents, consumers or advocates to know how to obtain an appropriate mix of quality services" (Crosson and Chavan, 1977, p. 48). Which professional within any one service delivery system knows what an appropriate mix of quality services for the autistic looks like?

The human delivery system is a complex of overlapping local, regional, state and national responsibilities. Viewed by the parent at the local level, this multilayered bureaucracy might resemble a huge onion. "No matter how many layers are stripped away, there always seems to be another layer . . . and a person is likely to be driven to tears before an accountable agent is found" (Neufeld, 1976, p. 100). Professional advocates or parents can intrude within these systems and find individuals who are at least concerned and willing to listen, but there seems to be a process, "dynamic inactivism," that operates within bureaucracies and is a formidable foe to any change influence (Arrell and Dickson, 1978). It seems quite ubiquitous and yet hard to confront directly. Dynamic inactivism means turning up the volume of agency activity in response to advocates — hearing them out, giving the appropriate answers, considering proposals, and basically passing the buck around in a circle. The advocate is held in limbo until the circle is completed and he knows for sure that nothing has been done. Everyone in the agency is working, moving, cooperating, but nothing happens as a result.

We can see the enormity of the task facing parents of autistic children and the challenge for advocates to bring expertise and coordination to the efforts of service providers. Parents and advocates are faced with the following:

1. Individual agencies that do not have basic, current knowledge about autism.
2. Individual agencies that cannot view the autistic person or his family "wholistically" because of limited jurisdiction.
3. Individual agencies that do not coordinate their services with other agencies or even know what other agencies can provide.
4. Individual agencies who each seem to perpetuate the *status quo*, even with concerned individuals working within it.

External vs. Internal

The CM/A, as piloted by the TSAC, operates outside the regulatory confines of public appropriations. He is *external* to the system in which he advocates. An internal advocate is paid by the system in which he works. The independent position of the CM/A does not preclude cooperative exchange, congeniality, diplomacy, and empathy for agency restraints. The advocate searches first for that common ground of concern from which parents and professionals may build. The external advocate has the additional recourse to confrontation if it is needed to facilitate the acknowledgement of legal responsibilities. Access to the media, parent groups and the courts often provides the needed impetus for conflict resolution. However, negotiated solutions are usually preferrable, especially for the autistic person receiving the services. The specter of the Independent Hearing Officer in Texas seems to facilitate an increase in negotiation at the local level.

The external position of the CM/A appears to be of preeminent importance at this particular stage in the evolution of services for the autistic individual. Even those "natural" advocates within the system must at some point bow to system maintenance (Neufeld, 1976). Because external advocates are hampered by limited access to the environments that serve the clients, the internal advocates can serve to relay accurate information to the external advocate about how the system works. Data related to program weakness is easier to obtain from inside a system, but internally funded advocacy mechanisms are limited in their ability to act on this data. If they adopt an external adversary style, they will be short-lived.

As agents of system change, advocates may do well to remain cognizant of these ideas (Eklund, 1978):

1. Bureaucrats are fixated on process rather than outcome.
2. Bureaucrats are usually decent people.
3. Bureaucrats can seldom exercise personal courage in making decisions.
4. Anyone can choose to be a bureaucrat as bureaucrats are not found exclusively within recognized bureaucracies.

Wolf Wolfensberger adds these concepts to our understanding of system change (Eklund, 1978):

1. When we seek change, that change must not be seen as synonymous with growth. In view of Proposition 13 consciousness, we must reduce fears of system growth by working with the generic services.
2. The predominant response to any change proposal will be negative; when there is an initial positive response, it probably means that people are confused or that the proposal does not really mean change.
3. Once a change strategy has been adopted by 10 percent to 20 percent of the people, it is impossible to reverse.

CM/A Cases: Issues, Problems, and Recommendations

There seems to be considerable momentum in the United States today to recognize the constitutionally guaranteed rights of our handicapped citizenry. Recent legislation mandating "free and appropriate" education and individual program planning has been the harbinger of hope for autistic individuals. Local school superintendents have proven to be pivotal in this regard. Depending upon their perspective, the shift in priorities implied within Public Law 94-142 has occurred on a continuum of swift actualization to conscious refusal. Drawing from the latter end of this continuum, the need for case management/advocacy services has been verified with fifty referrals to the Project over the course of fourteen months.

The problems have been comprehensive and diverse with no

clear solutions. The diagnostic ambiguity is the initial obstacle. There has not been professional consensus as to what symptoms must be present to establish the diagnosis of autism or guidelines for obtaining the data base to document the symptom picture. Fortunately, this situation appears to be changing. Clients of the Project have been referred to specifically designated evaluation centers. Predictably, parents lack confidence in the ability of local professionals to recognize the syndrome (or its absence) and to be sensitized to the need for further testing. One family of our Project has two "autistic like" daughters, ages two and four, and a long history of confusing diagnostic impressions. The children received more in-depth medical testing based on our recommendation and specific agency referral. The parents reported that the local pediatrician and treatment personnel dissuaded them against such an "unnecessary" evaluation. The testing revealed a rare oversight in the detection of PKU. The resulting dietary treatment, although dangerously delayed, had immediate ameliorative impact.

It has also been the exception to find diagnosticians and psychologists who were aware of the subtleties of administration and interpretation inherent in testing autistic individuals. We have dispersed much information related to new screening and prescriptive tools and have explored, with professionals, issues related to the guarded application of standard psychological testing. In our experience, audiological evaluations of the autistic child also need further refinement. This area is as gray as any in the morass of differential diagnosis.

The CM/A Project hopes to bolster its information and referral mechanism in the future as we continue to learn more about various evaluation and program services throughout the state. As our activities in the field increase, and with the concomitant increase in professional education and training, reliable and plentiful resources for referral can be compiled and a network of information sharing can begin. This is very much needed.

The advocate for the autistic individual must address the issue of diagnostic purity and its relevance to individual program planning. We are still in an embryonic stage in establishing a solid base of public and professional awareness. At this point, we must spotlight autism as at least a separate "genus" or "species" of neurological impairment (occurring concurrently with others) in order to sensitize funding sources, university special education departments, and service providers. The absence of an academic tract for autism has been reflected in our casework. Moreover, special education directors throughout the State of Texas are hard pressed to find teachers for the severely/profoundly multihandicapped and the emotionally disturbed (*Education for the Handicapped Children in Texas*, 1979, p. 61). The advocate's call for specialized services for the autistic is a springboard to an in-depth study of particular treatments and long-range planning. The management of individual cases compels the advocate to also recognize the advantage of heterogenous and normalized educational environments as well as the situation-specific context upon which issues of "least restrictive environment" and mainstreaming must be worked out.

Defining an "appropriate" education for the autistic individual, as the term is used in Public Law 94-142 (121a. 300), may stretch thin the credibility of the professional advocate. The CM/A cannot possibly be simultaneously on par professionally (at least on paper) with psychologists, educational diagnosticians, psychiatrists, teachers, and other adjunctive personnel. From a legal perspective, appropriateness in Public Law 94-142 is juxtaposed against those services "to be provided" in the I.E.P. (121a. 346), and tends therefore to be absorbed in subjective bias. We saw in one early case, for instance, that the appropriate duration of the school day was viewed more in terms of the teacher's lack of endurance and management skills rather than with a positive, proactive view of the autistic person's inherent capabilities and needs. Likewise, the need for a twelve month public school program for autistic individuals will soon be addressed in the context of appropriateness and agency endurance.

Designating those related services that are "required to assist" (121a. 13) the autistic individual in benefiting fully from special education is also a fertile field for advocate input. The phrase "required to assist" like "appropriate" leads once again to the same questions: How comprehensive or effective do you want to be? How much is enough? Parent training, complete with home visits and closely monitored homework assignments in behavior modification, has been demonstrated in our casework to be a service not provided and yet integrally related to the success of the school program. It is clear that an appropriate education does not equal the *best* education. The I.E.P. need not, as in the preliminary regulations promulgated by BEH, "specify all services needed by the child without regard to the local availability of the services."

The boundaries of a "free" education are inextricably tied to the issue of appropriateness. It is a real challenge for public school officials "to take primary responsibility for seeing that handicapped children who cannot be appropriately served by the district receive services in an alternate placement — such as other public or private facilities" (*Education for the Handicapped*, p. 148). Interagency planning of the Texas Education Agency with the Texas Department of Mental Health and Mental Retardation, the Department of Human Resources, and the Texas Rehabilitation Commission is a critical need but is confused by an opposing general momentum for other agencies and private facilities to place service and/or financing demands on the public schools.

The CM/A must help facilitate the recognition of treatment and funding responsibilities across several agencies. The prevention of institutionalization is of utmost importance. Alternative residential facilities such as the teaching home are more cost-effective as well as therapeutically beneficial. Interagency cooperation must be based on long-term planning for optimal independent functioning. Program planning meetings attended by the CM/A in support of parents often lacked any acknowledgement by the service personnel of what life might be like for the child several years later. Short-term objectives often seemed like ends in themselves with no connection to the concern of parents or prognostic probabilities. Based on his casework, the CM/A functions to give feedback to all service systems for the development of statewide planning and for a tract of appropriate services that provide lifetime care.

Conclusion

To conclude and summarize, the Case Manager/Advocate works in partnership with the families of autistic citizens to facilitate a truly interdisciplinary approach to program and life planning. He clarifies the access route to services and provides an unencumbered monitoring of their quality. The CM/A helps bring to life the recent legal mandates that signal a transformation of our country's relationship to the handicapped. The CM/A must be eclectic in his approach to the problems faced by families of autistic children. He engages many different agencies from the same client centered ideological perspective. The CM/A must proceed with a sense of history, a sense of purpose, and a sense of humor. The ultimate goal is the eventual passing away of the need for his service.

REFERENCES

Addison, M.: The theory and application of citizen advocacy. In Bensberg, G. J., and Rude, C. (Eds.): *Advocacy Systems for the Developmentally Disabled.* Lubbock, Texas, Texas Technological University, Research and Training Center in Mental Retardation, 1976.

Arrell, M. and Dickson, C.: Relating to the national advisory council. In Rude, C. and Baucom, L. (Eds.): *Implementing Protection and Advocacy Systems.* Lubbock, Texas, Texas Technological University, Research and Training Center in Mental Retardation, 1978.

Boggs, E.: Advocacy and protective services — Where are we coming from? In Bensberg, G. J. and Rude, C. (Eds.): *Advocacy Systems for the Developmentally Disabled.* Lubbock, Texas, Texas Technological University, Research and Training Center in Mental Retardation, 1976.

Crosson, J. and Chavan, A.: Individual program planning: a tool for monitoring. In Bensberg, G. J. and Baucom, L. (Eds.): *Advocacy Systems for Persons with Developmental Disabilities.* Lubbock, Texas, Texas Technological University, Research and Training Center in Mental Retardation, 1977.

Eklund, E.: *Systems Advocacy.* Lawrence, Kansas University Affiliated Facility, 1978.

Gold, M.: Vocational training. In Wortis, J. (Ed.): *Mental Retardation and Developmental Disabilities: An Annual Review,* vol. 7. New York, Brunner-Mazel, 1975, pp. 254-264.

Interagency Task Force on Autism: *Early Infantile Autism.* Austin, Texas, 1977.

Jessing, B. and Dean, S.: Case advocacy: ideology and operation. In Bensberg, G. J., and Baucom, L. (Eds.): *Advocacy Systems for Persons with Developmental*

Disabilities. Lubbock, Texas, Texas Technological University, Research and Training in Mental Retardation, 1977.

Moore, M.: A demonstration of three advocacy models for persons with developmental disabilities. In Bensberg, G. J. and Rude, C. (Eds): *Advocacy Systems for the Developmentally Disabled.* Lubbock, Texas, Texas Technological University, Research and Training Center in Mental Retardation, 1976.

National School Public Relations Association: *Educating All the Handicapped.* Arlington, Virginia, 1977.

Neufeld, G. R.: Advocacy: an examination of the interaction with the human service delivery system. In Bensberg, G. J. and Rude, C. (Eds.): *Advocacy Systems for the Developmentally Disabled.* Lubbock, Texas, Texas Technological University, Research and Training Center in Mental Retardation, 1976.

President's Committee on Mental Retardation: *Mental Retardation: Century of Decision,* Washington, D.C., U.S. Govt. Print. Office, 1976.

Report of the Joint Interim Committee on Special Education to the 66th Texas Legislature: *Education for the Handicapped Children of Texas.* Austin, Texas, 1979.

Roach, L.: Developmental disabilities advocacy projects. In Bensberg, G. J. and Rude, C. (Eds.): *Advocacy Systems for the Developmentally Disabled.* Lubbock, Texas, Texas Technological University, Research and Training Center in Mental Retardation, 1976.

State Planning Council of Texas: *State Plan for Developmental Disabilities and Facilities Construction Program.* Austin, Texas, 1978.

Sullivan, R.: *Keep Your Cool and Make the System Work for You.* Lawrence, Kansas University Affiliated Facility, 1978.

Wolfensberger, W.: *Toward Citizen Advocacy for the Handicapped, Impaired, and Disadvantaged: An Overview.* DHEW Publication No. (05) 72-42, Washington, D.C., U. S. Govt. Print. Office, 1972.

Chapter 11

INCREASING PARENTAL PARTICIPATION IN THE IEP PROCESS

RANDALL SOFFER AND RICHARD LaVALLO

Today, parents of autistic children have the opportunity to be involved in making decisions concerning their child's educational program. In the past, parents were frequently satisfied with the mere placement of their child into a public school program without questioning the appropriateness of such services. Those parents fortunate enough to have input into programmatic decisions viewed this as a privilege rather than a right.

Even though parent participation in developing educational plans is now mandated, a significant number of parents attending Individual Educational Planning (IEP) meetings are not involved in making the decisions related to their child's educational programs (SRI, 1977; Hoff et al., 1978). The law is a necessary but not sufficient condition for parent participation in developing their child's educational program. Therefore, other measures must be taken to maximize parental involvement. The purpose of this chapter is to explore and address specific problems associated with parent participation in the IEP process.

Rationale for Parent Involvement in the IEP Process

The importance of parent involvement in the IEP process is essential to the education of autistic children. Because of the low incidence of autism, i.e. 4 to 5 cases per 10,000, and, until recently, the unwillingness of public schools to educate severely handicapped children, educators do not possess the necessary experience or expertise to meet the needs of this population. Also, due to negative expectations, such as the unresponsiveness of autistic children, many public school programs fail to use

221

appropriate assessment devices and intervention strategies. Parent involvement can help to rectify this situation by achieving the following:

- More accurate identification of the child's individual educational needs and less traditional categorization and labeling of the child.
- Greater understanding of the whole child on the part of the school personnel.
- Reinforcement of the child's learning at home since parents are more familiar with exact goals and plans to be worked on at school.
- Long range planning in order to prepare adequately for the child's future.

By becoming full partners with professional educators, parents can review their child's progress and the appropriateness of education programs as well as judge program alternatives and help finalize decisions.

Obstacles to Parent Involvement in the IEP Process

Even though parent participation and input into the planning of educational programs for their children is highly regarded, it appears as though the level of parent involvement is minimal (Gilliam, 1976; Goldstein et al., 1977). This failure of parents to assume full partnership with professional educators in the IEP process is associated with the role perceptions of both parents and educators, i.e. the sets of behaviors that each group believes they should enact). That is, educators view programming decisions as being their exclusive responsibility (Nero, 1977; Yoshida et al., 1977); whereas parents see themselves more as information providers than as equal partners in decision making.

Role expectations of educators and parents toward each other are consistent with the aforementioned role perceptions. In other words, professionals feel that parents lack the knowledge and skills to participate actively in the IEP process. Nor do they believe that it is the parents' role to do so (Nero, 1977; Yoshida et al., 1977). Although research fails to indicate a clear pattern, parents generally view decision making related to their child's educational goals and objectives as being the role of educators (Nero, 1977). Thus, considering together the perceived roles of parents and educators and their expected roles of one another, it is of little surprise that the enacted roles of each, i.e. the sets of behaviors actually carried out, result in minimal parent participation.

In order to understand fully the relationship between these role perceptions and expectations, it is necessary to identify two factors that contribute to the undermining of parent involvement. They are as follows:

1. *The reluctance of educators to involve parents in programming decisions.* Traditionally, not only were educational decisions made by educators ("the experts"), but their decisions were seldom questioned by parents ("the nonexperts"). In *loco parentis* is the legal principle through which schools have gradually assumed many aspects of parental responsibilities. This role has been generally accepted by both parents and educators and significantly affects the attitudes of professionals toward parents and vice versa.

2. *The societal view of parents of the handicapped as well as their own self-perception.* This obstacle deals with the stereotyped maladaptive adjustment of parents to handicapped children. Consequently, parents lack "realistic positive growth" expectations for the development of their child. Guilt, denial, distrust, or an over/under demanding attitude of the parent towards the child can impede effective parent involvement. Many parents succumb to their "plight" and assume a passive nonparticipative role in meeting with intimidatingly "healthy" educators. On the other hand, the educators' expectations of such parental dysfunctions, whether present or not, can result in a negative attitude towards the role of parents in the decision-making process.

The combined impact of both these factors significantly constrains parental involvement.

Suggestions to Increase Parent Involvement in the IEP Process

Despite the intent of the law, the actual implementation of the IEP process has failed to establish a full partnership between parents and professionals. The educator's domination of educational program planning has caused not only a counterproductive breakdown in communication between parents and educators but also the token representation of parents in the IEP process. As stated earlier, the source of this problem is closely linked to the role perceptions and expectations of both parents and educators. That is, the limited expectations for parent responsibility and competence in formulating educational goals and objectives prevent parents from assuming a full partnership role. In order to reverse this detrimental self-fulfilling prophecy, the role expectations and role perceptions of both parents and educators must be changed.

There is no simple solution to this complex problem. However, any attempt at increasing the effectiveness of parent participation cannot be achieved without fostering a change in knowledge, attitudes, and skills of parents and educators. More specifically, the essential ingredients of such a change effort should incorporate:

For educators:

1. *Increasing their understanding and acceptance of parent involvement.* Educators must be informed of parents' rights under the laws as well as the potential benefits from such collaboration. Most importantly, educators need to recognize the interrelationship between the child's education and home environment. Not only does the child's home situation, i.e. parent-child relationship, influence the child's performance in school, but the school is also instrumental in resolving home-based problems. Therefore, if educators view parents as allies (Barsch, 1969), there is a greater likelihood for education to have a real impact on the developmental needs of the child at home as well as throughout his life.

2. *Changing attitudes and expectations regarding parent involvement.* To establish a viable relationship with parents, educators must recognize that parents have the following moral rights:

   —The right to have prescribed procedures followed as outlined in legislative or school manuals.

—The right to know about available services or facilities.

—The right to attempt to plan the best program for their child.

—The right to ask for explanations from professionals.

—The right to play the role of parent and child advocate and not to view things as an administrator or teacher.

—The right to be treated as a capable human adult and not to be patronized.

—The right to use one's judgment to help decide priorities and schedules.

—The right to refuse inappropriate requests or pressure without feeling guilty, selfish or ignorant.

—The right to have one's opinions given the same respect and consideration that others are given (Markel, 1976, p. 6).

3. *Training in group dynamics.* By developing communication and group process skills, educators could reduce the feelings of intimidation and anxiety commonly felt by parents in IEP meetings and promote an atmosphere that would be more sensitive to direct parent input. For example, if the educators could "actively" listen to the parents in a supportive and nonjudgmental manner, they would gain a better understanding of what parents are actually thinking and feeling.

4. *Developing more opportunities for parents and educators to participate in the school decision-making process.* This would reinforce the value of parent input into school decisions as well as undermine the barriers existing between parents and educators. An example of this would be to have teachers, parents, and other concerned citizens serve on curriculum advisory committees.

5. *Increasing the frequency and nature of contacts between parents and educators.* Parents could be encouraged to serve as classroom aides, attend staffings, and participate in parent-teacher associations. In addition, because many parents perceive the school as a formidable and disapproving setting, educators could plan off-campus get-togethers for parents and themselves. Such gatherings could take place

in comfortable environments such as community meeting rooms. The purpose of these "nonmeetings" would be to encourage spontaneous and relaxed communication between parents and educators. One possible way to accomplish this is by showing slides of autistic children involved in various program activities. This could serve as a stimulus for informal discussion.

For Parents:

1. *Developing a more realistic perception of their role.* Parents must be advised of their rights, their responsibilities, and the benefits derived from their participation in the IEP meeting. For instance, parents must be aware of their right to due process — which includes being adequately notified of any changes in their child's school program; examining all of their child's school records and evaluations; having the opportunity to call an impartial hearing to appeal any decisions concerning their child's placement; and having access to legal counsel.
2. *Gaining knowledge and confidence to question professionals.* Parents must be informed about the IEP process, special education programs and related service alternatives proposed for their child. By knowing not only what services are available, but also what services their child is entitled to, parents can more effectively advocate for their child. Furthermore, parents must be cognizant of decisions actually made in the IEP meeting. For example, the areas covered in the IEP should include self-help/basic living skills, social/behavioral development, career/vocational development, and academics.
3. *Communicating more effectively with educators.* Parents must be familiarized with basic educational terminology and jargon. It is helpful for parents to understand concepts and terms such as *affective domain, psycho-pharmacological intervention* and *diagnostic testing.* When parents are unfamiliar with an educator's usage of a particular term, they should not hesitate to ask for clarification.
4. *Acquiring a more realistic attitude towards professional roles.*

Parents must be aware of the roles and responsibilities of the other participants in the IEP process. In other words, it is essential for parents to be familiar with the various persons in attendance at the IEP meeting, such as the school administrator (principal), resource teacher, diagnostician, speech therapist, psychologist, and others. A basic understanding of the school's organizational chart and chain of command would also enhance parents' effectiveness in the IEP meeting.

5. *Interacting more effectively in the actual development of their child's individualized education plan.* Parents must know how to prepare for and conduct themselves in IEP meetings. By being proficient in goal planning, assertiveness and negotiation, parents would be able to provide support and justify a firm, consistent stand for what they feel is best for their child.

6. *Developing realistic positive attitudes toward the capabilities and potential of their autistic child.* Parents must be aware of the most recent innovations in the treatment and education of autistic children. Parents must assess their values and expose themselves to a variety of programs and facilities serving autistic children. Knowledge acquired from such experiences would help parents clarify their position on the future of their child.

7. *Increasing contacts with other parents.* It is essential for parents to recognize that parents of other handicapped children can be a valuable source of support, information, and power. By communicating with parents in their child's program as well as in parent associations, parents will obtain a broader perspective of the special education program and school district.

Conclusion

This chapter focuses on the problem of parents who attend, but minimally participate, in IEP meetings. The writers have attempted to help those concerned with IEP meetings to understand and cope more effectively with this specific problem associated with the IEP process.

It should be pointed out, however, that this lack of parental participation is neither inevitable nor omnipresent. It is the writers' contention that this problem can be completely avoided. The key ingredient is informal home-school communication, which is another aspect of parental involvement. Through informal communications, an accepting and open relationship can be established between parents and educators. This will naturally lead to spontaneous participation of parents in IEP meetings. Therefore, informal communications between parents and educators should be encouraged. The time and place of such communications can vary greatly. Parents can chat with educators when they pick up their children from school. Casual telephone conversations will also help. Teachers can send home progress notes to parents. Parents can invite their child's teacher to their home for coffee. All these activities can be easily and inexpensively initiated.

One final caution needs to be articulated. It is not the intent of the writer to imply that a totally harmonious or conflict free IEP meeting will result from greater parent participation. However, it is our firm belief that the best interests of autistic children will be served by parents assuming an active role in the IEP process. Furthermore, to accomplish the intent of P.L. 94-142, parents and educators need to appreciate their respective areas of expertise. The result can and should be increased sharing of information about the child and, consequently, increased parental impact on the individualized education plan.

REFERENCES

Barsch, R. H.: *The Parent Teacher Partnership.* Arlington, Va., Council for Exceptional Children, 1969.

Gilliam, J.: *The Contributions, Influence, and Status Rankings of Educational Planning and Placement Committee Meetings.* Unpublished doctoral dissertation, The University of Michigan, 1976.

Goldstein, H., Arkell, C., Ashcroft, S. C., Hurley, O. L., and Lilly, M. S.: Schools. In N. Hobbs (Ed.): *Issues in the Classification of Children.* Washington, Jossey-Bass, 1975.

Hoff, M.K., Fenton, K. S., Yoshida, R. K., and Kaufman, M. J.: Notice and consent: the school's responsibility to inform parents. *J School Psychol, 16(3):*265-273, 1978.

Markel, G.: *Assertive Training for Parents of Exceptional Children.* ERIC Document Reproduction Service No. ED 122 569, Reston, VA, 1976.

Nero and Associates, Inc.: *Project IEP*. Roslyn, Va., 1977.
SRI International: Study results. In National Association of State Directory of Special Education: *Summary of Research Findings on Individual Education Programs*. Washington, D.C., 1977.
Yoshida, R. K., Fenton, K. S., Maxwell, J. P., and Kaufman, M. J.: *Parental Involvement in the Special Education, Pupil Planning Process: The School's Perspective*. Washington, D.C., U.S. Office of Education, Bureau of Education for the Handicapped, 1977.

Chapter 12

THE HIGH LEVEL AUTISTIC
Parents' Views and Concerns

ANONYMOUS

IN RECENT YEARS, books, articles, and workshops covering a wide range of subjects relating to autism abound. Yet one area has been greatly neglected — that of the near-normal autistic. After struggling to bring their autistic children close to normal in their development, parents find themselves groping in the dark for direction. Many people, even professionals, think of autism only in terms of the most severe cases. The purpose of this chapter is to bring attention to the problems of the near-normal autistic person and his/her family. The following is a description of a near-normal autistic girl as related by her mother. Included are descriptions of many of her characteristics and the mother's interpretation of some of these characteristics. Concluding this article are questions asked by parents of near-normal autistic children. It is hoped that we may soon see more articles that attempt to answer these questions.

"LINDA"

At age twelve, Linda is above average in intelligence and academics, and below average in social skills. After apparent normal development during the first two years of life, she suddenly lost all speech and developed the characteristics typical of autism: no eye contact, resistance to change, withdrawal, disinterest in people, hyperactivity, sleeping and eating problems, spinning, rocking, tantrums, obsessive interest in certain objects, etc. Diagnosed as autistic before the age of three, she was placed in a regular nursery school with a very understanding teacher. A behavior modification program was started at home. Beginning efforts were slow, but, once eye contact was established, she made rapid progress. Limited speech began again at age three and one-half and speech therapy was initiated at age four and one-half.

At the age of five, Linda was placed in a private school, primarily for children with learning disabilities. The school had a strong behavior modification approach. At age eight, she was moved to a regular, private school and then changed to another private school a year later. After these attempts at mainstreaming failed, she was returned to the school for LD children. Individual therapy with the school psychologist began at age nine. Group therapy with other students has been included in her school program. Recently, her individual therapy was taken over by a psychologist not involved in the school program. She also has private tutoring in handwriting and organizational skills. Currently, Linda is in the seventh grade. She attends eighth grade math and science classes and is capable of reading on an eleventh grade level.

Unlike many near-normal autistic children, Linda's speech is fairly normal. Problems with pronunciation are slightly noticeable, and she still has some difficulty with volume control. Because of extensive reading, her vocabulary is large, though some words are mispronounced. The greatest difficulty seems to lie in talking too much, usually about her favorite subjects. She seems to be unaware that others may not be interested in what she has to say. People find it necessary to cut her off very abruptly. Her conversations may be inappropriate for the situation. Frequently, she is uninterested in the conversation of others, unless it is one of her favorite topics.

Probably the one word that would best describe Linda is single-minded. Once she becomes interested in a subject, it becomes an obsession. Occasionally, obsessive subjects have related to pleasurable activities such as swimming and science. Interest in the subject of astronomy led to a Science Fair award in the fourth grade. However, I believe that these obsessive interests are often related to fears or internal conflicts. Fire was an early obsession. After being given eye glasses, optometry was the favorite subject. At age ten, she was preoccupied with disease and medicine. Encyclopedia articles and medical books were read again and again. Conversations centered around medical problems. She once inquired of an acquaintance, "How are your kidneys working today?" Later, in therapy we learned that she feared that she might have an incurable disease. She was not sure exactly what autism might include.

Last year, the obsessive topics were Russia and Hitler. She became an authority on these subjects. Some encyclopedia articles were even memorized. While neighborhood kids modeled animals and flowers out of clay, Linda made a tombstone for Hitler — not exactly typical play for an eleven-year-old. During this year, Linda was involved in a conflict with her teachers and with us over control of her life. She wanted all control with no responsibilities. Her art work was a daily series of drawings that showed one country gaining control of another. Dictatorships were always established. She developed an imaginary country, complete with a constitution and strict laws, which were strictly black or white with no gray areas. Torture chambers were carefully drawn for punishment of lawbreakers. Of course, she was absolute dictator of this country.

Linda's favorite activities are reading, drawing, cooking, and swimming. She prefers reading fact to fiction and finds reference materials especially appealing. Artwork seems to be far more than a pleasurable pastime for her as it often is for other near-normal autistic children. It is as though she is working out thoughts and feelings in her pictures. I was amazed to find that her drawings were very different from most children her age, but were very similar to other near-normal autistics. The people in her drawings are very primitive; yet buildings, streets, and houses show incredible detail. A constant flow of dialogue accompanies the drawing of each picture. During her obsession with medicine, she drew children with various stages of unknown diseases. Often, she would invent medicines to cure these diseases.

Lately, her drawings have been replaced by play during which she uses small beads and Lego® building blocks. The blocks have been set up to represent large bodies of land and water. Various sizes and colors of beads represent nations of people, food, animals, and so on. Bead nations conquer other bead nations. Some nations become industrialized while others with poor nutrition develop diseases. Beads in wheelchairs are made by putting small safety pins through the beads. This play is intricate and has been ongoing for many months. It is very similar to her series of drawings, only more concrete and continuous. Perhaps it is a form of self-stimulation. The more stress that Linda feels, the more hours per day are spent in this solitary bead play. She seems to be constantly organizing things in her drawings and bead play, yet she is very disorganized in other areas of her life. I have also observed that she tries to organize activities on paper if several guests are expected to visit. If the guests fail to follow her plans, she becomes very frustrated.

One major problem for her and for the family is her ritualistic, compulsive behavior. Although it is much more subtle than that exhibited by other autistic children, it definitely causes problems. She moves at her own pace in her own way, regardless of the problems caused for other family members. The fact that she may cause a family member to be late to an important appointment seems to have little effect on her. Each daily activity has its own ritual. For example, the Eskimo Pie® Eating Ritual goes as follows: The chocolate is stripped from the ice cream bar and placed under a high intensity lamp to melt. The ice cream bar is placed in a bowl and the ice cream is eaten from the stick with a special spoon. Then the melted chocolate is consumed. Any variation in this ritual brings frustration and anger. As family members, we find our lives revolving around her rituals.

Obsessions with food have continued since childhood. Linda will eat two or three kinds of food for months, almost to the exclusion of all other food. Then suddenly, she will switch to another food. Attempts to vary her diet have not been successful. Recently, the subject of nutrition has become an obsession. After months of struggling to lose twenty pounds on a low carbohydrate diet, she suddenly declared herself a junk food addict and stopped the diet. Devious methods were used to avoid taking vitamins, yet she was reading several books on nutrition. In her bead play, bead nations were dying from poor nutrition. It seems that this behavior may be a subtle form of self-abuse. In a sudden about-face, she has decided to take large numbers of vitamins. However, her diet has not yet changed.

As she enters adolescence, our greatest problem with Linda is her conflicts with authority. Although this is not uncommon in early adolescence, she carries it to the extreme. Throughout her early years, behavior modification was used successfully to control her behavior. Now any obvious attempts at behavior control meet with great resistance and usually fail. Much of her energy seems to be spent in trying to counter-control. Her desire to be in total control of every aspect of her life, with others revolving around her wishes, is not unlike that of other autistic children. Appropriate dress, manners, actions, etc., are far down on her scale of importance compared with maintenance of her ritualistic way of life. Even following a simple recipe in cooking meets with resistance. She always wants to change the recipe in some way. Following directions meets with similar resistance. Getting in step with the rest of the world is not one of her high priorities; however, being out of step does not make her happy.

Linda is going through conflicts about her handicaps. She knows that she is autistic, but she does not understand what it all means. She wants to attend a regular school, yet her unwillingness (or inability) to act in an appropriate manner has caused her to be placed in a special school. Earlier attempts at mainstreaming failed. Although she was able to handle the academic work, the behavior problems became too difficult for the untrained teachers to handle. With a label of autism, her teachers were frightened of her behavior. Instead of coming down hard when she got out of line, they preferred to let her get by with behaviors not tolerated in other students. They seemed to be afraid to discipline her. Knowing her reaction to discipline, I can understand why. It was easier to drop her from the school.

Social situations with normal children are very difficult. She is frequently teased and abused. Although she wants to be part of the group, Linda usually ends up befriending other outcasts. The influence of some of these troubled friends is not always beneficial. She does have one fairly close friendship that was made during her years at the regular school. Her friend, a very intelligent and creative girl who is not really in the rest of the group, seems to recognize and admire the intellectual qualities about Linda. Her friendship has had a very positive influence on Linda.

Linda is an accomplished manipulator. She is very dependent on others and is unwilling to take responsibility for her own actions. She thinks that her problems are always caused by someone else, an attitude which is a major concern. Authority figures are enemies. She spends endless hours plotting the demise of her teachers. Linda seems to be torn between being a normal, independent, responsible person and being irresponsibly handicapped. At times, her thinking and behavior is very logical and responsible. At other times, nothing else matters except her desires, regardless of the consequences.

Adolescence has brought her much unhappiness thus far. In spite of her high intelligence, she seems to find little pleasure in academic achievements, with the possible exception of science. She complains that her classes with LD students are boring. Yet she has been unable to function in a regular classroom. The moral values of our family are being challenged. She talks constantly of drugs, alcohol, violence, and suicide. I realize that normal adolescent children also rebel, but her self-destructive attitude bothers me. She does not seem to fear the consequences of rebellious, self-destructive actions. Under peer pressure, she might try anything.

To the casual observer, Linda appears normal, but somewhat peculiar. It is very difficult for others to see and understand her ever-present handicaps. I am optimistic about her future. She has come so far, yet we still have much to accomplish. Her progress seems to go in cycles, three steps forward and two backward. Adolescence is definitely a backward step! We have had great support from the professionals working with us. The problems of the near-normal autistic often seem to be more subtle forms of the problems of severe autistics. Dealing with these problems can be just as difficult, and little guidance is available. Linda seems close, yet so far from being normal.

QUESTIONS ASKED BY PARENTS

1. How do you tell your child about autism? How much do you tell him and when?
2. Will he use autism as an excuse for inappropriate behavior? How do you prevent this?

3. How do you help him understand about the differences in himself?
4. How do you teach judgment, values, and decision making?
5. How do you teach about the gray parts of life when everything seems black and white to him?
6. How do you handle his obsessions with certain subjects? Do you encourage or discourage them?
7. Do you stress academics or vocational skills?
8. How do you teach social skills when he doesn't learn them naturally?
9. How do you help him build self-esteem when social situations frequently go wrong?
10. How do you help him express emotions in an acceptable manner?
11. Is it best to mainstream him or keep him in a sheltered and smaller classroom?
12. How restrictive is a least restrictive classroom?
13. How do you know when he is ready to be mainstreamed?
14. Do you tell a regular classroom teacher about his autism and try to explain his problems or do you keep quiet so that the teacher will not prejudge him?
15. What can parents and speech therapists do to help him with voice inflection and sentence structure?
16. At what point do you drop the label of autism and change to LLD?
17. How do you deal with a self-destructive attitude?
18. Is psychotherapy helpful? How do you know when it should begin? Where do you find a therapist knowledgeable about this subject?
19. How do you balance time given to an autistic child as opposed to other children?
20. How do you explain autism to a sibling? How do you help a sibling handle his embarrassment or his angry feelings about the autistic child?
21. What kind of adult living arrangements should be made for him?
22. What type of sex education should he have? How do you teach him about socially acceptable sexual relationships?

23. Should girls be given birth control methods at puberty?
24. How do you handle inappropriate sexual advances toward a parent?
25. How do you motivate him to act in an appropriate manner?
26. How do you teach him concern for others? How do you help him become aware of other people's feelings?
27. How do you handle inappropriate self-stimulating behaviors such as hand flapping? Do you allow him to do them privately?
28. If he shows outstanding talent in one particular area, should you encourage this talent, even if it takes him away from social situations?
29. How do you know if you are being overprotective or are pushing him beyond his capacity?
30. Should he be allowed to marry and have children? How would you prevent it? If he had children, would they be normal? Should he be sterilized?

IV.
RESEARCH

Chapter 13

RESEARCH ON AUTISM AND CHILDHOOD SCHIZOPHRENIA

BRUCE BALOW

R ESEARCH HAS PROVEN little, if anything, thus far regarding autism. It has, however, narrowed the choices in a number of areas. To adequately consider research findings and conclusions, and put those in proper perspective, one must be well steeped in knowledge of the methodological problems that plague almost all of the research dealing with autistic children. Therefore, this chapter begins with a description of some of the more obvious methodological problems, moves to an illustration of the problem by a rather detailed illustration of one area of research on autistic children, and closes with a discussion of some things we appear to know about autism.

METHODOLOGICAL PROBLEMS IN THE REPORTED RESEARCH

Design

Autism is one of those low prevalence problems. With a reported rate of about one autistic child per 2500 population and with identification of the problem in the neonatal period no simple matter, one may readily understand that the researcher will have an extraordinarily difficult time assembling a group of autistic children large enough to be separated into experimental and control samples or even large enough to follow longitudinally in a prospective design. For those reasons, the typical research on autistic children is either a very small sample study (usually one or several children) conducted not as an experimental study in which a contrast is made between research and control children, but rather as an evaluation study in which one or several children are provided some kind of intervention followed by

241

evaluation of the outcome. Another major type of study design is retrospective, wherein for example, children from ages six to twelve are identified as being autistic and then their early histories are investigated or their diets, or blood, or neurological status is tested and conclusions are reported.

Single subject research is perfectly legitimate, provided that it is done in appropriate fashion, as in the procedure commonly followed by behavior modifiers. That is, a baseline is established by counting a given behavior under normal circumstances, an experimental intervention is applied, that same behavior is again counted, and finally the intervention is removed and the behavior of interest is again counted. Changes in the pattern of behavior related to intervention suggest the value of the intervention. Such research must be tightly controlled and there are highly detailed procedures to be followed if the research is to be considered legitimate; it is not simply a matter of reporting a case study. This design seems to work very well for specific bits of behavior, as in teaching an autistic child to use pronouns appropriately, but appears much more difficult to properly manage in research with broader goals, such as teaching volitional language.

The typical retrospective study is fraught with design difficulties. The likelihood of error that attaches to retrospective investigations is almost 100 percent and certainly not trivial in import. The birth and infancy characteristics of a sample of autistic children who survived to ages sixteen to twenty would probably be quite different from the infancy and birth characteristics of a sample of autistic children selected at ages six to ten. Thus if one starts with the sixteen to twenty year olds and uses them to investigate the preschool characteristics of "autistic children" one is likely to have a considerable sampling bias. Typically, in retrospective studies, the mother is asked information about behaviors of the child many years earlier. Maternal recall is biased by knowledge of the present problem and, as has been shown (Weiner, 1963), by fashions in child rearing.

If one traces the child's medical records or early school records, these written materials will reflect the observations and judgments of a number of people made under a variety of conditions with little reliability in their observations and without any uniformity in the types of observations made. Finally, with specific reference to retrospective studies, the result cannot be a prediction that children with a set of characteristics that may have been identified in the study will turn out to show autistic behaviors, but rather that children identified as autistic at the given age level and in the given geographic area and with given socioeconomic levels of their families, will show as infants a given set of stresses or negative factors. That is, in such retrospective studies one is not making forward contingencies but rather backward contingency probabilities. For example, it is a different thing to show a high probability that a newborn with a specific blood factor will show autistic behaviors at three years of age (a forward contingency) than it is to show that a child with autistic behaviors at three had, at birth, the specific blood factor (a backward contingency).

The final design problem that commonly shows up is that of single variables. Many studies attempt to relate a single independent variable to a single dependent or outcome variable, while others try multiple independent variables with a single outcome, or the reverse of that. It doesn't matter much, the basic problem is the same throughout. Connected with such a design is an assumption of linear or straight-line relationships. At this point in our knowledge it seems quite clear that autism is far too complex to be understood by single variable, linear relationships. Such studies do not reflect the possible interactions of input variables, of intervention variables, or of outcomes. Beware the linear connection.

When one considers the nature of autism and the associated difficulty of getting a sizable number of subjects for research it is not surprising that researchers in this field follow the designs that are typically reported. It is crucial to understand the problems associated with the three kinds of designs; to wit, problems associated with single subject and clinical evaluations as against experimental designs, problems associated with retrospective designs, and problems associated with single variables and linear connections rather than multivariate designs looking for interactions. Because those designs tend to be quite weak, one might expect the researchers to be extra cautious in interpreting their results and in making claims or conclusions based upon those results. Despite the prevalence of such problems in the reported research, any degree of humility about the interpretations and conclusions drawn from that research is hard to find. Overstated conclusions abound where understatement would seem to be indicated.

Definitions

As everyone knows who has read any of the literature on autism, there is a great deal of disagreement about the diagnostic signs characteristic of autism and of childhood schizophrenia. Differential diagnosis between the two is difficult and different diagnostic systems for each syndrome have been utilized, but agreement among the various systems is not overly encouraging. DeMyer et al. (1971) made a comparison of five systems of diagnosing autism and schizophrenia and found that the different systems, while significantly correlated, have an overlap of no more than 35 percent.

Infantile autism was originally described by Leo Kanner (1943) who lists twelve characteristics of the syndrome, with four of the characteristics of particular importance. These were extreme autistic aloneness, an obsessive desire for sameness in the environment, stereotypical or repetitive actions, and echolalia. Later writers have developed their own lists, but all owe a debt to Kanner. Creak (1961; 1964) reports on a British Working Party that proposed nine characteristics for "schizophrenic syndrome in childhood," with two of the characteristics of major importance. These were gross and sustained impairment of emotional relations with people and serious retardation with islets of normal or above normal skills. The DeMyer paper mentioned previously indicates that this syndrome is essentially what other writers have called *autism*. Rimland (1964) has also put forward nine characteristics of autism and selected two as major indicators; these are autistic aloneness and insistence on being left alone in an unchanging environment. Rutter (1969) lists five diagnostic indicators of autism with some highlighting of problems relating to others, distortions in language and stereotypical or repetitive behaviors.

The point of these brief mentions of four different sets of diagnostic criteria is to show that major workers in the field use different descriptors to identify the syndrome and, as DeMyer has indicated, the percentage of agreement of the criteria is far from total. Secondly, it should be clear that all of these definitions are simply aggregates of descriptors, thus the definitions at this point are simply lists of signs or symptoms having general agreement at the core but general disagreement on the edges. Thirdly, from the standpoint of selecting a research sample, how much of any one characteristic does a child need to be considered autistic? How often must a child show the particular sign or symptom? Is the child autistic if he shows two out of nine or three out of five? Does it matter whether the child shows one or two major symptoms and none of the minor ones? Is a child who is considered autistic following Doctor Kanner's symptoms also considered autistic by a person following Doctor Rimland's criteria? If child A shows the first three symptoms on the British Working Party list and child B shows the last three, but there are no overlapping symptoms found between them, are both autistic? Is neither autistic? Reading the research one will not find answers to those questions. Further, rarely will the research studies specify what particular criteria each child in the sample may have met or may not have met. Thus, children described as autistic in study X could be totally different from children described as autistic in study Y and yet the research is written (and we read it) as if autism was rather clearly defined when it would appear to be not defined at all.

Finally, in the matter of definition, even with one specific set of descriptors the problem of how much of a particular characteristic the child shows is still at issue. Rarely will you find a description of a sample of autistic children that indicates, with any degree of precision, the extent to which the child shows the various characteristics claimed to represent autism.

Measurement of Dependent and Independent Variables

A significant problem in the research on autism is that many, possibly most, of the measures of behavior (usually outcome, or dependent variables) and often the measures of independent variables are derived from observations, rating scales, and other subjective estimates. We know that the reliability and validity of such measures is always in doubt. Rarely does the researcher help to allay our generalized doubts by producing a reliability coefficient, a percentage of agreement among observers, an internal consistency correlation, or any other data that would demonstrate the extent to which the evidence produced can be believed. Reliability is not always easy to obtain but researchers do have a responsibility to establish and to report the reliability of their measures. When reliability is demonstrated there yet remains the question of validity, which is often also taken for granted, but which has absolutely no business being treated so cavalierly either by the researcher or by the reader of research.

In general terms, one should expect to find correlation coefficients of reliability or validity in the neighborhood of 0.80 or better to be considered high enough for decisions about individuals. It is unlikely, however, for one to find much research on autism that shows reliability or validity coefficients anywhere near that level, but even coefficients of the magnitude of 0.30 would be extremely helpful for understanding what autism is all about, if researchers would only report such information. To put it bluntly, most of the measures applied are quite crude or their use with autistic persons is crude (often inherent in the device), resulting in rough estimates at best and misleading results at worst.

Nonadditivity and Nonreplicability

Perhaps for these reasons — low incidence, definitional problems, and measurement weaknesses — research on autistic children is rarely replicated. There are studies that attempt to do things in a fashion similar to certain other studies and there may be more similarities than differences among certain groups of studies, but replication is a rather precise repeat of the original study, an undoubtedly difficult and certainly quite rare procedure in this field. Unfortunately, in the absence of replication, it is most difficult to prove anything, because one study is rarely sufficient to establish a fact. Thus, on that score, we are left with a great deal of clinical judgment based on experience and spurious or quasievidence to buttress our biases.

Coupled with the absence of replication is the nonadditivity of the published research studies. One could make an argument that replications are not necessary in research on human subjects, that efficiency in areas of low incidence would call for little if any replication, but in making that argument one would have to accept the principle of additivity. That is, that the research ought at least to build from one study to the next: later studies should logically grow out of earlier studies, and a careful reading of a large amount of research in the particular field would demonstrate a solid foundation of theory and early empirical research, from which emanates a stairway of fairly solidly established steps toward a particular end result. Reading the research on autism and childhood schizophrenia shows nothing of the sort.

As an example, the review to follow focuses on one very small aspect of the research on autism and child schizophrenia in an area in which the studies are likely to show better than average attention to problems of design, definitions, and measurement. Yet, this review reveals a plethora of problems and may in fact raise more questions than it answers. It may be as Gertrude Stein has so aptly stated, "When you get there, there is no there there."

COMPLICATIONS OF PREGNANCY AND BIRTH AS CONTRIBUTORS TO AUTISM AND CHILDHOOD SCHIZOPHRENIA

This section has been adapted from Balow, Rubin and Rosen (1977) and is one very small piece from a rather large report.

The possibility that childhood schizophrenia and infantile autism have at least partially organic etiologies underlies the work of researchers investigating the presence of perinatal problems in the histories of children so diagnosed. The evidence thus far suggests that perinatal problems do play a role in the etiology of these afflictions. Many of the studies to follow were reviewed by Mura (1969), who came to a similar conclusion.

Using hospital records and information from maternal interviews, Lotter (1967) compared the prevalence of pregnancy and birth complications (PBCs) in the histories of forty-nine autistic children, sixty-seven of their siblings, and twenty-two non-autistic, but psychologically handicapped, children who showed disturbed behavior, but received lower scores on the behavior rating scale used in the diagnosis of autism. More non-autistic disturbed children had severe PBCs than did autistic children; more autistic children had severe PBCs than did their siblings (respectively 33%, 22%, 7%), but these differences were not statistically significant.

Lotter, of course, used the British Working Party criteria in diagnosing autism, although he made an adaptation of those criteria. Lobascher, Kingerlee, and Gubbay (1970) compared twenty-five western Australian children diagnosed as autistic, using the British Working Party criteria, with a group of control children matched for age, sex, socioeconomic status, and cultural group. Medical histories from an unspecified source were available for twenty-five of the autistic children. Among the autistic children, there were significantly more labor complications, use of forceps, assisted deliveries, abnormal conditions at birth, and neonatal complications. That significantly more autistic children had a gestation period of over 287 days is an item of importance because abnormally long gestation periods are associated with increased risk of intrauterine anoxia.

Another Australian study, combining the criteria for autism from Rutter and the British Working Party, matched 131 children diagnosed as autistic with a group of children hospitalized for medical conditions (Harper and Williams, 1974).

Subjects in the study ranged in age from three to twenty-two years, with a mean of 10.8 years, but the diagnoses had been made some time earlier, apparently. The groups were matched for age, sex, socioeconomic status, and several birth order factors and were compared on seventeen perinatal variables drawn from parental questionnaires. The autistic group differed significantly from the disturbed group on seven factors: virus infection during pregnancy, severe prenatal emotional strain, prenatal depression, induced labor, difficult labor, cord around neck, and stimulated breathing. The autistic and physically ill children differed significantly on all seventeen factors, including those listed above plus history of miscarriage, rubella, other pregnancy disorders, threatened miscarriage, toxemia, excessive maternal weight gain, high maternal blood pressure, prenatal physical strain or accident, baby held back, and oxygen administered. This study gives rise particularly to questions about the reliability of recall and of medical service notes on such matters as emotional strain, depression, threatened miscarriage, prenatal physical strain, and similar highly subjective matters.

Knobloch and Pasamanick (1975) report on fifty autistic children with a mean age of eighteen months, who were seen in child development clinic and diagnosed following Kanner's criteria. They were compared with fifty abnormal, but not autistic, children who had organic central nervous system dysfunction and with fifty children without neuropsychiatric disorder who were examined for teaching, adoption, or similar purposes. The groups did not differ in sociocultural factors, motor and intellectual deficits, antecedent complications, or associated disorders. They were significantly different in the frequency of toxemia and/or bleeding during pregnancy (55% vs. 39% vs. 15%) and neonatal complications (57% vs. 60% vs. 27%), but not in the frequency of low birth weight.

Harper and Williams (1974) found an excess of rubella among their autistic subjects. Two other recent publications have suggested that autism should be added to the list of abnormalities that can be caused by maternal gestational rubella. Using Kanner's criteria for diagnosing autism, Chess, Korn, and Fernandez (1971) found ten autistic children and eight children with a partial syndrome of autism among 243 whose mothers contracted rubella during pregnancy, a prevalence rate of 741 cases per 10,000 children, roughly 180 times higher than the usual estimate for the general population.

Pinsky, Mendelson, and Lajoie (1973) tested blood serum samples from three groups of children for the presence of rubella antibodies. They found that the combined group of twelve children diagnosed as autistic (diagnostic criteria not stated) or with autistic-like traits and twenty-one children with language delay were significantly more often seropositive (had rubella antibodies) than twenty-six children referred to a child psychiatric clinic for problems not involving language (33% vs. 8%). The autistic and language-delay children were also significantly more often seropositive than the general population. All mothers of seropositive children were themselves seropositive. Although there was not historical evidence of maternal gestational rubella within this sample and there were only a few minor congenital anomalies of the type associated with such a diagnosis, this study supports the findings of Chess and her colleagues.

It has been suggested that autistic-like behavior may occur with unusual frequency among children blind due to retrolental fibroplasia (RLF), which appears mainly among premature children exposed to excessive concentrations of oxygen while incubated (Lowenfeld, 1963). Chase (1974) examined the relations between affective development, especially autistic-like symptoms, and early medical and environmental variables among 263 people with RLF born from 1939 to 1959. Two diagnostic checklists for autistic symptomatology were used — one filled out by parents and one by professional workers.

According to the parents' checklist, no individuals were clearly autistic, while four showed autistic-like behavior. One person appeared autistic according to the counselor's checklist. A prevalence rate of one case in 263 is much higher than that found among unselected children, thus supporting the clinical impressions cited by Lowenfeld. There were not significant correlations in Chase's sample between birthweight or length of gestation and autistic symptomatology, which was significantly correlated with parental educational level and neurological impairment. It may be that a complex relationship exists in this sample among the subjects' perinatal and neurological histories, their home environments, and the emotional effects of essentially congenital blindness.

Schizophrenic Children

Taft and Goldfarb (1964) compared the frequency of prenatal and perinatal complications on the basis of maternal interviews, physician interviews and records, and hospital records among twenty-nine institutionalized child schizophrenics, thirty-nine of their siblings, and thirty-four public school students roughly matched with the schizophrenics for age, race, socioeconomic status, and cultural background. They found significantly more evidence of possible and definite complications among the schizophrenic boys than among their controls and a similar trend among the girls. Results were similar when evidence of complications drawn from hospital records alone was used.

Data drawn from maternal interviews and, when available, birth and hospital records were used by Vorster (1960) to compare fifteen child schizophrenics and thirty-three of their siblings. Among the schizophrenics, there were significantly more traumatic prenatal and perinatal factors on the basis of all the evidence and on the basis of birth record data alone.

Rutt and Offord (1971) compared thirty-five hospitalized child schizophrenics with eighty-three of their siblings. Their medical information was drawn from hospital birth records, state hospital records, and birth certificates. The perinatal events they studied included prematurity (undefined), toxemia, bleeding, breech presentation, placenta previa, mid or high forceps use, induced labor, first stage of labor over twenty-four hours, newborn distress and resuscitation, projectile vomiting, and serious neonatal illness. More prenatal and perinatal complications were found among the schizophrenics than among the controls, a trend significant for the perinatal complications alone and for the combined perinatal and prenatal complications. The severely impaired schizophrenics tended to have more complications and lower birth weights than the less impaired schizophrenics.

The birth certificate records of 466 child schizophrenics found in the records of Bellevue Hospital's child psychiatric service were compared by Terris, Lapouse, and Monk (1964) with the records of the next single birth in the same hospital, matched for sex, race, and maternal age. A total of 463 controls were obtained. There were no significant differences in the incidence of prematurity as defined by birth weight; length of gestation; manual, instrumental, or operative delivery procedures; or pregnancy complications. There were no birth weight differences between the groups. Among the 187 pairs in which the mothers were multiparous, previous stillbirth or spontaneous abortion had occurred among 28.6% of the mothers of the schizophrenics and 17.6 percent of the mothers of the controls, a significant difference.

It is not clear why the major findings of this study are so at variance with those reported in similar studies of psychotic children. The study design is similar to most others, the sample appears not unlike the urban poor sample of many other studies, and the data are probably no more nor no less reliable than those used by other investigators.

Osterkamp and Sands (1962) compare the prevalence of birth difficulties (anoxia, induced labor, instrumental delivery, severe hemorrhaging, breech delivery, and attempted abortion) and of breast feeding among forty-one schizophrenic children and forty-one neurotic children in a psychiatric unit, using data from maternal interviews done at admission. They find that neither factor alone differentiated the groups, but that schizophrenics were more likely to have had both birth difficulties and a short period of breast feeding. They interpret these findings as reflective of the mothers' rejection of their children.

An alternate causal chain that might underlie these findings was discussed by Pasamanick and Knobloch (1963), who point out that many cases of shortened periods of breast feeding are due to neonatal sucking difficulties, which may be related to neurological abnormality. They also pointed out that, although Osterkamp and Sands give no data about the socioeconomic status of their subjects, it is known that both breast feeding and birth difficulties are more frequent in low socioeconomic status families.

Using data from parental interviews, Gittelman and Birch (1967) report the prevalence of pregnancy and birth complications among eighty-three of ninety-seven schizophrenics enrolled in a day school for severely disturbed children. Data were presented separately for children "ever enrolled," and children "presently enrolled," because changes in record-keeping procedures made the more recent case records more uniform than earlier records. Among the children "ever enrolled," pregnancy complications were present in 16.8 percent and pregnancy or birth complications in 34.9 percent of the records. Among the forty-nine "presently enrolled," 18.3 percent had had pregnancy complications and 36.7 percent had had pregnancy or birth complications. Children with either type of complication had significantly lower IQs than the other children. However, in the absence of data on a control sample or comparison with the base rate of PBCs for this socioeconomic group, these percentages have little meaning.

The development of eighteen schizophrenic children, thirty-seven children with mild behavior disorders or neurosis, and twenty-eight children with no known emotional disturbance was compared by Patterson, Block, Block, and Jackson (1960). Mothers completed questionnaires concerning pregnancy events including nausea, vomiting, exhaustion and fatigue, excessive weight gain, hemorrhage, bleeding or infection, feelings of depression, and irritability. No relation was found between the number of symptoms and the children's diagnoses. The subjects were evidently all from relatively high socioeconomic status families. As is too often true in this research area, the lack of background information on the subjects and the use of retrospective maternal data limits the value of these results.

High Risk Studies

The one exception to the common application of retrospective designs in the study of the antecedents of psychosis is the increasing use of prospective designs to study children at high risk for developing psychosis. An impressive body of evidence pointing toward a genetic propensity for schizophrenia has been developed in recent years; thus, the children of schiozphrenic parents form such a high-risk group. The rationales, methodologies, and findings to date of a number of such studies have been summarized by Garmezy (Garmezy, 1974; Garmezy & Streitman, 1974).

One investigator (Mednick, 1970) has developed a hypothesis of the role that perinatal complications may play in the development of schizophrenia, using findings from his study of 207 Danish children of chronic, severely schizophrenic mothers. He is comparing them with a control group of 104 children, matched for sex, age, social class, education, rural or urban residence, and assignment to children's homes. By the time the children reached a mean age of 15.1 years, twenty of the high-risk children had suffered severe psychiatric breakdowns; there was no mention of outcome for the controls.

These disturbed or psychotic children were differentiated from the well children (high-risk children who had not suffered breakdowns) and control children by the following factors: some characteristics of the maternal illness; certain personality traits; performance on a continuous association test; performance on physiological conditioning tests involving conditioning of heart rate, muscle tension, respiration, and galvanic skin response to a tone; and birth records, based on the detailed, standardized form that Danish midwives are legally required to complete.

No single birth complication significantly differentiated the disturbed children from the others, but 70 percent of them had one or more serious pregnancy or birth complication (PBC), while 15 percent of the well group and 33 percent of the control group had such complications. These serious PBCs included anoxia, prematurity, prolonged labor, placental difficulty, umbilical cord complications, maternal illness during pregnancy, multiple birth, and breech presentation, all of which could lead to oxygen deprivation to which neural tissue is sensitive.

By relating the perinatal findings, the results from the physiological conditioning tests, and data from the performance of brain-injured rats on similar conditioning tasks, Mednick formed an hypothesis of a possible etiology of schizophrenia. According to this hypothesis, PBCs damage the hippocampus, which is very vulnerable to anoxia, resulting in behavioral anomalies that are in some way predispositional to psychiatric breakdown and schizophrenia in individuals with schizophrenic mothers. Such hippocampal dysfunction, which may be linked to ACTH secretion and thus to arousal mechanisms, may be important only in certain types of schizophrenia. Genetic factors, postnatal injuries, and high fever might produce equivalent hippocampal dysfunction.

This theory has been criticized on three counts. Garmezy (1974) points out problems in the perinatal data; Kessler and Neale (1974) summarize a number of studies that run counter to Mednick's interpretation of the function of the hippocampus; and Van Dyke (1973) failed to confirm Mednick's psychophysiological findings, although there were differences between his and Mednick's subjects. Although both Mednick's data and his interpretations thus far have been criticized, further data can be expected from his study; additionally, his work should prove heuristically valuable, even if his hypothesis is ultimately rejected.

Conclusion

In view of the work summarized here, it would be difficult to claim that perinatal problems and psychosis are unrelated. However, the nature of the relationship is unclear and its magnitude appears relatively low. The pregnancy, birth, and neonatal anomalies present in the histories of some psychotic children and the significant correlations sometimes found between the two types of condition can only suggest, rather than define, an association. The low magnitude of the relation suggests that the influence of PBCs is quite likely interactive with other circumstances in the child's environment or genetic endowment. It does appear, however, that the occurrence of perinatal complications raises slightly a child's chance of developing a psychosis. It remains for researchers to isolate either the direct mechanisms through which perinatal problems relate to psychotic thinking and behavior or else the ultimate cause that leads to both perinatal problems and psychotic behavior.

Occasionally, some first rate research is done. Despite the difficulty of doing good research in this area and all critical comments notwithstanding, there are some things about autism and autistic children that appear to have a reasonably solid foundation based upon relatively consistent observation and a reasonable amount of relatively consistent research. It should also be noted that there are some outstanding studies in this field, carefully and wisely done, but, for the most part, they do not claim anything momentous. They do provide, however, the building blocks out of which an understanding of autism might one day be built.

One such paper is that of Hanson and Gottesman (1976) in which they point out that the majority of gene influenced human variability arises not from Mendalian genes of major effect or chromosomal errors, but from polygenic effects, the simultaneous occurrence of several genes of small effect that combine with environmental effects. They suggest that the bulk of genetic evidence and the characteristics and behaviors observed in childhood psychoses indicate that (A) early childhood psychoses are different from postpubescent psychoses, (B) no strong evidence exists for genetic causation, although mutations and polygenetic inheritance cannot be ruled out, (C) psychogenic causation of autism and childhood schizophrenia is simply not credible, and (D) biological etiology, probably congenital but not genetic, is likely, given: (1) the similarities in symptoms of children diagnosed as infantile psychotics with those diagnosed as suffering from central nervous system trauma, (2) the known central nervous system pathology in autistic children, including increased pregnancy and birth complications, epilepsy, electroencephalogram abnormalities, perceptual abnormalities, etc., and (3) the 1975 evidence of Hauser, Delong, and Rosman that fifteen of seventeen autistic children showed enlarged left temporal ventrical horns, which strongly suggests organic involvement and dysfunctioning in the language center in particular.

Hanson and Gottesman go on to indicate that when adult schizophrenics are retrospectively studied, only about 50 percent of them show histories of unusual behavior including irritability, excitability, anxiety, unsocialized aggression, apathy, and withdrawal. Shyness, even when extreme, does not forecast schizophrenia. They then go on to describe, briefly, a study in which Hanson identified thirty children of schizophrenic parents, of whom five were found to show special problems including "schizoid" behaviors (apathy, withdrawal, emotional flatness) during the first seven years of life. The five target children along with the twenty-five others of schizophrenic parents who were not found to show schizoid behaviors were followed as part of a major prospective study of child development. The five children, over a number of years, showed continuing patterns of malajustment, but none were reported to have delusions or hallucinations and none fit the syndrome of adult schizophrenia, according to Hanson. It turned out rather clearly that these children of schizophrenic parents were definitely not childhood schizophrenics and whether they become adult schizophrenics remains to be seen.

SOME THINGS WE APPEAR TO KNOW/BELIEVE

1. Autism is not just another intrapsychic emotional disturbance. The behaviors are quite clearly bizarre in many instances and it hasn't yet been demonstrated quite what autism is, but we do know it does not correspond to the typical pattern of emotional disturbance in which environmental overload appears to play a significant role in blowing a fuse.

2. Autism is found throughout the world and in all social classes in otherwise physically healthy families and among physically healthy children.

3. Some persons appear to feel "better" about the autism label than about a retardation label. Since the data so far suggest that the vast majority of retarded persons can live independently in the community, a smaller but sizable number can live semi-independently and only a very small percentage of the retarded require twenty-four hour a day care, that feeling or belief is not fully rational because the reverse is true for autistic children: the vast majority require twenty-four hour a day care. It may be that persons who believe the autism classification is "better," have faith that a cure or breakthrough of some sort is at hand and, once the key is found and the lock is opened, the autistic person will become normal. The unfortunate, but true, evidence thus far is that the long term prognosis for autistic children is terrible; there are no breakthroughs obvious on the horizon and, for some time to come, the adaptability and acceptability of retarded persons will likely be much better than will be true for autistic persons.

4. Thus far, the only treatment that consistently produces positive results is education. Medical treatment, including drugs, electroconvulsive shock, and surgery, have been shown to be "negatively" useful in that they can control gross behaviors so that the child is less troublesome to adults, but they have not yet demonstrated positive effects that move the child forward in the development of expected behavior. It is argued that appropriate control of unwanted behavior allows the child to be better taught by other therapeutic procedures, but the evidence for that is quite mixed with little consistent evidence to support that notion.

Talking therapy has not been shown to be helpful.

Nutrition, hypoallergenic diets, and megavitamins have not been shown to be helpful. With all such interventions, there are reports of clinical cases that claim to have been greatly helped by treatment, but there is little or no research, even N = 1 studies, showing positive results.

When educational treatments are producing excruciatingly slow progress and you want to break out and try something wild and new and faddish, go ahead, and do it so long as (a) the marvelous new treatment does not disrupt your carefully planned educational program, (b) that this marvelous new treatment does not provide risk to the child, or at most a very minimal risk, and (c) that the treatment does not insult the person within. Among currently used treatments, drugs provide the most likely agent having negative aspects. When we are really straight about the use of drugs we ask, "To what extent are drugs needed to benefit the child and to what extent to fit the convenience of adult caretakers?"

Lastly, with respect to unproven but glamorous treatments, keep in mind the history of research on psychotherapy and the many decades during which psychotherapy was claimed to be the only truly effective treatment for emotionally disturbed persons. Hans Eysenck (1952; 1965) exploded the myth by simply reviewing the research reported by the psychotherapists themselves, which showed that the effectiveness of psychotherapy was extremely limited.

5. The treatment of speech and language difficulties is absolutely critical in autistic children. Virtually all such children show speech and language problems; perhaps 50 percent are mute; those who are not mute commonly have little functional language and the extent to which autistic children accurately receive is oftentimes questionable. Some promising work is going on in the use of sign language, communications boards, behavior modification shaping procedures and the like, but since this is a central problem in the development of the autistic child we need an enormous amount of work in this area. Hamblin et al. (1971), Stuecher (1972), and Patterson (1978) all contain important material on the development of

language skills; the former two among autistic children and the latter a highly interesting, provocative and useful piece on the development of volitional language (and possibly thought) in a gorilla.

6. The final item we know is represented by a term from a book by Walker Percy. Percy described in his novel, *Love in the Ruins*, a characteristic which is very common among professionals dealing with handicapped children. In that book he has his character, Doctor Thomas More make the following judgement, "It is not uncommon now days to see patients suffering from angelism-bestialism." He goes on to suggest that people come up with all kinds of grandiose generalizations such as *Love thy neighbor* and *Make the world safe for democracy.* At the same time as we make such grandiose generalizations we show ourselves to be mean, crude or insensitive in our specific everyday dealing with other human beings. That is, while we love mankind in general we are bestial with particular individuals, including ourselves. Walker Percy suggests that this is the great puzzle that ought to haunt us; the central, glaring, yet largely unacknowledged fact that every single utopian promise, whether its origin is in the natural or social sciences or in politics or philosophical theory, has ultimately floundered on the condition that he has his character describe, angelism-bestialism. Angelism is proposed, but bestialism persists. Century after century we've proclaimed new sources of salvation, yet throughout demonstrate a remarkable consistency of behavior.

As we ride this particular wave that has made autism suddenly popular, let us do the best we can to be sure that we stay focused on angelism and ward off as best we can the bestialism that seems always ready to arise.

REFERENCES

Balow, B., Rubin, R., and Rosen, M.: Complications of pregnancy and birth as contributors to personality development and aberrant behavior. USOE, Bureau of Education for the Handicapped, *Interim Report No. 26,* Project 6-1176, November, 1977.

Chase, J. B.: A retrospective study of retrolental fibroplasia. *The New Outlook for the Blind, 68:*61-71, 1974.

Chess, S., Korn, S. J., and Fernandez, P. B.: *Psychiatric Disorders of Children With Congenital Rubella*. New York, Brunner-Mazel, 1971.

Creak, E. M.: Schizophrenic syndrome in childhood: progress report of a working party. *Cerebral Palsy Bull, 3:*501-504, 1961.

Creak, E. M.: Schizophrenic syndrome in childhood: further progress report of a working party. *Dev Med Child Neurol, 6:*530-535, 1964.

DeMyer, M. K., Churchill, D. W., Pontius, W., and Gilkey, K. M.: A comparison of five diagnostic systems of childhood schizophrenia and infantile autism. *J Autism Child Schizophr, 1:*175-189, 1971.

Eysenck, H. J.: The effects of psychotherapy: an evaluation *J Consult Psychol, 16:*319-324, 1952.

Eysenck, H. J.: The effects of psychotherapy. *Int J Psychiatry, 1:*99-178, January, 1965.

Garmezy, N.: Children at risk: the search for the antecedents of schizophrenia: II. Ongoing research programs, issues, and intervention. *Schizophr Bull, 9:*55-125, 1974.

Garmezy, N. and Streitman, S.: Children at risk: the search for the antecedents of schizophrenia: I. Conceptual models and research methods. *Schizophr Bull, 8:*14-90, 1974.

Gittelman, M., and Birch, H. G.: Childhood schizophrenia: intellect, neurologic status, perinatal risk, prognosis, and family pathology. *Arch Gen Psychiatry, 17:*16-25, 1967.

Hamblin, R., Buckholdt, D., Ferritor, Kozloff M., and Blackwell, L.: *The Humanization Processes*. New York, Wiley and Sons, Inc., 1971.

Hanson, D., and Gottesman, I.: *J Autism Child Schizophr, 6:* , 1976.

Harper, J., and Williams, S.: Early environmental stress and infantile autism. *Med J Australia, 1:*341-346, 1974.

Kanner, L.: Autistic disturbances of affective contact. *Nerv Child, 2:*217-250, 1943.

Kessler, P. and Neale, J. M.: Hippocampal damage and schizophrenia: a critique of Mednick's theory. *J Abnorm Psychol, 83:*91-96, 1974.

Knobloch, H. and Pasamanick, B.: Some etiological and prognostic factors in early infantile autism and psychosis. *Pediatr, 55:*182-191, 1975.

Lobascher, M. E., Kingerlee, P. E., and Gubbay, S. S.: Childhood autism: an investigation of aetiological factors in twenty-five cases. *Br J Psychiatry, 117:*525-529, 1970.

Lotter, V.: Epidemiology of autistic conditions in young children, II. Some characteristics of the parents and children. *Soc Psychiatry, 1:*163-173, 1967.

Lowenfeld, B.: The impact of retrolental fibroplasia. *The New Outlook for the Blind, 57:*402-405, 1963.

Mednick, S. A.: Breakdown in individuals at high risk for schizophrenia: possible predispositional perinatal factors. *Mental Hygiene, 54:*50-63, 1970.

Mura, E. L.: Perinatal differences: a comparison of child psychiatric patients and their siblings. *Psychiatr Q, 48:*239-255, 1974.

Osterkamp, A. and Sands, D. J.: Early feeding and birth difficulties in childhood schizophrenia: a brief study. *J Genet Psychol, 101:*363-366, 1962.

Pasamanick, B., and Knobloch, H.: The epidemiology of reproductive casualty. In von Krevelan, B. A.: *Child Psychiatry and Prevention*. Bern, Verlag Hans Huber, 1964.

Patterson, F.: Conversations with a gorilla. *Nat Geog*, October:438-465, 1978.

Patterson, V., Block, J., Block, J., and Jackson, D. D.: The relation between intention to conceive and symptoms during pregnancy. *Psychosom Med*, *22:*373-376, 1960.

Percy, W.: *Love in the Ruins*, New York, FS&G, 1973.

Pinsky, L., Mendelson, J., and Lojoie, R.: Can language disorder not due to peripheral deafness be an isolated expression of prenatal rubella? *Pediatr*, *52:*296-298, 1973.

Rimland, B.: *Infantile Autism: The Syndrome and Its Implication for a Neural Theory of Behavior*. New York, Appleton-Century-Crofts, 1964.

Rutt, C. N., Offord, D. R.: Prenatal and perinatal complications in childhood schizophrenics and their siblings. *J Nerv Ment Dis*, *152:*324-331, 1971.

Rutter, M.: A tri-axial classification of mental disorders in childhood. *J Child Psychol Psychiatry*, *10:*41-61, 1969.

Stuecher, U.: *Tommy: A Treatment Study of an Autistic Child*. Council for Exceptional Children Publication, 1972, Reston, VA.

Taft, L. T. and Goldfarb, W.: Prenatal and perinatal factors in childhood schizophrenia. *Dev Med Child Neurol*, *6:*32-43, 1964.

Terris, M., Lapouse, R., & Monk, M. A.: The relation of prematurity and previous fetal loss to childhood schizophrenia. *Am J Psychiatry*, *121:*476-481, 1962.

Van Dyke, J. L.: Electrodermal functioning in adopted-way offspring of schizophrenics: A study of the inherited diathesis in schizophrenia (Doctoral dissertation, The George Washington University, 1972). *Dissertation Abstracts International*, 1973, *33*, 3965B-3966B. (University Microfilms No. 73-4028).

Vorster, D.: An investigation into the part played by organic factors in childhood schizophrenia. *J Ment Sci* (The British Journal of Psychiatry), *106:*494-522, 1960.

Weiner, C.: The reliability of developmental history: summary and evaluation of evidence. *Psychosom Med*, *25:*505-509, 1963.

Chapter 14

A REVIEW OF LEARNING RESEARCH IN AUTISTIC CHILDREN

Melvin E. Kaufman and Helen M. Clark

Until quite recently, research in autistic learning was almost nonexistent (Hintgen & Bryson, 1972). The major emphasis in the field involved identification, differential diagnosis, and etiology. However, the past decade has seen an increased amount of interest in the study of the learning process in this group of children. This chapter deals with some of the more important trends in learning research with autistics as well as a comparison of similarities and differences observed in retarded and normal groups. Specific emphasis is placed on the available studies dealing with the process of overselectivity, conditionability, memory, and a pot pourri of other aspects of the learning process. Finally, a critique of past studies is offered with some suggestions for future research.

Overselectivity

During the present decade, a number of researchers have been investigating the attentional deficits of severely disturbed children primarily using operant techniques. The results of these studies indicate that many of these children attend to environmental stimuli in a highly selective fashion. From a learning viewpoint, the behavior of psychotic children comes under the control of very select stimuli. Since these highly select stimuli control responses, the more obvious stimuli usually controlling the child's behavior may, in fact, be totally ignored by the autistic

From Melvin E. Kaufman and Helen M. Clark, *A Review of Learning Research in Autistic Children.* In Rutherford, R. B., and Prieto, A. G., Severe Behavior Disorders of Children and Youth: *Monograph in Behavioral Disorders.* Council for Children with Behavioral Disorders of the Council for Exceptional Children, Reston, Va. 1979.

child, i.e. some minute detail may be actually controlling the response. The implications of the behavioristic theory of selective attention may explain many of the difficulties encountered in the attempts to teach discrimination tasks to autistic children.

Lovaas, Schreibhan, Koegel, and Rehm (1971) report the results of the first study on stimulus overselectivity. This study used a discrimination learning task in which autistic, retarded, and normal children participated. All subjects received reinforcement for pressing a bar in the presence of a complex stimulus consisting of the simultaneous presentation of visual, auditory, and tactile components. After the response to the complex stimulus was established, each of the specific sensory component cues were presented separately in order to assess which cue had acquired control over the child's response. It was found that autistic children characteristically responded to only one of the components, to the exclusion of the others. By contrast, normal children responded to all three components and retarded subjects responded to at least two.

In a second study, Lovaas and Schreibman (1971) narrowed the stimulus complex to just an auditory component (white noise) and a visual component (red floodlight). The two groups studied were classified as autistic and normal. The experimental procedure was essentially the same as in the original Lovaas et al. study. In the second study, each child was presented with auditory, visual, and a combination of auditory-visual stimuli. Results indicate that both groups were able to learn the task, with most autistic children requiring substantially longer time periods to master the task (a few minutes for the normals as compared with two days to six weeks for the autistic group). In most instances the normals responded only to the stimulus complex, while the autistic children showed stimulus overselectivity demonstrated by their differential response to one of the two stimulus components. It was interesting to note that the unused cue could become functional for the autistic children if specific training sessions were provided for the former nonfunctional cue. Of further interest was the lack of evidence that one specific sensory modality was impaired in the autistic children or that they preferred a particular modality.

Further studies of the phenomenon of overselectivity generally confirm the hypothesis that autistic children tend to respond to only a sparse number of potentially relevant cues available in the learning situation. The range of experiments include studies that demonstrate overselectivity not only across sense modalities, but within a single modality (Koegel & Wilhelm, 1973; Reynolds, Newsom, & Lovaas, 1974).

The 1973 study of Schreibman and Lovaas illustrated the extent to which severely autistic children responded to just a restricted number of possible cues. In this research, autistic and normal children were trained to discriminate between girl and boy doll figures. Further examination of the cues determining responses in the autistic children revealed that this group responded only to a very specific aspect of the total visual cue. That is the autistics selected the doll on the basis of a single detail, e.g., an article of clothing worn, rather than on the basis of responding to the entire doll, as was the case with the normal subjects.

Schreibman and Lovaas suggest that since the autistic group did not respond to the totality of the doll figure, then perhaps this lack of response implied that autistic children discriminated in the same basic manner in social situations. Autistic children may attend to some detail of a person's dress, and when that person appeared in different dress the child no longer recognized him due to loss of the necessary stimulus cue. Autistic children could be taught to discriminate the facial features of the boy and girl dolls, but this discrimination was maintained only for brief periods. The authors speculated that the human face may be too complex a stimulus for the discrimination skills of the autistic child and recommended additional research with respect to this hypothesis.

Schreibman (1975) indicated that one of the implications of overselectivity in autistic children was the necessity to carefully consider the fact that, in many learning situations, the subject was presented simultaneously a prompting cue as well as the stimulus to be discriminated. This resulted in the autistic child being presented a rather complex stimulus which he was required to respond to. Schreibman designed a study to assess the effectiveness of an ordinary prompting technique such as pointing to or placing a light in front of the correct stimulus to be discriminated. This type of *extra-stimulus prompt* was to be compared with a *within-stimulus prompt* such as intensifying the stimulus to be discriminated. Schreibman investigated prompting in visual discrimination learning of autistic children. The extra-stimulus cue consisted of pointing to the correct stimulus. The within-stimulus prompt consisted of an exaggeration of the relevant component of the training stimulus itself and therefore did not require the child to respond to multiple cues. The results showed that the children usually failed to learn the discrimination without any prompt. Further the children always failed to learn a discrimination when an extra-stimulus prompt was used. Most importantly, the discrimination was achieved only when a within-stimulus prompt was used. Similar findings were reported as well by Schreibman for auditory discriminations involving within- or extra-stimulus prompts.

Schreibman's earlier findings were recently corroborated by Arick and Krug (1978) indicating that extra-stimulus prompts were relatively ineffective with autistic children as compared to within-stimulus prompts. The task used by these investigators involved matching ten differentially shaped symbols with randomly presented picture cards of noun labels. All of the subjects in the within-stimulus group reached criterion within 200 to 300 responses, whereas the extra-stimulus group failed to reach criterion after a mean of 1,100 responses.

Memory

In a series of experiments on higher functioning autistic children, some of whom functioned in the normal range on nonverbal tests of intelligence, O'Connor (1970) reported on a number of the unusual characteristics of memory in this group. Generally speaking, meaning played a minimal role in memory processes. Autistic children tended to remember best what they heard last. Hermelin and Frith (1971) report a rather representative finding within their high functioning autistic population. These authors studied verbal recall in autistic, normal, and retarded children. They found that the normal and retarded subjects showed significantly better recall of words in sentence form than did the autistics and that the latter group frequently showed better recall of random strings of words. The authors found evidence of clustering during recall in retarded and normals, but not in autistic children. Further, the autistics demonstrated categorization deficits. In a test of rule-finding (remembering lists containing systematic repetitions), the retarded and normal subjects performed at a significantly higher level than did the autistic. When quasirandom lists were presented, the autistics performed at a higher level than did normal or retarded subjects. Hermelin and Frith concluded that there was clearly delineated cognitive pathology in autistic children, a state of affairs that interfered with normal learning and memory processes. One additional finding in an autistic group reported by Hermelin and O'Connor (1970) was that recall of words was more frequently dependent on the sound of the words rather than meaning or grammatical usage.

Based upon more recent research, Hermelin (1976) reported that autistic children functioning in the above IQ 50 range had unimpaired short-term memories. However, she added that "Much of the encoding and restructuring of information, which apparently occurs normally in the short-term non-modality-specific, abstract memory store, may be absent in childhood autism" (p. 163). Rather these children tended to use an extended form of their uncoded immediate memory system.

A final note on memory of these children is provided by Kozloff (1973) who reported that four autistics had an unusual memory for songs — a finding frequently found in the clinical literature, but by no means universally reported.

Conditionability

Churchill (1972; 1973; 1978) has studied conditionability in autistic children in a most unique and ingenious fashion. Let us move directly to the conclusions and then return to an examination of this investigator's novel research. Churchill concluded that the conditionability in low functioning members of the autistic group was highly variable. The common denominator was the extensive evidence of low level conditionability, with the specific nature of the difficulty being extremely individualistic. He found low functioning autistics conditionable to some point. However, no level of additional training experience could overcome the barrier to advancing beyond that particular level.

To assess conditioning in autistic children, Churchill (1972) developed a nine word experimental language. The basic nine word language (9WL) contained three different parts of speech, including three objects (block, ring, and stick), three adjectives (red, yellow, and blue), and three verbs (give, tap, and slide). If the individual components were learned, the child received additional training on two-word phrases and basic grammar involving three word sentences with a noun, adjective, and verb. Through the use of specific hand signs for each of the 9WL, the autistic's visual as well as auditory reception was evaluated. Thus the 9WL provided a way of evaluating the conditioning of receptive visual, receptive auditory, expressive vocal, and expressive motor modalities.

The subjects consisted principally of thirteen autistic children classified by the use of the DeMyer et al. (1971) system. Of the thirteen children, five were higher functioning autistics (presumably on the basis of overall intellectual functioning). The eight low functioning children experienced a wide variety of difficulty in the basic aspects of the 9WL. Churchill could identify individualized patterns of abilities and handicaps. While some exhibited specific modality impairments, others did not.

The five higher functioning children were able to learn the various components of the 9WL, but showed impairment in higher order tasks such as cross-referencing, manipulating syntactical structures, and handling prepositions.

The conclusion to be drawn from Churchill's work was that the conditioning of various aspects related to language development tended to be highly variable and highly individualistic. In addition, it was clear that lower functioning autistics showed more problems in conditionability than higher functioning autistics. This finding points to the need to carefully consider the general characteristics of the population, including degree of intellectual impairment, when attempting to do research with autistics. Further discussion of the lack of control for intellectual factors is to be found later in this chapter.

Additional Findings

Cowan et al. (1965) studied the discrimination of colors and shapes with 12 autistic children, only 2 of whom had any degree of language development. The tasks included selecting red objects from a multicolored array; likewise the children had to select square objects from a tray rather than selecting circles or triangles. Only the two autistics with language development mastered the task. The remaining ten children performed significantly below chance. Concerning their findings, Cowan et al. state "No hypotheses concerning loose thought associations or other perceptual or conceptual distortions of color and form can possibly explain the low number of correct choices given by most children . . . The children *knew* the correct responses; they were able to emit them but did not do so on demand. This is negativism by definition" (p. 919).

Hermelin and O'Connor (1970) studied various aspects of discrimination learning in relatively bright autistics. They concluded that size was the easiest discrimination to be made by these subjects, as compared to shape and color discrimination.

Bryson (1970), in an investigation of matching-to-sample tasks involving visual, auditory, and fine motor components, found that the area of most difficulty involved cross-modal tasks. Matching was used instead of discrimination because memory was not required and thus felt to be more effective. Bryson reported that auditory-to-visual and visual-to-vocal performances were extremely poor. She suggested that this may account for some of the observed language problems in many autistics. Further, Bryson failed to confirm the oft-reported clinical finding that autistic children have well developed fine motor skills.

Rutter (1978) reviewed a number of cognitive defects that need to be considered in terms of assessing learning potential in autistic children. The impairments noted by available research findings to date included verbal understanding, sequencing, abstracting, comprehending gestures, and written language. Further, Rutter cited Hermelin's (1976) research, pointing to the problems of temporal sequencing, which were found to be substantially greater than spatial sequencing. Likewise, Rutter concluded that the observed disabilities were not restricted to any given sensory modality. Finally, the observed evidence did not point to the presence of any significant degree of visuo-spatial defects in autistic children.

Present Status

Based upon presently available research, there are at least two significant problems in drawing firm conclusions about the learning characteristics of autistic children. The first problem lies in the unsatisfactory job many investigators have done in specifying the nature of the population they are purporting to study. Too many of the studies have used the term *autistic* without further elaboration. At times the authors have referred to the fact that the children were "carefully diagnosed" as autistic by a psychiatrist or psychologist. Since these professionals differ radically with respect to which children should or should not be included in such a group, it is not surprising to find that the subjects of various studies have been markedly dissimilar. As Rutter (1978) points out, there is a need to determine which particular symptoms are both universal and specific to the autistic group. Rutter suggests three general sets of symptoms including: (1) a profound and general failure to develop social relationships: (2) language retardation with impaired comprehension, echolalia, and pronominal reversal; and (3) ritualistic or compulsive phenomena as suggested by Kanner's term *preservation of sameness*.

Our own learning research with Doctor Paul Alberto and Doctor David Center, presently underway at Georgia State, is based upon classification of subjects using a series of observable and measurable behaviors. Thus the autistic group clearly demonstrates known deficiencies unique to that group and not present in a comparison group of severely mentally retarded children. We are using a combination of teacher rated behaviors as well as direct observation. We are finding that we can reliably identify severely autistic children in this fashion. That is, we are only willing to accept into the autistic group children who exhibit unique and specific deficits not found in severely retarded subjects. Thus, in all instances, we are using behavioral criteria for distinguishing between autistic and retarded children within a severely handicapped population. Of the eight behaviors we are using, we find that absence of maintaining eye contact for periods of 3 seconds or more and preservation of sameness (behaviorally defined[1]) are the most consistently occurring discriminanda within a sample of 20 autistic children found throughout the Metropolitan Atlanta area.

A second criticism of much of the existing research involves the frequent lack of equating the groups on some measure of cognitive functioning. The consequence of not controlling for differences in intellectual functioning is to restrict the meaningfulness of conclusions drawn from much of the presently available research. As Rutter (1978) states "Unfortunately, a large number of otherwise sound pieces of research are virtually uninterpretable because they fail to take mental age into account either in defining symptoms or in comparing groups" (p. 6). Not controlling for mental age (MA) within autistic populations has fairly serious consequences. This is particularly cogent when we consider that children labelled as autistic have been classified as ranging in intelligence from above average (based primarily upon the English view) through the profoundly retarded level. The fact that a number of very low functioning or "untestable children" are sometimes thrown together in a sample which also includes subjects who are functioning at significantly higher levels is an unpardonable experimental error.

In summary, the past decade has been characterized by more studies of the specific learning characteristics of groups of autistic children. However, because of the fact that researchers have generally not concerned themselves with operational definitions of subjects and likewise have not adequately controlled for differences in MA, the generalizations made at this point must be considered to be tentative.

---

1. Preservation of sameness is defined as follows: (a) child is upset by minor changes in the environment, e.g. changes in scheduling of daily activities, rearrangement of furniture, personnel changes; or (b) child adopts complicated rituals which make him very upset if not followed, e.g. putting many dolls to bed in a certain order, taking exactly the same route between two places, dressing according to a precise pattern, or insisting that only certain words be used in a given situation. Child is rated by his teacher as either characteristically exhibiting or not exhibiting this phenomenon.

REFERENCES

Arick, J. R. & Krug, D. A. Autistic children: A study of learning characteristics and programming needs. *American Journal of Mental Deficiency*, 1978, *83*, 200-202.

Bryson, C. Q. Systematic identification of perceptual disabilities in autistic children. *Perceptual Motor Skills*, 1970, *31*:239-246.

Churchill, D. The relation of infantile autism and early childhood schizophrenia to developmental language disorders of childhood. *Journal of Autism and Childhood Schizophrenia*, 1972, 2, 182-197.

Churchill, D. An experimental nine-word language: Strategies and errors of autistic children. Paper presented at *Conference on Severe Psychopathologies in Childhood*, New York, NYU-Bellevue Medical Center, December 1973.

Churchill, D. Language: The problem beyond conditioning. In Rutter, M., & Schopler, E. (Eds.) *Autism: a reappraisal of concepts and treatment*. New York: Plenum Press, 1978.

Cowan, P. A., Hoddinott, B. A. & Wright, B. A. Compliance and resistance in the conditioning of autistic children: An exploratory study. *Child Development*, 1965, *36*, 913-923.

DeMyer, M., Churchill, D., Pontius, W., & Gilkey, K. A comparison of five diagnostic systems for childhood schizophrenia and infantile autism. *Journal of Autism and Childhood Schizophrenia*, 1971, *1*, 175-189.

Hermelin, B. Coding and the sense modalities. In Wing, L. (Ed.) *Early Childhood Autism*, New York: Pergamon, 1976.

Hermelin, B., & Frith, U. Psychological studies of childhood autism: Can autistic children make sense of what they see and hear? *Journal of Special Education*, 1971, *5*, 107-117.

Hermelin, B., & O'Connor, N. *Psychological Experiments with Autistic Children.* Oxford: Pergamon, 1970.

Hingten, J. N. & Bryson, C. Q. Recent developments in the study of early childhood psychoses: Infantile autism, childhood schizophrenia, and related disorders. *Schizophrenia Bulletin*, 1972, *5*, 8-53.

Koegel, R. L. & Wilhelm, H. Selective responding to the components of multiple visual cues in autistic children. *Journal of Experimental Child Psychology*, 1973, *15*, 442-453.

Kozloff, U. A. *Reaching the Autistic Child: A Parent Training Program.* Champaign: Research Press, 1973.

Lovaas, O. I. & Schreibman, L. Stimulus overselectivity of autistic children in a two-stimulus situation. *Behavior Research and Therapy*, 1971, *9*, 305-310.

Lovaas, O. I., Schreibman, L., Koegel, R. L. & Rehm, R. Selective responding by autistic children to multiple sensory input. *Journal of Abnormal Psychology*, 1971, 77, 211-222.

Reynolds, B. S., Newsom, C. D., & Lovaas, O. I. Auditory overselectivity in autistic children. *Journal of Child Psychology*, 1974, 2, 253-263.

Rutter, M. Diagnosis and definition. In Rutter, M., & Schopler, E. (Eds.) *Autism a Reappraisal of Concepts and Treatment.* New York: Plenum Press, 1978.

Schreibman, L. Effects of within-stimulus and extra-stimulus prompting on discrimination learning in autistic children. *Journal of Applied Behavior Analysis,* 1975, *8,* 91-112.

Schreibman, L., & Lovaas, O. I. Overselective response to social stimuli by autistic children. *Journal of Abnormal Child Psychology,* 1973, *1,* 152-168.

Chapter 15

A STUDY OF AUTISTIC CHILDREN'S RESPONSES TO VISION, AUDITION, GUSTATION, OLFACTION, PRESSURE, TOUCH, PROPRIOCEPTION, VIBRATION, AND TEMPERATURE

Maureen Ivey, Beverly Sutton, and Donald Marburg

L ITERATURE RELATING to the autistic child frequently begins with a description of their bizarre adaptation to their environment. A typical description would include the following characteristics: lack of response to loud noises such as slamming door, but immediately discerning the rustle of candy paper; attending to minute visual details, such as finger gazing rather than the entire visual spectrum; fascination with spinning objects; lack of fear about realistic dangers; and failure to develop responsiveness to people. These are a few of the descriptive hallmarks that have led researchers to probe the perceptual processes of autistic children. One area of focus has been autistic children's ability to receive and integrate sensory information. What messages are autistic children receiving? What integrative functioning occurs to produce such bizarre adaptive responses?

Tanguay (1977) at the National Society for Autistic Children's Conference postulated a theory of etiology based on a disruption in the maturation of the tertiary functions of the brain causing extensive disturbance in abstracting ability. DeLong's (1975) research also focused on a disruption of brain functions as shown in his pneumoencephalographic findings of disproportionate enlargements of the left temporal horn. Sutton (1969) as well as DeLong (1975) describe the similarities between autism and the Kluver-Bucy syndrome, which is caused by damage to the temporal lobes and has a distinctly similar behavioral symptomatolo-

273

gy to autism. These researchers focused on disturbances of brain function as the underlying etiology. What effect would this dysfunction have on the sensory processing in the brain?

Early studies looked at the issue of sensory preferences. Did the autistic child prefer one sense modality more than another? Could the autistic child respond to a particular sense modality and not to others? Goldfarb (1964) examines the possibility of receptor preference in a one stimulus display and reports autistic-like children prefer the near receptors rather than the far receptors of vision and audition. Rimland (1964) also demonstrates that visual, auditory, and pain stimuli are less likely to elicit a response than tactile, olfactory, and gustatory stimulation. A third study by Schopler (1965) also supports a theory of sensory preference and reports that autistic children avoid the far receptors and use the near receptors of touch, taste, and smell to a greater degree.

Lovaas et al. (1971) explores the issue using two stimulus and three stimulus displays. Their results changed the focus from sensory preferences to the area of selective attention. They report an overselection theory and suggest that autistic children do not respond to multiple sensory displays because of overloading, such that only one cue is functional and has acquired control over the child's behavior. When Lovaas trained the sense modality in a one stimulus display, the child learned the correct response, thereby making a once nonfunctional cue (when presented in association with other cues) functional upon one stimulus training.

This study explores the area of sensory input and motor output in a one stimulus display using an operant paradigm for all nine sense modalities. If all the variables remained the same and only the sense modalities changed, how would an autistic child respond? As Lovaas reported, would the autistic child respond to each sense modality in the same fashion? Or, as Goldfarb, Rimland and Schopler reported, would the autistic child have a greater functioning in, or preference to, some sense modalities more than others?

Methods

An operant conditioning model was used to explore this question. Vision, pressure, proprioception, touch, audition, vibration, temperature, smell, and taste were trained and tested in a one stimulus display. Subjects were required to respond in the presence of the stimulus and not to respond in the absence of the stimulus. Each correct response was rewarded with a primary reinforcer; each incorrect response during testing was ignored. An operant discrimination paradigm was used to test smell, temperature, and taste in order to insure a one stimulus display. This was a three level discrimination in which the subject had to discriminate the response as well as inhibit a response.

Subjects

Five autistic children and five nonpsychotic, nonorganic hospitalized controls comprised the subjects. The autistic subjects were two girls and three boys with a mean chronological age of 10.5 years (range 7.6 to 13.4 years). The controls were one girl and four boys with a mean chronological age of 11.9 (range 10.8 to 13.1 years). The autistic subjects were diagnosed upon admission to the hospital using the Rendle-Short diagnostic checklist. All subjects had twelve or more of the fourteen behavioral characteristics manifested before the age of three. The following is a list of the fourteen behavioral characteristics defined by the Rendle-Short checklist:

1. Difficulty in mixing and playing with other children.
2. Acts as if deaf — does not react to speech or noise.
3. Strong resistance to any learning, either new behavior or new skills.
4. Lack of fear about realistic dangers, e.g. may play with fire.
5. Resists change in routine — a slight change may produce disproportionate anxiety.
6. Prefers to indicate needs by gestures — speech may or may not be present.
7. Laughs and giggles for no apparent reason.
8. Not cuddly as a baby.
9. Marked physical overactivity.
10. No eye contact — persistently looks past or turns away from persons.

11. Unusual attachment to a particular object or objects.
12. Spins objects, especially round ones.
13. Repetitive and sustained odd play, e.g. rattling stones in a can.
14. Standoffish manner — treats persons as objects rather than as persons.

Two of the autistic subjects were mute and used gestures and guttural noises to communicate; one had a very limited repertoire of signs for communication; one was echolalic with minimally comprehensible speech; and one had functional speech with mild echolalia. The controls were outpatients and inpatients in the hospital day and residential programs. All were diagnosed by the hospital evaluation team as having various behavioral disorders with no organic involvement. A brief description of the autistic subjects follows.

S_1, a 7.6 year-old female, had been in an institutional setting since the age of three. She was mute and had numerous self-stimulatory behaviors including hand and leg flapping, hyperventilating, and finger gazing. She was not toilet trained and had minimal self-help skills. For the most part, her time was occupied in self-stimulatory activity in isolation from peers and staff unless consistent and positive intrusion was maintained. A seizure disorder was controlled through medication. On the Vineland Social Maturity Scale she received a functional age of 1.4 years and a Social Quotient of 19.7.

S_2, an 11.9 year-old male, had been in an institutional setting since the age of four. He was mute and his self-stimulatory repertoire included finger flicking and high-pitched screams while twirling at a slow or fast pace. At times he was aggressive and bit, pulled hair, and hit peers as well as staff. He was easily overstimulated and had a short attention span. He was toilet trained and had marginal self-help skills. On the Vineland Social Maturity Scale he received a functional age equivalent of 2.4 years and a Social Quotient of 28.

S_3, a 13.2 year-old male, had been in an institutional setting since the age of nine. He was mute, but had recently begun using a limited number of signs to communicate basic needs. Self-stimulatory behavior involved flapping, and he would go to concentrated and unusual lengths to obtain objects of various descriptions (from spoons to baseboards) to use as flappers. This behavior was ritualistic, but often became aggressive when his flapping was interrupted by peers or staff. He was toilet trained and had functional self-help skills. On the Vineland Social Maturity Scale he received a functional age equivalent of 2.7 years and a Social Quotient of 21.4.

S_4 was a 13.4 year-old female who had been in an institutional setting since the age of eleven. She had limited functional speech and was echolalic. Her self-stimulatory behavior involved elaborate water play rituals and spitting. When she was not engaged in self-stimulatory activities, she interacted with the staff using repetitive garbled vocalization and enjoyed receiving individual attention. She was sometimes aggressive and pinched and hit her peers and the staff. She was toilet trained and had fair self-help skills. On the Vineland Social Maturity Scale she received a functional age of 3.3 years and a Social Quotient of 25.7.

S_5 was a 12.7 year-old male who had never been institutionalized but had remained at home for the most part without a formal educational program. He had functional speech, but was mildly echolalic. He was an outpatient in the affiliated dayschool program. His self-stimulatory behavior involved ritualistic use of language in a "sing-song" fashion and rhythmic finger banging. He was preoccupied with radios and repeated disc jockeys and programs he heard. He had exceptional self-help skills and fair socialization skills. On the Vineland Social Maturity Scale he received a functional age equivalent of 6.6 years and a Social Quotient of 55.

Apparatus

The subjects were seated at a 3 by 6 foot wood testing booth in a 9 by 12 foot room. A white, floor-to-ceiling curtain divided the testing booth from the rest of the area. The visual field was neutral with white walls and ceiling. Illumination from a fluorescent fixture was above the subject and experimenter. A white formica shelf 30 inches high was attached to the testing booth. A 3 by 5 inch buzzer box was fastened to the right front corner adjacent to the subject. The buzzer box was connected to an electromagnetic programming device designed by William

Porcher, M.D. to regulate the timing intervals for the stimulus presentations. The subject and experimenter were separated by an opaque screen 18 inches high attached to the shelf. Three types of interchangeable screens were designed (these will be described in the following paragraph on stimulus display). The experimentation room was sound attenuated and white noise from a Grason-Stadler generator #455B at 7 db was fed from a tape into a speaker situated above the subject. Primary reinforcers were given manually by the experimenter for correct responses.

Nine sense modalities were trained and tested using a one-stimulus display presentation. The following is a list of the apparati designed for each of the nine sense modalities. The *visual* stimulus consisted of a 40 watt light bulb encased in an opaque box with a transparent screen placed in front of the subject. The *auditory* stimulus consisted of a pure tone of 1,000 hertz emitted from a tape recorder placed behind the opaque screen. The noise level generated was 80 db as measured by a Breur and Keur sound level meter. The *pressure* stimulus consisted of a sphygmomanometer attached to the subject's left calf delivering 20 mm of mercury pressure. The *touch* stimulus consisted of strokes applied to the right index finger placed face up on the testing booth shelf through an opening in the opaque screen. A one-half inch 120 Artista natural fiber flat easel brush manufactured by Binney and Smith Co. was used to administer the stimulus. The *proprioceptive* stimulus consisted of slow, even, up-and-down movement to the third joint of the right index finger placed palm down on the testing booth shelf through an opening in the opaque screen and out of view of the subject. The subject's right index finger was held at the first joint along the sides by the experimenter's thumb and index finger. The *vibratory* stimulus consisted of a Sears model #63104 electric vibrator attached to the underside of the subject's chair encased in a sound attenuated box. The last three stimulus display presentations employed an operant discrimination paradigm to ensure a one stimulus display. The *olfactory* stimulus consisted of identical cotton swab presentations from behind the opaque screen of musk oil for thirty trials, and distilled water for fifteen trials using random sequencing. The gustatory stimulus consisted of identical medicine droppers filled with either a 5% saline solution or distilled water. The subjects were trained to open their mouths and three drops of either solution were placed on the front portion of the tongue. The saline solution was presented for 30 trials and the distilled water for 15 trials in a random sequence. The *temperature* stimulus consisted of identical General Electric Automatic Heating Pads (Model P55/5455040). One heating pad was on *high* for thirty trials and the second heating pad was on *off* for fifteen trials using random sequencing. The subject was trained to place his hand palm down through an opening in the opaque screen onto the heating pad.

Training Sessions

The subjects began with acclimation sessions allowing them to explore the experimentation room, testing booth and apparatus in order to become comfortable with the surroundings. A count was taken of the number of free operant button-presses emitted by the subjects during the acclimation sessions. Each subject had three acclimation sessions lasting twenty minutes each. Training sessions for the operant testing procedure began after the completion of the acclimation sessions. During training sessions the subjects were seated at the testing booth and instructed to press the button; the response was then rewarded with a primary reinforcer. If the subject failed to respond to the verbal cue, a manual prompt was given. Once the subject made two unassisted button presses within one minute, the one stimulus display presentations were introduced for training. During training sessions the subjects were reinforced with primary reinforcers for pressing the button in the presence of the stimulus. If the verbal cue failed to elicit the desired response, a manual prompt was given and a fading technique was used to shape the desired response. The stimulus was presented for ten seconds or until terminated by a button press. Upon termination of the stimulus display a twenty second interval period occurred. If a subject pressed the button during the last five seconds of the twenty second interval, a response-contingent delay lag of five seconds occurred.

The training sessions lasted approximately twenty to forty-five minutes, depending on the amount of time each subject required to complete thirty trials in the case of the straight stimulus displays or forty-five trials in the case of the discrimination displays. Not more than two sessions a day took place and the sessions were no more than three days apart. The electromagnetic programming device automatically regulated the timing of the ten second stimulus presentations, the twenty second interval periods, and the five second response-contingent delay lags. The data recording, reinforcing, and individual stimulus presentations were accomplished manually by the experimenter. The training sessions were terminated after the subject correctly responded without verbal or manual cues to two successive individual stimulus presentations. If the subject failed to meet criterion for the training sessions after completion of ten training sessions, then sessions were terminated and testing sessions were not begun since the subject apparently could not learn the required task. Training sessions occurred before testing in each of the nine sense modalities.

Testing Sessions

Upon meeting criterion for training, the subjects began the testing sessions. These sessions followed the same paradigm as the training sessions except that verbal or manual prompts were not used. For vision, audition, touch, pressure, proprioception and vibration, thirty trials constituted a session. In the case of gustation, olfaction and temperature, a discrimination paradigm was employed and forty-five trials constituted a session. When the subject completed two successive sessions with 90 percent correct responses the test sessions were terminated. Again, not more than two test sessions a day occurred and the test sessions for each sense modality were not more than three days apart.

Results

Results from the training and testing sessions are presented in Tables 15.I and 15.II. Formal data analysis was not performed due to the very small sample, which would render any estimates of statistical significance open to serious question.

TABLE 15.I
SUBJECT 1A, 1B, 1C, 1D, 1E

Sense	# of Training Sessions	# of Testing Sessions	% Errors of Test Score
Vision	0	2	0%
Pressure	0	2	0%
Proprioception	0	2	0%
Temperature	0	2	0%
Touch	0	2	0%
Smell	0	2	0%
Audition	0	2	0%
Taste	0	2	0%
Vibration	0	2	0%

Table 15.I outlines the results for all five nonpsychotic, nonorganic hospitalized controls. The subjects, referred to as 1A, 1B, 1C, 1D, and 1E all exhibited the same pattern of response. Training criterion was met immediately upon instruction and testing criteria were met in the first two consecutive sessions. The task for the controls was simple and they completed all testing sessions without hesitation. The controls in this experiment served primarily to underscore the discrepancies in the sensory input and output mechanisms of the autistic subjects. A comparison between controls and autistic subjects was not feasible due to the distinctly different nature of the two subject groups studied.

Table 15.II outlines the number of training sessions, the number of testing sessions, and the percent error scores for each autistic subject in each sense modality. In reviewing the five autistic subjects' tables, the variability of their responses can be seen. Each autistic subject presented a unique pattern of responses that will be briefly described. S_1 required extensive training sessions with an average of 7.4 training sessions per sense modality. On temperature, smell, audition, taste, and vibration, S_1 was not able to meet criterion after ten training sessions. It appears that these sense modalities were not functional for S_1 since after extensive training she could not respond. The touch modality required the fewest training and testing sessions and she met criterion relatively quickly in comparison to her difficulties with the other sense modalities. Vision also had a low percent error score but S_1 required the total number of 10

TABLE 15.II

Sense	# of Training Sessions	# of Testing Sessions	% Errors of Test
	Subject 1		
Vision	10	10	30.7%
Pressure	3	10	59.7%
Proprioception	3	8	53.3%
Temperature	10	—	—
Touch	1	4	27.5%
Smell	10	—	—
Audition	10	—	—
Taste	10	—	—
Vibration	10	—	—
	Subject 2		
Vision	2	3	6.7%
Pressure	6	2	3.3%
Proprioception	1	2	3.3%
Temperature	10	—	—
Touch	3	2	5 %
Smell	10	—	—
Audition	0	4	24.2%
Taste	10	—	—
Vibration	0	3	11.1%
	Subject 3		
Vision	0	3	4.4%
Pressure	2	2	3.3%
Proprioception	10	—	—
Temperature	10	—	—
Touch	2	2	0 %
Smell	10	—	—
Audition	0	2	1.6%
Taste	10	—	—
Vibration	0	8	39.5%
	Subject 4		
Vision	0	2	3.3%
Pressure	0	2	1.6%
Proprioception	10	—	—
Temperature	9	2	3.3%
Touch	0	6	10.6%
Smell	10	—	—
Audition	0	2	0 %
Taste	0	2	0 %
Vibration	0	2	0 %
	Subject 5		
Vision	0	2	0 %
Pressure	0	2	0 %
Proprioception	10	—	—
Temperature	2	2	0 %
Touch	0	2	1.6%
Smell	10	—	—
Audition	0	2	0 %
Taste	0	2	0 %

training and testing sessions before meeting criterion. One possible explanation could be that this was the first sense modality trained and tested and S_1 needed extensive acclimation to the expected task. Pressure and proprioception were similar for S_1 in that they required few, but extensive, training sessions and both had relatively high percent error scores. It appears that S_1's responses to the majority of sensory stimuli were nonfunctional, with vision and touch yielding the greatest response and most proficient learning. Behaviorally, through the training and testing periods S_1 engaged in continual self-stimulatory behavior

TABLE 15.III

FUNCTIONALITY OF SENSE FOR AUTISTIC SUBJECTS

High	*Moderate*	*Non*
	S_1	
Touch	Pressure	Smell
Vision	Proprioception	Temperature
		Vibration
		Audition
		Taste
	S_2	
Proprioception		Temperature
Pressure		Smell
Touch		Taste
Vision		
Vibration		
Audition		
	S_3	
Touch	Vibration	Proprioception
Audition		Temperature
Pressure		Smell
Vision		Taste
	S_4	
Audition		Smell
Taste		Proprioception
Vibration		
Pressure		
Vision		
Temperature		
Touch		
	S_5	
Vision		Proprioception
Pressure		Smell
Temperature		Taste
Audition		
Vibration		
Touch		

that substantially blocked her attending behavior. On a developmental continuum, S_1 would be placed in the severely impaired area.

S_2's profile as seen in Table 15.II, and Table 15.III shows another unique pattern of response. In reviewing the number of training sessions, it appears that when S_2 understood the task required, he could proceed. This was seen in his response to vision, proprioception, touch, audition, and vibration, which took an average of 1.2 training sessions and 2.8 testing sessions to meet criterion. Most discrepant was the pressure modality, which took six training sessions. S_2 had great difficulty adjusting to the format of this stimulus presentation. He would not allow the pressure cuff to remain on his calf. For some reason, this was very disconcerting for S_2 and he would get out of his chair and walk away from the testing booth with the apparatus on, thereby pulling the cuff from his calf in the process. It took four sessions just to acclimate S_2 to the pressure stimulus presentation, thereby skewing his training session data since once he adjusted, he met testing criterion immediately with a very low percent error score. S_2 was not able to respond to the discrimination paradigm, thereby making temperature, smell, and touch nonfunctional. The sense modality requiring the least number of training and testing sessions and one of the lowest percent error scores was proprioception. (It is interesting to note that S_2's self-stimulatory behavior involved completely proprioceptive input.)

S_3's profile as seen in Table 15.II and Table 15.III again points out the comprehension factor as mentioned in S_2's profile. When S_3 understood the stimulus presentation task, he could respond to the stimulus display. His response to vision, audition, touch, and pressure required an average of one training session and 2.25 testing sessions and a 2.325 average percent error score. Clearly, S_3 was responding to these sensory inputs and was able to integrate the senses for motor output. Vibration was a discrepancy in this comprehension factor since S_3 needed no training sessions, but required eight testing sessions. An environmental factor could have affected S_3's performance on the vibration modality. During the testing session S_3 had a serious viral infection with a cold sore on his lip, which distracted him, and he was often not attending to the task. S_3 did not respond at all to the three discrimination tasks for temperature, smell, and taste. Proprioception was a fourth sense modality that S_3 did not respond to after ten training sessions. (The incongruity between S_2 and S_3 responses to proprioception cannot be explained by this research project.) Intervention programs for S_3 begun during the research project centered on simultaneous communication, and S_3 responded significantly. As noted in the subject description section, S_3 was mute with a few basic signs at the start of the research project. Over a year's period S_3 developed over a hundred word sign vocabulary and began signing in sentences. Simultaneous communication involves all four of the sense modalities to which S_3 responded with the lowest percent error scores.

S_4's profile as seen in Table 15.II and Table 15.III shows a lower percent error score to more of the sense modalities than the previous three autistic subjects. For vision, pressure, touch, audition, taste, and vibration, S_4 required no training sessions and responded immediately to the instructions. On the aforementioned sense modalities S_4 required an average of 2.6 testing sessions and an average percent error score of 2.58. Unlike the previous subjects, S_4 was able to discriminate both temperature and taste. The first discrimination sense modality was temperature, which took nine training sessions to meet criterion. It appeared at first that S_4 did not understand the task, but once she comprehended the correct response and could inhibit a response, S_4 needed only the required two testing sessions and had a percent error score of 3.3. The taste discrimination was trained and tested immediately with a zero percent error score. The two unexplainable factors in S_4's profile were her inabilities to respond to the proprioception or smell modalities. Clearly S_4 could discriminate, but she could not apply this ability when the sense of smell was involved. On a diagnostic continuum of autism S_4 would be considered less severe than the previous three subjects.

S_5's profile in Table 15.II and Table 15.III showed the highest level of functioning when compared to the other autistic subjects tested. For vision, pressure, touch, audition, and vibration, S_5

required no training sessions, met testing criterion immediately, and had a .32 percent error score. For the first discrimination sense modality of temperature, S_5 required two training sessions to comprehend the task required of him; he then immediately met testing criterion with a zero percent error score. S_5 along with S_4 could not meet criterion after ten training sessions for proprioception or smell. Again, it appears that it was not S_5's inability to understand the task since he was quite capable for the majority of senses tested; however, it appeared that proprioceptive and smell inputs could not be integrated. The taste modality presented aother problem for S_5 due to his peculiar problems with eating. Ten training sessions were attempted, but S_5 adamantly refused to participate. He would turn his head, swear, and yell, push the experimenter away, and, in general, not allow either the water or saline solution to be placed in his mouth. S_5's eating problems consisted of refusing edible objects unless they were untouched by human hands other than his own. For example, he would not accept an M&M® from the experimenter's hand, but if he saw them being poured from the bag into a cup he would accept the cup. For this reason, S_5 data for taste cannot be used since it only indicated his own peculiarity rather than his ability to respond to the sense modality.

Table 15.III presents a summary of the data elaborated in Table 15.II, and provides a vehicle to address the question of sensory preference in autistic children. As seen in the table, the subjects responded very differently across modalities: when comparing percent error scores, it is evident that some senses were considerably more functional than others. Indeed, some of the senses seemed totally nonfunctional for some of the autistic

TABLE 15.IV
COMPARISON OF FUNCTIONAL AGE TO MEAN PERCENT ERROR SCORE

Subjects	Functional Age	Mean Percent Error
S_1	1.4	48.8
S_2	2.4	8.9
S_3	2.7	9.7
S_4	3.3	4.1
S_5	6.6	.26

subjects. These results do not correspond to the work of Gold-farb (1964), Rimland (1964), or Schopler (1965), indicating that the dichotomy between near and far receptors was not present for these five subjects.

Table 15.IV illustrates the interesting finding of a direct correlation between the functional age of each autistic subject as scored on the Vineland Social Maturity Scale (SMS) and the mean percent error scores. S_4 and S_5 had a higher functional age and a lower percent error score, and, on a developmental continuum, their behavioral characteristics depict a higher level of functioning. S_2 and S_3 have a lower functional age as scored on the Vineland SMS and their ability to respond to the sensory inputs of the research project showed a lower functionality and greater percent error score. S_1 presents both the lowest functional age and the highest percent error score, and her behavioral characteristics place her at the severely impaired end of the developmental continuum. The three developmentally higher level subjects, however, could not respond to the low level sensory input of proprioception. It is interesting to note that proprioception is the only sense modality completed by two of the developmentally low subjects and not by the three other autistic subjects. One possible hypothesis is that this low level sensory response drops out for higher level autistic subjects when other senses become more functional. This research project can not effectively deal with the discrepancies found in proprioception, and additional research would be necessary to further explore this question.

Table 15.V presents the third factor for discussion: the difficulty autistic subjects displayed when presented with the discrimination paradigm. Out of a possible fourteen discrimination

TABLE 15.V
ABILITY TO DISCRIMINATE

Sense	Subjects Able to Discriminate
Temperature	S_4 and S_5
Smell	None
Taste	S_4

Autism

tasks presented, in only three cases were the autistic subjects able to successfully discriminate. As indicated in the Methods section, this task was a three level discrimination. The subject had to discriminate the stimulus, discriminate the response, and inhibit a response. The question, therefore, becomes "were the autistic subjects not responding to the stimulus display or to the discrimination paradigm?" The data available from this study cannot assess the question. The difficulty with the smell modality is particularly puzzling, however, since S_4 could respond to the two other discriminations, and S_5 could respond to one other with taste being a problem of refusal. It would be tempting to report that the data shows autistic subjects incapable of responding to smell, but the limited scope of this research could not substantiate such a statement. Further research is necessary to explore the factors involved in the autistic subject's difficulty with the discrimination paradigm and their lack of responsiveness to smell.

In conclusion, the data demonstrate that these five autistic subjects did not respond to all nine sense modalities in the same fashion. Each autistic subject presented a unique pattern of response, clearly indicating sensory preferences. The patterns of response correlated with the subjects' developmental level, seems to illustrate a continuum of severity in autism. Unlike previous researchers' findings, there was not a preference for near rather than far receptors, and each sense modality did not become functional with separate training.

As an exploratory study, this research has raised some interesting questions as well as possibilities for further research. It would be advisable to repeat this same procedure (in effect, expand the subject population) in order to see if the findings remain consistent. Also, other interesting questions regarding the discrimination ability of autistics would be well worth studying.

REFERENCES

Clancy, H., Dugdale, A., and Rendle-Short, J.: The diagnosis of infantile autism. *Dev Med Child Neurol, 11:*432-442, 1969.
Delong, G. R.: Temporal lobe lesions may play part in autism. *JAMA, 234:*584, 1975.

Goldfarb, W.: An investigation of childhood schizophrenia. *Arch Gen Psychiatry,* 11:620-634, 1964.

Lovaas, O. I. and Schreibman, L.: Stimulus overselectivity of autistic children in a two stimulus situation. *Behav Res Ther, 9:*305-310, 1971.

Lovaas, O. I., Schreibman, L., Koegel, R., and Rehm, R.: Selective responding by autistic children to multiple sensory input. *J Abnorm Psychol, 77:*211-222, 1971.

Rimland, B.: *Infantile Autism.* New York, Appleton-Century-Crofts, 1964.

Schopler, E.: Early infantile autism and receptor processes. *Arch Gen Psychiatry, 13:*327-335, 1965.

Schopler, E.: Visual versus tactual receptor preference in normal and schizophrenic children. *J Abnorm Psychol, 71:*108-114, 1966.

Sutton, B.: The Autistic Psychotic Child and the Kluver-Bucy Syndrome. Unpublished manuscript, 1969.

Chapter 16

AUTISM
Caregivers' Questions and Concerns

James E. Gilliam and Pamela A. Kimbrough

The formulation of a problem is far more often essential than its solution, which may be merely a matter of mathematical or experimental skill. To raise new questions, new possibilities, to regard old problems from a new angle requires creative imagination and marks real advance in science.

A. Einstein and L. Infield,
The Evolution of Physics,
Simon and Schuster, 1938

RESEARCH AND EVALUATION studies of any subject are derived from a process of inquiry. A question is posed and an answer is sought. Research and evaluation is most relevant when it builds upon and involves the people directly affected. While there is an army of researchers investigating autism, too often the topics under study are narrow in scope and esoteric in nature. The results of these studies are unlikely to have great impact on the autistic population to be served nor significance to the caregivers responsible for providing service. Before relevant studies on autism can be attempted, attention must be given to the questions and concerns posed by parents and other caregivers. This report represents one effort to ascertain these questions and concerns.

In a recent project to train primary caregivers to screen for early infantile autism, 1365 caregivers were surveyed to determine their immediate questions and concerns relative to autism. These data were collected at the beginning of the training sessions, thus the responses were not generated as a result of the

290

training received, but represent questions and concerns the caregivers brought with them to the training sessions.

The caregivers represented over sixty different occupational roles. For purposes of analysis, the most frequently occurring roles were selected and organized into subgroups. The following roles comprised these subgroups:

Role	N	Percent of Total Sample
Nurses	179	13.1
Teachers	246	18.0
Psychologists	55	4.1
Students	246	18.0
Speech clinicians	82	6.0
Counselors	44	3.2
Educational diagnosticians	70	5.2
Social Workers	64	4.7
Teacher Aides	52	3.8
Administrators/supervisors	53	3.9
Physicians	15	1.1
Parents	18	1.3
Associate psychologists	17	1.2
Total	1141	83.6

The questions varied in content according to the level of professional experience of the respondent. However, the types of questions asked were comparable within the thirteen subgroups analyzed. It became apparent after further study that the questions asked could be grouped into distinct categories, i.e. Etiology, Diagnosis, Education, Treatment/Management, Prognosis, and Miscellaneous. For the sake of brevity, the questions posed were paraphrased and are presented here by category in order of frequency asked (most frequent to least frequent).

Etiology

What are the current theories on *cause?*
Is the cause —
developmental?
organic?
chemical imbalance?
allergic reaction?
genetic factors?
peri- post- prenatal factors?

What is the incidence of familial autism?

If one theory of etiology supports an organic brain disorder, why then is it not treatable physiologically?

Has the current research on serotonin levels produced anything significant?

Education

Language:

If an autistic child has not developed speech by age six, what chance does he have for acquiring meaningful language?

Is signing (manual communication) appropriate for working with autistics?

How is echolalia extinguished?

How does one elicit spontaneous speech?

Programming:

What type of educational program is best suited for autistics?

Are there other methods besides behavior modification (operant conditioning) being used successfully in the classroom?

How effective is the use of time-out?

What are the effects of a multidisciplinary approach to educating autistics?

Curriculum:

What functional skills can be taught that will be used in later life?

How is an autistic child taught to read?

How can schools and parents work cooperatively on what the child is to be taught?

Professional Preparation:

Can paraprofessionals be trained to work with autistics?

What doctoral programs are available for training one to work with autistics?

Treatment/Management

Management Issues:

How should self-injurious behavior be treated?

How should verbal tantrums be treated?

How does one effectively deal with constant giggling or laughter that occurs for no apparent reason?

Treatment Issues:

How can autistics be taught to overcome their fear of people or objects?

How are autistics taught to show and release their emotions appropriately?

Is there an age when autistics are no longer treatable?

Is play therapy appropriate for young autistic children?

What does current research conclude about the use of behavior controlling drugs with autistic children?

Is vitamin therapy an effective treatment of autism?

Prognosis

Have any autistic children been cured?

Can one outgrow autism?

Can autism be overcome?

What percentage are able to function on their own?

What signs point to a positive prognosis?

What happens to these children when they become adolescents? Adults?

What federal legislation provides for continual care of autistic children outside the institution?

How does autism fit into the new educational concept of severely and profoundly handicapped?

Miscellaneous

Can a correlation be made between masturbation and self-stimulation?

Do autistics that spin do so in the same direction as their handedness?

What is the divorce rate among parents of autistic children?

From all the questions asked, the one common denominator that seemed a part of each subgroup was the primary concern for researchers to determine a specific cause, thereby gaining some basis or rationale for developing a method for preventing the occurrence of autism. Also apparent was an attitude of frustration and state of confusion among caregivers from their numerous unresolved questions. This, in part, may be attributed to the fact that autism is a relatively new field, having been identified as recently as 1943. Information contained in the current literature indicates that to date there is no known cause or cure for autism. That in itself is frustrating: however, once resolved, the core issues of treatment, management, and education were addressed.

In addition to listing any questions they might have, the caregivers were asked to comment on any additional concerns regarding autism. The concerns mentioned were somewhat more specialized than the questions with respect to addressing areas of interest. It was often unnecessary to note from which subgroup the questionnaire came, as it was frequently apparent by the type of comment voiced. For example, teachers discussed behavior management, parents were concerned with the limited number of available services, diagnosticians stated a need for standardization of assessment procedures, nurses asked about controlling self-abusive behavior.

Although the questions presented earlier seemed to fall into categories, the concerns raised did not take on such organization. However, the issues shared were repeated throughout the questionnaires and are worthy of mention.

General Concerns

More research into finding a cure and/or prevention for autism.
A more nonbiased presentation of the literature so that myths won't be taken as facts.
A wider distribution of standardized checklists so that doctors and schools can recognize autistic symptoms for early identification.

Parent/Social Service/Community Concerns

More public awareness as to the problem of autism and materials to educate parents, schools, and communities.
More parental involvement and training in home management for an autistic child.
More relevant placement alternatives (e.g. group homes) than residential care.
More vocational training for autistic children.

More placement opportunities for living and working autistic adults.

More provisions for respite care.

Making public schools assume their educational responsibility.

Educational Concerns

Relevant teacher-training that includes:

Preparation of volunteers.

Academic assessment techniques and task analysis procedures.

Controlling compulsive, self-stimulating, or self-abusive behaviors.

Curriculum specifically designed for working with autistics.

Speech therapy and sign language for developing communication skills in autistics.

The information gained from examining the caregivers' questions and concerns indicates that there remains much work to be done, from educating the general population about autism, to providing teachers with more "how to" materials, to ensuring parents of other placement alternatives than institutions. More importantly, it provides direction for researchers, administrators, and service providers as they examine questions and topics related to autism. Hopefully, these data will allow them to address issues of relevance and significance to large numbers of primary caregivers.

NAME INDEX

297

SUBJECT INDEX

301